P9-DZZ-205

WITHDRAWAL

University Libraries, University of Memphis

Careers in Sales, Insurance & Real Estate

Careers in Sales, Insurance & Real Estate

Editor

Michael Shally-Jensen, Ph.D.

SALEM PRESS

A Division of EBSCO Information Services, Inc.

Ipswich, Massachusetts

GREY HOUSE PUBLISHING

Copyright © 2016 by Grey House Publishing, Inc./Salem Press, A Division of EBSCO Information Services, Inc.

All rights reserved. No part of this work may be used or reproduced in any manner whatsoever or transmitted in any form or by any means, electronic or mechanical, including photocopy, recording, or any information storage and retrieval system, without written permission from the copyright owner. For information, contact Grey House Publishing/ Salem Press, 4919 Route 22, PO Box 56, Amenia, NY 12501.

∞ The paper used in these volumes conforms to the American National Standard for Permanence of Paper for Printed Library Materials, Z39.48-1992 (R1997).

Publisher's Cataloging-In-Publication Data
(Prepared by The Donohue Group, Inc.)

Names: Shally-Jensen, Michael, editor.
Title: Careers in sales, insurance & real estate / editor, Michael Shally-Jensen, PhD.
Other Titles: Careers in sales, insurance and real estate | Careers in--
Description: [First edition]. | Ipswich, Massachusetts : Salem Press, a division of EBSCO
        Information Services, Inc. ; Amenia, NY : Grey House Publishing,
        [2016] | Careers in-- | Includes bibliographical references and index.
Identifiers: ISBN 9781619258921 (hardcover)
Subjects: LCSH: Sales personnel--Vocational guidance--United States. | Insurance--
        Vocational guidance--United States. | Real estate business--Vocational
        guidance--United States.
Classification: LCC HF5439.5 .C375 2016 | DDC 658.85023--dc23

First Printing

PRINTED IN THE UNITED STATES OF AMERICA

CONTENTS

Career
HF
5439.5
.C375
2016

CCS #945199931

4/4/2019

PUBLISHER'S NOTE

Careers in Sales, Insurance & Real Estate contains twenty-five alphabetically arranged chapters describing specific fields of interest in these industries. Merging scholarship with occupational development, this single comprehensive guidebook provides building construction students with the necessary insight into potential careers, and provides instruction on what job seekers can expect in terms of training, advancement, earnings, job prospects, working conditions, relevant associations, and more. *Careers in Sales, Insurance & Real Estate* is specifically designed for a high school and undergraduate audience and is edited to align with secondary or high school curriculum standards.

Scope of Coverage

Understanding the wide net of jobs in these fields is important for anyone preparing for a career within it. *Careers in Sales, Insurance & Real Estate* comprises twenty-five lengthy chapters on a broad range of occupations including traditional and long-established jobs such as Cashier and Real Estate Sales Agent, as well as in-demand jobs: Pharmaceutical Sales Representative, Financial Analyst, and E-commerce Specialist. This excellent reference also presents possible career paths and occupations within high-growth and emerging fields in these industries.

Careers in Sales, Insurance & Real Estate is enhanced with numerous charts and tables, including projections from the US Bureau of Labor Statistics, and median annual salaries or wages for those occupations profiled. Each chapter also notes those skills that can be applied across broad occupation categories. Interesting enhancements, like **Fun Facts**, **Famous Firsts**, and dozens of photos, add depth to the discussion. A highlight of most chapters is **Conversation With** – a two-page interview with a professional working in a related job. The respondents share their personal career paths, detail potential for career advancement, offer advice for students, and include a "try this" for those interested in embarking on a career in their profession.

Essay Length and Format

Each chapter ranges in length from 3,500 to 4,500 words and begins with a Snapshot of the occupation that includes career clusters, interests, earnings and employment outlook. This is followed by these major categories:

- **Overview** includes detailed discussions on: Sphere of Work; Work Environment; Occupation Interest; A Day in the Life. Also included here is a Profile that outlines working conditions, educational needs, and physical abilities. You will also find the occupation's Holland Interest Score, which matches up character and personality traits with specific jobs.

- **Occupational Specialties** lists specific jobs that are related in some way, like Online and Social Media Advertising Agents, Portfolio Managers, Commercial Account Underwriters, and Copywriter. Duties and Responsibilities are also included.

- **Work Environment** details the physical, human, and technological environment of the occupation profiled.

- **Education, Training, and Advancement** outlines how to prepare for this field while in high school, and what college courses to take, including licenses and certifications needed. A section is devoted to the Adult Job Seeker, and there is a list of skills and abilities needed to succeed in the job profiled.

- **Earnings and Advancements** offers specific salary ranges, and includes a chart of metropolitan areas that have the highest concentration of the profession.

- **Employment and Outlook** discusses employment trends, and projects growth to 2020. This section also lists related occupations.

- **Selected Schools** list those prominent learning institutions that offer specific courses in the profiles occupations.

- **More Information** includes associations that the reader can contact for more information.

Special Features

Several features continue to distinguish this reference series from other career-oriented reference works. The back matter includes:

- Appendix A: Guide to Holland Code. This discusses John Holland's theory that people and work environments can be classified into six different groups: Realistic; Investigative; Artistic; Social; Enterprising; and Conventional. See if the job you want is right for you!

- Appendix B: General Bibliography. This is a collection of suggested readings, organized into major categories.

- Subject Index: Includes people, concepts, technologies, terms, principles, and all specific occupations discussed in the occupational profile chapters.

Acknowledgments

Special mention is made of editor Michael Shally-Jensen, who played a principal role in shaping this work with current, comprehensive, and valuable material. Thanks are due to Allison Blake, who took the lead in developing "Conversations With," with help from Vanessa Parks, and to the professionals who communicated their work experience through interview questionnaires. Their frank and honest responses provide immeasurable value to *Careers in Sales, Insurance & Real Estate*. The contributions of all are gratefully acknowledged.

EDITOR'S INTRODUCTION

Overview

People who make a living in sales are paid to persuade others to purchase goods and services. Virtually every product or service, from car tires to city tours, benefits from having an intermediary on the scene—a go-between—to help buyers understand the product or service being offered and make the best choice for their needs. That go-between is the salesperson.

Sales jobs are quite numerous. In 2014, there were over 14.2 million sales workers (both hourly and salaried) in the United States, according to the U.S. Bureau of Labor Statistics (BLS). Not all sales occupations are high paying, but many of them provide individuals with solid financial rewards and satisfying careers. The wages of many sales occupations are higher than the median for all occupations across the spectrum. Moreover, top performers often make more than $100,000 per year. As is true in any occupation, wages generally increase with experience. But a salesperson's pay is typically based on how much he or she sells, so good performance leads to high earnings in sales more quickly than in other occupations. Sales workers often also receive financial bonuses and other incentives for meeting or exceeding sales targets. And, positions in sales provide good experience for individuals hoping to move into management.

Sales occupations encompass a wide variety of industries, from real estate and insurance to financial services and technology. For this reason, the sales field as a whole continues to expand. BLS expects job growth to be faster than the average for most sales occupations through 2024, resulting in good opportunities for job seekers in sales.

Outlines of a Career in Sales

Sales careers provide options for people with diverse interests, strengths, and experience. For example, if engineering is your passion, then working as a sales representative for technical and scientific products could be a good match. If you have strong skills in business and economics, you might have an aptitude for selling financial services. And if you have work experience in agriculture, you might do well selling farm equipment or agricultural products.

Whatever you choose to sell, you will undoubtedly practice a variety of tasks that come with the territory when serving as a salesperson. You will likely identify new sources of business and develop customer relationships. You may make cold calls, research potential clients, attend trade shows, give sales presentations, negotiate contracts, and prepare sales reports.

In many ways, sales work is about building relationships. Sales professionals must be excellent communicators, with an ability to develop a strong rapport with customers. They become experts on the product or service they promote so that they can explain its benefits to potential buyers. Salespersons are also skilled listeners who ask questions to better understand their customers' needs and preferences. Besides being persuasive and having the ability to negotiate, salespeople are good at networking, which helps them develop and maintain customer contacts.

Sales work can be competitive—and stressful. Some workers must meet sales quotas to keep their jobs. Because many work on commission, usually earning a base salary plus a percentage of total sales, limited selling means limited income. Work schedules are irregular in many sales jobs, often requiring nonstandard hours or work on weekends. Some jobs, especially those with sales territories covering a broad geographic region, include significant travel.

Yet salespeople often have flexibility in their jobs that other workers do not. Some salespeople are self-employed or work as independent contractors, which allows them a certain amount of freedom to determine when and how they do their jobs. Even those who work for a company usually are free to schedule their own sales calls and appointments, leave the office as necessary to pursue business prospects, or perform certain duties from home or on the road.

The educational backgrounds of sales workers tend to be as varied as the products and services they sell. Some have a high school diploma; others have a bachelor's degree or higher qualifications. Many have something in between: some college, perhaps an associate's degree, but little beyond that. The good news is that employers have a broad range of expectations when it comes to the educational background of sales personnel.

Product Sales Representatives

Product sales representatives typically sell goods for wholesalers and manufacturers. They most often sell to businesses rather than to individual consumers. Some product sales representatives sell goods for more than one company or product line; others work for only one company or specialize in selling a particular type of good. About 5 percent of product sales reps were self-employed in 2014.

These professionals sell a variety of products, from raw materials to finished goods, and work in many different industries. There are two separate categories of product sales representatives: those who sell technical and scientific products, and those who sell all other types of products.

Sales representatives for technical and scientific products. These sales professionals sell or promote prescription drugs, medical devices, computer equipment, and other technical or scientific products. A technical or scientific background is often necessary for these workers to understand customers' needs and to explain how a product works. As a result, many wholesale and manufacturing technical and scientific product sales representatives must have expertise about the products they sell. This usually means that they need a bachelor's degree in a related subject, such as chemistry, computer science, or engineering.

Other product sales representatives. With more than 1.4 million workers in 2014, other product sales representatives— known officially as sales representatives, wholesale and manufacturing (except technical and scientific products)—is the largest of the occupations discussed in the present book. These representatives sell many different products, including groceries, home furnishings, and motor vehicle parts.

Services Sales Representatives

Sales professionals who sell services to businesses and individuals are known as services sales representatives. Three types of services sales representatives are commonly recognized: advertising sales agents; insurance sales agents; and securities, commodities, and financial services sales agents. Other examples include workers who sell travel, telecommunications, and consulting services.

Advertising sales agents. Also called advertising sales representatives, advertising sales agents sell or solicit advertising on television and radio stations, in newspapers and magazines, and on websites. They also help to place advertising on billboards, in direct mail materials, on social media sites, and in other advertising venues.

These sales agents explain to customers which types of advertising are best for promoting a particular business, product, or service. Some sales agents work for media representative firms, which sell advertising slots for media companies; others are employed directly by media outlets, such as newspapers, magazines, and radio stations. About 5 percent of these sales workers were self-employed in 2014.

Insurance Sales Agents. Insurance sales agents sell insurance policies and other financial services to businesses and individuals. Some of these agents specialize in a particular type of insurance, such as life or health insurance, although many sell a variety of policy types. Agents might represent one insurance company or multiple companies. Qualified agents may also sell other financial services. About 15 percent of these sales professionals were self-employed in 2014.

Insurance sales agents need a license from the state in which they work. Licensure requirements vary by state. Workers who offer other financial services must meet the licensure requirements of securities, commodities, and financial services sales representatives.

Securities, commodities, and financial services sales agents. These agents sell securities—such as stocks, bonds, and mutual funds—and commodities to individuals or businesses. They also sell financial services, such as portfolio management, and advise customers about these products and general financial market conditions. Others trade securities or commodities in investment and trading firms. Specific job titles vary but include stock broker, investment banker, and financial representative. Nearly 10 percent of these professionals were self-employed in 2014.

Securities, commodities, and financial services sales agents must be licensed. In most states, agents must have been an employee of a registered securities firm for at least four months and must pass written exams to become licensed. On-the-job training, including preparation for these exams, is often provided by employers. Specialty licenses may be required for some positions.

Other Sales People

Some sales professionals do not fit into either of the above categories. Among them are real estate brokers and sales agents and sales engineers.

Real estate brokers and sales agents. Real estate brokers and sales agents help clients sell, buy, or rent property. Both are experts on local real estate markets. They research and show properties that will best fit prospective buyers' or renters' needs. They also meet with property owners to obtain listings of properties to put on the market. In addition, they assist buyers or sellers with tasks such as running title searches, negotiating prices, and scheduling property inspections. Brokers and agents might specialize in a particular type of property, such as residential or commercial real estate.

Although similar, real estate brokers and sales agents are slightly different. Real estate brokers are licensed to operate their own real estate firm. Real estate sales agents, on the other hand, often work as independent contractors for brokers, receiving a portion of the commission earned on each sale. More than one-fourth of all brokers and agents were self-employed in 2014.

Real estate brokers and agents must be at least 18 years old and have a high school diploma. Some firms prefer to hire workers who have a college degree. Many real estate agents start as sales trainees in a brokerage firm, learning on the job from more experienced agents.

Both real estate brokers and sales agents need a state license: either a broker's license or an agent's license. Licensure requirements vary by state but often include a pre-license education course and passage of a written exam. To qualify for licensure, brokers must have previously worked as real estate agents.

Sales engineers. Sales engineers provide technical expertise and support for the installation and use of industrial equipment. Sales engineers might sell highly technical goods or services and install, configure, or help to customize products to fit customers' needs. (Because of the small number of workers in this occupation, self-employment data are not available from BLS.)

These workers usually need a bachelor's degree in engineering or a related field. Many work as engineers before beginning a sales career, an experience that gives them a better understanding of the products and services they later sell.

Preparing for a Career in Sales

Self-motivation, persistence, and self-confidence are central to a salesperson's success. Rejection is a reality of sales jobs, so sales reps should have enough confidence to allow them to be comfortable in dealing with rejection.

Students can start preparing for a sales career in high school or college. Many schools offer courses in sales-related subjects, such as business and marketing. And some student organizations focus on helping members learn about sales, selling techniques, and building a network.

Getting an internship or entry-level job with a company of interest while still in school is a good way to make contacts and gain experience—and could lead to a job after graduation. Product sales representatives, for example, might test their selling skills and learn more about a company's products by first working in telemarketing or customer service. Securities and commodities sales agents frequently intern with a company during college. Career placement offices or academic departments often keep internship listings; other resources, such as organizations' websites, also describe opportunities.

There are other ways to gain sales experience. Some companies provide training to people who demonstrate certain aptitudes or skills. A prospective employer might look for candidates who have ambition, for example, or whose backgrounds relate to the products or services they will sell.

Many employers want workers who can sell to other businesses. For these sales positions, workers might start in inside sales— jobs that do not involve leaving the office— perhaps by helping to develop leads for the sales representatives who meet with prospective customers offsite.

Not every entry-level sales position is the same. Certain industries and employers may have fewer requirements than others and are, therefore, easier for launching a career. These jobs, which are usually lower paying or less prestigious, may provide good training and might lead to better opportunities in the future.

Related Occupations

This book also contains detailed information on occupations related to sales in industries like real estate, insurance, and financial services but not directly involving a sales per se. Occupations such as insurance claims adjuster or property and real estate manager, for example, do not entail "selling" as such but nevertheless relate to sales in that they concern customer service and satisfaction. Thus, career seekers inclined to something other than sales in the usual sense will find useful information herein as well.

—M. Shally-Jensen, Ph.D.

Sources

Bureau of Labor Statistics. *Occupational Outlook Handbook*. Washington, DC: BLS, 2014. http://www.bls.gov/ooh/

Torpey, Elka. "Paid to Persuade: Careers in Sales," *Occupational Outlook Quarterly* (Summer 2011): 24-33. http://www.bls.gov/careeroutlook/2011/summer/art03.pdf

Actuary

Snapshot

Career Cluster(s): Business, Finance, Insurance
Interests: Mathematics, statistics, finance, financial analysis, risk analysis
Earnings (Yearly Average): $96,700
Employment & Outlook: Faster than Average Growth Expected

OVERVIEW

Sphere of Work

Actuaries use statistics and data to assess the likelihoods of future risks such as death, sickness, injury, disability, environmental catastrophe, property loss, or investment loss. In some instances, the job of an actuary will include risk assessment and risk reduction through policy or business decisions. Actuaries design risk-based financial systems such as insurance and pension plans with specific premium costs, age and health requirements, and payout schedules in order to minimize an organization's potential financial losses and maximize organizational sustainability.

Work Environment

The majority of actuaries work in the insurance industry—in areas such as property insurance, life insurance, health insurance, and disability insurance. Other fields requiring actuarial skills include the financial industry, health care industry, and government programs such as Social Security and Medicare. Actuaries work as full-time salaried and contract employees in insurance companies, hospitals, investment firms, and social service government agencies. The actuarial profession, being in high demand and involving complex statistical analysis of data, tends to require long hours and great dedication.

Profile

Working Conditions: Work Indoors
Physical Strength: Light Work
Education Needs: Bachelor's Degree
Licensure/Certification:
Recommended
Opportunities For Experience:
Apprenticeship, Part-Time Work
Holland Interest Score*: ISE

* See Appendix A

Occupation Interest

Individuals drawn to the actuarial profession have an interest in and an affinity for mathematics, analysis, statistics, and business processes. Actuaries are detail-oriented people who have the ability to analyze complex data. They use their findings to make big picture business and policy assessments and recommendations. Actuaries find satisfaction in solving complex problems and making informed predictions about future risk-based events.

A Day in the Life—Duties and Responsibilities

An actuary's occupational duties and responsibilities focus on gathering and analyzing statistical data to assess the probable risk of events such as accidents, sickness, disability, death, property loss, retirement, and natural or man-made disasters. Actuaries determine probable risk and then use this data to make decisions about insurance premiums, pension plan payouts, and tax rates. Actuaries are responsible for ensuring that an organization can make payments to beneficiaries without risk of present or future financial loss to the organization.

An actuary's daily tasks may include compiling economic and social data on organizational stakeholders, using a computer for data analysis and communication, and creating databases for statistical data. Actuaries may also assess financial risk of different business decisions and models; draft probability charts for events such as accidents, sickness, disability, death, property loss, retirement, and natural or man-made disasters; and calculate insurance and deductible rates. Actuaries may meet with stakeholders to explain the relationship between statistical data and company policies or with insurance carriers and management to discuss insurance rates.

Ultimately, an actuary's daily duties and responsibilities are diverse, challenging, and weighty. Actuaries have a central role in making decisions about insurance premiums, insurance payments, employee benefits, and pension amounts that affect daily life.

Duties and Responsibilities

- Making sure that the price charged for the insurance will enable the company to pay all claims and expenses as they occur
- Calculating rates and determining policy contract provisions for each type of insurance offered
- Helping to determine company policy
- Being called upon to explain complex technical matters to company executives, government officials, policyholders and the public
- Helping companies develop plans to enter new lines of business

WORK ENVIRONMENT

Physical Environment

Most actuaries work in office environments. The work of an actuary requires sitting at a desk and using computers for long periods each day. Actuaries who work on a contract basis may be required to travel to client offices to analyze data and attend meetings.

Relevant Skills and Abilities

Communication Skills
- Speaking effectively
- Writing concisely

Organization & Management Skills
- Making decisions
- Paying attention to and handling details
- Performing duties which change frequently

Research & Planning Skills
- Developing evaluation strategies
- Using logical reasoning

Technical Skills
- Performing scientific, mathematical and technical work

Unclassified Skills
- Having knowledge of historical, social, legislative and political issues

Plant Environment

Actuaries working in plant or manufacturing environments might be responsible for assessing in-house risk, such as work-place safety and employee health, or external risk to the company, by measuring the safety of products and the company's liability to its customers.

Human Environment

An actuary's work involves interaction with clients, colleagues, supervisors, and employees. Actuaries use interpersonal skills to interact with fellow workers, communicate findings, and propose new ideas.

Technological Environment

Actuaries must have a strong familiarity with spreadsheets, databases, and statistical analysis software. Internet communication skills are usually required. Computer programming skills are generally not required for actuarial employment but are considered useful. Actuaries are usually required to keep their technology skills up to date as a condition of continued and successful employment.

EDUCATION, TRAINING, AND ADVANCEMENT

High School/Secondary

High school students who are interested in pursuing an actuarial career should prepare themselves by developing strong organizational skills, building good study habits, and exhibiting confidence in the study of mathematics, economics, and business. Students should consider applying for actuary-related internships to learn more about an actuary's daily work, skills sets, and challenges.

Suggested High School Subjects
- Accounting
- Calculus
- College Preparatory
- Computer Science
- Economics
- English
- Humanities
- Mathematics
- Statistics

Famous First

The first actuarial system of rating insurance risks was created by New York Life Insurance Company in 1903. Factors affecting the insurability of an applicant were assigned numerical values and tallied up to help the company determine whether the applicant was insurable under its rules and, if so, at what rate he or she would be charged for coverage.

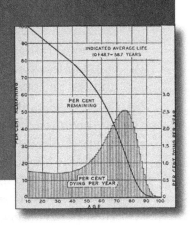

College/Postsecondary

Actuaries generally earn a bachelor's degree prior to beginning professional actuarial work. College students interested in pursuing an actuarial career should study mathematics, computer science, and business. Particularly important areas of college study and coursework include finance, economics, calculus, algebra, probability and statistics, business, computer science, and technical writing. Due to the human impact of actuarial work, college students interested in actuarial careers will also benefit from studying sociology and political science, as well as keeping abreast of current events. Interested college students should consider pursuing actuarial internships and part-time actuarial related work, as well as educating themselves about the requirements of the actuarial exams.

Related College Majors
- Actuarial Science
- Finance, General

Adult Job Seekers

Adults seeking actuarial jobs have generally earned a bachelor's degree and passed a series of actuary exams. Adult job seekers will benefit from joining professional actuarial associations, including Casualty Actuarial Society (CAS) and the Society of Actuaries (SOA), as a means of professional networking. Professional actuarial associations often hold career-finding workshops and maintain job lists advertising open actuary positions. Actuarial recruiters and internships may also prove useful resources for adult job seekers. Supervisors and mentors can help junior actuaries to plan their career, exam schedule, and education choices.

Professional Certification and Licensure

The actuarial profession requires that individuals pass a series of examinations administered by the Casualty Actuarial Society (CAS) and the Society of Actuaries (SOA). Both societies sponsor the same entry-level exams, which include the Probability Exam, the Financial Mathematics Exam, Financial Economics Exam, Life Contingencies Exam, and Construction and Evaluation of Actuarial Models Exam. A candidate seeking a career in life insurance, health benefits systems, retirement systems, or finance and investment would pursue the certification process developed by the SOA. A candidate seeking a career in property and casualty liability (auto, home, malpractice, workers compensation, and personal injury), would follow the requirements outlined by the CAS. Those involved in the federal pension field must follow requirements outlined by the federal government.

Professional actuaries usually take the series of required exams over the course of their careers. Mid-career actuaries who have passed the beginning exams may choose to pursue Actuarial Associateship or Fellowship status. These ranks are clearly defined by the CAS, SOA, and the federal government and require a combination of work experience and the satisfactory completion of professional workshops and exams

Additional Requirements

Individuals who find satisfaction, success, and job security in the actuarial profession will be knowledgeable about the profession's requirements, responsibilities, and opportunities. Successful actuaries engage in ongoing development of their mathematical, financial, and business skills. Written and verbal communication skills are also important for actuaries, as is proficiency with computer spreadsheets and databases. High levels of integrity and ethics are required of actuaries, as actuaries often work with confidential and personal information. Membership in professional actuary associations is encouraged among junior and senior actuaries as a means of building status within a professional community and networking.

Fun Fact

Believe it or not, there's a website called actuarialjokes.com. Here's one: An actuary is someone who'd rather be completely wrong than approximately right.

Source: http://actuarialjokes.com

EARNINGS AND ADVANCEMENT

Median annual earnings of actuaries were $96,700 in 2014. The lowest ten percent earned less than $58,080, while the highest ten percent earned more than $180,680.

Earnings and Advancement are tied to the number of actuarial exams a candidate has passed. Insurance companies and consulting firms give merit increases to actuaries as they gain experience and pass examinations. Some companies offer cash bonuses for each professional designation achieved.

Actuaries may receive paid vacations, holidays, and sick days; life and health insurance; and retirement benefits. These are usually paid by the employer.

Metropolitan Areas with the Highest Employment Level in this Occupation

Metropolitan area	Employment	Employment per thousand jobs	Annual mean wage
New York-White Plains-Wayne, NY-NJ	2,510	0.47	$139,290
Philadelphia, PA	940	0.51	$120,970
Hartford-West Hartford-East Hartford, CT	900	1.59	$114,810
Kansas City, MO-KS	860	0.85	$130,960
Chicago-Joliet-Naperville, IL	770	0.20	$96,890
Boston-Cambridge-Quincy, MA	750	0.42	$110,460
Minneapolis-St. Paul-Bloomington, MN-WI	600	0.33	$96,290
Santa Ana-Anaheim-Irvine, CA	520	0.35	$116,960
San Francisco-San Mateo-Redwood City, CA	460	0.43	$112,570
Denver-Aurora-Broomfield, CO	450	0.34	N/A

Source: Bureau of Labor Statistics

EMPLOYMENT AND OUTLOOK

Actuaries held about 25,000 jobs in 2014. Employment of actuaries is expected to grow faster than the average for all occupations through the year 2024, which means employment is projected to increase 15 percent to 20 percent. Most job openings arise to replace actuaries who transfer to other occupations or retire. The most favorable opportunities are for college graduates with strong backgrounds in mathematics and statistics who have passed at least two actuarial exams. Because insurance coverage is considered to be a necessity, actuaries are unlikely to be laid off even during recessions.

Employment Trend, Projected 2014–24

Mathematical science occupations: 28%

Actuaries: 18%

Total, all occupations: 7%

Note: "All Occupations" includes all occupations in the U.S. Economy. Source: U.S. Bureau of Labor Statistics, Employment Projections Program

Related Occupations

- Auditor
- Budget Analyst
- Economist
- Energy Auditor
- Financial Analyst
- Financial Manager
- Insurance Underwriter
- Management Analyst & Consultant
- Mathematician
- Personal Financial Advisor
- Statistical Assistant
- Statistician

Conversation With . . .
WILLIAM HINES

Principal & Consulting Actuary, Milliman, Inc.
Wakefield, Massachusetts
Actuary, 28 years

1. What was your individual career path in terms of education/training, entry-level job, or other significant opportunity?

I received an undergraduate degree in business from the University of Massachusetts/Amherst. My major was finance, with a minor in math. UMass didn't have a formal actuarial science major, but a professor in the math department was promoting an actuarial career path for math and business majors. (They now offer a concentration in actuarial science.) He identified the courses that allowed me to take several actuarial exams while I was still in college.

I did an internship that helped me understand a bit more about what it was like to work in a company and what type of work an actuary might be asked to do. I believe it's vital that prospective actuaries get this type of experience.

Upon graduation, I joined the actuarial training program at John Hancock Life Insurance Company and spent the first half of my career there. I worked in a program that required me to rotate from one department to another, which I found to be an invaluable experience later in my career as a consultant. I've been consulting since I left John Hancock after fourteen years there.

2. What are the most important skills and/or qualities for someone in your profession?

I believe that the most important skills and qualities are an interest in problem-solving, the ability to listen, and the ability to adapt and apply your skills to new and different areas. Communication skills are often a challenge for people who have high quantitative aptitude, but an actuary has to be able to communicate well both orally and in writing. A key aspect of what an actuary does is very technical, and the actuary needs to be able to communicate technical, sometimes complex, information to non-technical people. Continuing to learn new things is absolutely critical in any profession, and definitely so for actuaries.

3. What do you wish you had known going into this profession?

Because I was lucky enough to have that professor pointing out the right classes to take and because I had done an internship, I felt quite prepared when I took my first job. My biggest issue was having so many good options for lunch in the cafeteria that it was difficult to stay awake in the early afternoon! I always ate too much.

4. Are there many job opportunities in your profession? In what specific areas?

There are good jobs for people with actuarial skills. Actuarial skills are applicable in a large number of areas, not just in insurance. Risk management is a rapidly emerging area where actuarial skills are well suited. Data analytics is also an emerging area for actuaries.

5. How do you see your profession changing in the next five years? What role will technology play in those changes, and what skills will be required?

I believe that there will be a significant increase in the use of external data to enhance the predictability of policyholder behavior and claim activity in all types of insurance. Actuaries will need to think more broadly about the types of information that can be brought to bear on any particular problem and the most effective ways of using such data.

I also believe there will be more reliance on the actuary's judgment, rather than relying on a rule. That means there will be more pressure on actuaries to provide a thorough and clear rationale for and documentation of their work. An emphasis on standards of practice is a hallmark of the actuarial profession and sets it apart from many other types of jobs.

6. What do you enjoy most about your job? What do you enjoy least about your job?

I enjoy the variety of work, the ability to help clients solve business problems, and the opportunity to develop new skills and areas of expertise. I enjoy being a volunteer in professional organizations such as the American Academy of Actuaries and the International Actuarial Association. Through these organizations, I've been able to see the variety of work that actuaries perform. I've also been able to see how our professional standards provide significant value to the U.S. and international economies and the financial well-being of all people.

Probably the part that I liked least were the exams. It took me longer than it should have to go through them.

7. Can you suggest a valuable "try this" for students considering a career in your profession?

I suggest that students considering an actuarial career participate in an internship or co-op placement with an insurance company or actuarial consulting firm. I would also suggest that they shadow an actuary for a day. Many large cities have actuarial clubs that may be able to coordinate such an activity.

Teach someone about math. Become a tutor. Give presentations about things you know. Learn how to communicate ideas and concepts by starting with a topic you know well.

SELECTED SCHOOLS

Most colleges and universities offer programs related to careers in business, insurance, or sales; a variety of them more specialized programs. For a list of schools with actuarial programs, visit the website of the Society of Actuaries (see below).

MORE INFORMATION

American Academy of Actuaries
1850 M Street NW, Suite 300
Washington, DC 20036
202.223.8196
www.actuary.org

American Society of Pension Professionals & Actuaries
4245 N. Fairfax Drive, Suite 750
Arlington, VA 22203
703.516.9300
www.asppa.org

Casualty Actuarial Society
4350 N. Fairfax Drive, Suite 250
Arlington, VA 22203
703.276.3100
www.casact.org

Society of Actuaries
475 N. Martingale Road, Suite 600
Schaumburg, IL 60173
847.706.3500
www.soa.org

Simone Isadora Flynn/Editor

Advertising Sales Agent

Snapshot

Career Cluster: Business, Marketing, Sales & Service

Interests: Marketing and sales, creating new media, working with clients, analyzing surveys and data

Earnings (Yearly Average): $47,890

Employment & Outlook: Decline Expected

OVERVIEW

Sphere of Work

Advertising sales agents plan, develop, and create advertising campaigns to promote client products or services. Their responsibilities include generating sales for and building relationships with current clients, as well as acquiring new clients. Advertising sales agents develop a full understanding of a client's products and services before they plan a campaign. Campaigns cover a range of advertising types, from ads in print and on radio and television broadcasts to various

applications on websites. Advertising sales agents are continually reviewing trends in advertising through consumer surveys and competitive analysis.

Work Environment

Advertising sales agents generally work in busy offices where there is a great deal of pressure to meet advertising campaign deadlines and monthly sales goals. Depending on the size of the agency, advertising sales agents may work independently or with a team; most agents do a combination of both. Although much of their time is spent in meetings, doing research, or making phone calls to current clients, they must also spend a significant amount of time away from the office visiting prospective clients. Advertising is a field that is sensitive to changes in the economy, and prosperous times tend to be extremely busy, requiring agents to work extra hours. Economic downturns, on the other hand, can cause companies to cut advertising budgets, resulting in layoffs at some advertising agencies.

Profile

Working Conditions: Light Work
Physical Strength: Light Work
Education Needs: Bachelor's Degree
Licensure/Certification: Usually Not Required
Opportunities For Experience: Internship, Apprenticeship, Part-Time Work
Holland Interest Score*: ESA

* See Appendix A

Occupation Interest

Advertising sales agents help transform an idea to promote a product or service into a well-developed campaign that generates increased sales for a client. Those attracted to the advertising industry are usually energetic, curious, and creative individuals who understand how to generate persuasive messages.

Advertising sales agents tend to be good communicators, both verbally and in writing, and enjoy interaction with a variety of people from a range of industries. They are fast learners and must understand clients' products and wishes before tailoring advertising to meet those needs. Advertising sales agents maintain current knowledge of popular culture and trends in order to understand which themes or images may resonate with consumers and affect spending habits. Using this skill, advertising sales agents can transform an unknown product into one that is widely recognized and purchased.

A Day in the Life—Duties and Responsibilities

Typical daily work tasks of an advertising sales agent revolve around developing a multidimensional media campaign that will generate sales of a client's products or services. Advertising sales agents familiarize themselves with client products and services, review advertising trends, and analyze information from consumer surveys. They present sample advertising work and submit budget estimates to clients for approval before beginning campaigns. Advertising sales agents work with creative teams to develop the strategic messages to be communicated in their campaigns. In addition, advertising sales agents interact with customers, company executives, and sales departments to put together promotional plans that will be transmitted through different media.

Advertising sales agents are also involved in the preparation and use of marketing and advertising brochures, pamphlets, text copy, and graphics for Internet campaigns, and website advertising formats. They evaluate an advertising campaign's success in direct relation to the amount of sales it has generated. Tracking these sales is an important part of an advertising sales agent's job, because the timing of increased sales may indicate that the advertising campaign was effective. Clients periodically re-evaluate their relationship with an advertising agency in terms of overall sales trends. To retain clients over long periods of time, an advertising sales agent must be attentive to short- and long-term sales trends.

When traveling to visit clients, advertising sales agents represent their company; however, they also make an effort to identify with the client's company or organization in order to understand what type of content will best represent the client to consumers. Advertising sales agents often travel to client locations to present campaign recommendations, meet with executives, and discuss the success or failure of previous advertising efforts. Advertising sales agents should be able to communicate to consumers what it is that their client does or sells in the form of persuasive promotional messages that attract attention and increase product or service sales. Often, the persuasive messages used in an advertising campaign are the result of communication between the client and the advertising firm. A client usually knows his or her product or service very well, while the advertising sales agent understands the language, imagery, and consumer behavior patterns that may be beneficial to sales of that particular product.

Duties and Responsibilities

- Studying the products or services of the client
- Reviewing advertising trends and consumer surveys
- Organizing facts in order to plan the advertising campaign
- Consulting with customers
- Budgeting and submitting estimates of costs
- Preparing sales contracts
- Reviewing and proof-reading layout and copy before printing
- Preparing advertising brochures and manuals for publication

OCCUPATION SPECIALTIES

Online and Social Media Advertising Agents

Online and Social Media Advertising Agents work with clients to promote products and services over the Internet and mobile digital media platforms.

Radio and T.V. Time Sales Representatives

Radio and T.V. Time Sales Representatives contact prospective customers to sell radio and television time for advertising on broadcasting stations or networks.

Signs and Displays Sales Representatives

Signs and Displays Sales Representatives solicit and draw up contracts for signs and displays.

Sales-Promotion Representatives

Sales-Promotion Representatives persuade customers to use sales promotion display items of wholesale commodity distributors.

WORK ENVIRONMENT

Physical Environment

Advertising sales agents usually work in office environments that are pleasant and comfortable. Unlike many business offices, advertising offices may contain eclectic work rooms or areas meant to inspire creativity and innovative thought in work projects. Advertising sales agents work at computers and have a significant amount of variety in their daily tasks, as they are frequently networking with current and prospective clients or working with creative teams to help build campaigns.

Relevant Skills and Abilities

Communication Skills
- Persuading others
- Speaking effectively
- Writing concisely

Interpersonal/Social Skills
- Being able to work independently
- Cooperating with others
- Working as a member of a team

Organization & Management Skills
- Managing time
- Meeting goals and deadlines

Human Environment

The job of an advertising sales agent involves a great deal of interaction with others. Advertising sales agents work in busy environments where different members of an agency perform different tasks to meet a common goal, often on a tight deadline. Advertising sales agents generally work forty hours per week, but evening or weekend work is not unusual during busy periods.

They may travel extensively to client locations both nationally and internationally.

Technological Environment

Advertising sales agents work with computers, the Internet, and word processing, graphic design, and spreadsheet software. They must familiarize themselves with clients' products as needed, which often involves using a new product on a daily basis for a short period of time to evaluate its features.

EDUCATION, TRAINING, AND ADVANCEMENT

High School/Secondary

High school students interested in becoming an advertising sales agent may find it useful to study art, business, communications, English, foreign languages, and applied math. It is beneficial for interested students to take summer jobs with advertising agencies and work on high school publications such as the yearbook and newspaper. Participation in extracurricular organizations geared towards marketing or advertising will give students some familiarity with business situations and formulating marketing solutions.

Suggested High School Subjects
- Applied Math
- Arts
- Business
- College Preparatory
- Composition
- English
- Graphic Communications
- Journalism
- Mathematics
- Merchandising
- Psychology
- Social Studies
- Speech

Famous First

The first banner ads on the Internet appeared on the site hotwired.com starting on October 25, 1994. The format used (460 x 60 pixels) subsequently became the industry standard. The inaugural banner was for the telecommunications company AT&T. It asked, "Have you ever clicked your mouse right here?"

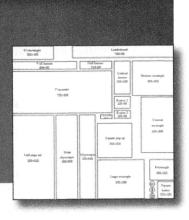

College/Postsecondary

Postsecondary students interested in pursuing a career as an advertising sales agent will benefit from building a foundation in communications and marketing courses. Other classes should include journalism, advertising, print layout, graphic design, new media, market research, economics, psychology, marketing communications, and advertising history, theory, and ethics. Postsecondary students can gain practical experience through internships at advertising agencies or with any company that has a marketing department or advertises. Entry-level opportunities in advertising or marketing departments give students hands-on experience that can help them learn new skills and make them attractive to future employers.

Related College Majors

- Advertising
- Business & Personal Services Marketing Operations
- Communications, General
- Mass Communications
- Public Relations & Organizational Communications

Adult Job Seekers

Adults interested in working as advertising sales agents can look for entry-level, part-time, or seasonal jobs in the advertising, marketing, or sales fields. It may also be useful to obtain practical experience through a specialized education, volunteer experience, internships, or mentors in professional advertising organizations who can provide guidance about existing career opportunities.

Professional Certification and Licensure

There are no licensing requirements for advertising sales agents. Prominent industry organizations give annual awards to recognize highly successful agency campaigns.

Additional Requirements

Prospective advertising sales agents should have excellent interpersonal skills and be able to work independently and cooperate with others in a team environment. They must be able to influence others, use their knowledge of consumer behavior to influence buying habits, sell their ideas to current and prospective clients, and communicate clearly. Creativity and the desire to stay informed about trends in popular culture are all assets in this occupation.

Fun Fact

Online ad revenue escalated by more than $31 billion between 2011 and 2013 and is on track to double between 2011 and 2016.

Source: http://blog.wishpond.com/post/70908774557/online-advertising-25-stats-and-facts-that-break-it

EARNINGS AND ADVANCEMENT

Earnings depend on the size and geographic location of the advertising agency, type of accounts handled and gross earnings of the agency. Earnings are also based on the employee's educational background, talent and experience. Median annual earnings of advertising sales agents were $47,890, including commissions, in 2014. The lowest ten percent earned less than $23,050, and the highest ten percent earned more than $113,120 a year.

Advertising sales agents may receive paid vacations, holidays, and sick days; life and health insurance; and retirement benefits. These are usually paid by the employer.

Metropolitan Areas with the Highest Employment Level in this Occupation

Metropolitan area	Employment	Employment per thousand jobs	Annual mean wage
New York-White Plains-Wayne, NY-NJ	20,190	3.75	$88,710
Chicago-Joliet-Naperville, IL	8,110	2.16	$61,980
Los Angeles-Long Beach-Glendale, CA	7,480	1.84	$78,850
Atlanta-Sandy Springs-Marietta, GA	5,710	2.39	$78,510
Tampa-St. Petersburg-Clearwater, FL	3,000	2.54	$47,430
Philadelphia, PA	2,920	1.57	$57,210
San Francisco-San Mateo-Redwood City, CA	2,520	2.32	$71,770
Miami-Miami Beach-Kendall, FL	2,100	2.00	$66,390
Dallas-Plano-Irving, TX	2,090	0.93	$59,320
Boston-Cambridge-Quincy, MA	2,040	1.14	$76,770

Source: Bureau of Labor Statistics

EMPLOYMENT AND OUTLOOK

There were about 168,000 advertising sales agents employed nationally in 2014. Employment is expected to decline somewhat through the year 2024, which means employment is projected to decrease around 3 percent. Employment of advertising sales agents is strongly affected by general business conditions and the state of the economy. Some growth is expected to occur in the areas of online advertising sales and cable television sales, while less demand is expected in the newspaper, periodical and directory publishing industries.

Employment Trend, Projected 2014–24

Sales representatives, services: 7%

Total, all occupations: 7%

Advertising sales agents: -3%

Note: "All Occupations" includes all occupations in the U.S. Economy. Source: U.S. Bureau of Labor Statistics, Employment Projections Program

Related Occupations
- Advertising & Marketing Manager
- Advertising Director
- Copywriter
- Online Merchant
- Public Relations Specialist
- Real Estate Sales Agent
- Services Sales Representative

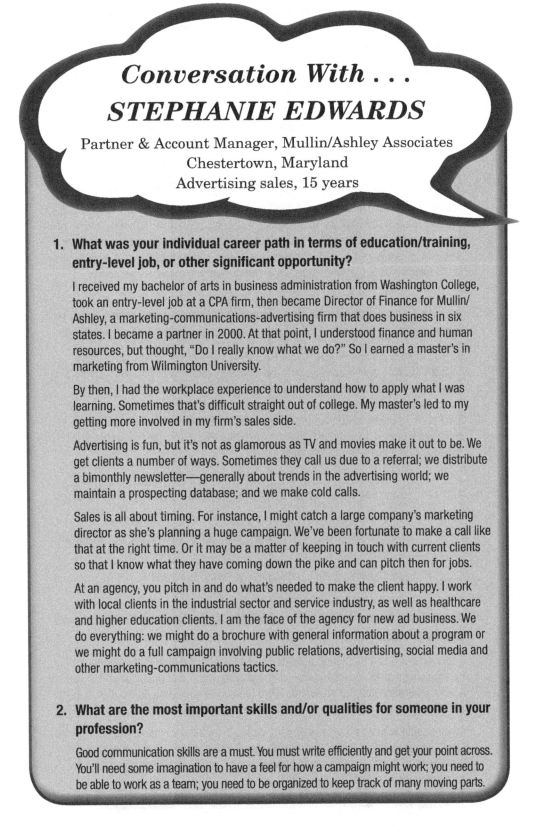

Conversation With . . .
STEPHANIE EDWARDS

Partner & Account Manager, Mullin/Ashley Associates
Chestertown, Maryland
Advertising sales, 15 years

1. What was your individual career path in terms of education/training, entry-level job, or other significant opportunity?

I received my bachelor of arts in business administration from Washington College, took an entry-level job at a CPA firm, then became Director of Finance for Mullin/Ashley, a marketing-communications-advertising firm that does business in six states. I became a partner in 2000. At that point, I understood finance and human resources, but thought, "Do I really know what we do?" So I earned a master's in marketing from Wilmington University.

By then, I had the workplace experience to understand how to apply what I was learning. Sometimes that's difficult straight out of college. My master's led to my getting more involved in my firm's sales side.

Advertising is fun, but it's not as glamorous as TV and movies make it out to be. We get clients a number of ways. Sometimes they call us due to a referral; we distribute a bimonthly newsletter—generally about trends in the advertising world; we maintain a prospecting database; and we make cold calls.

Sales is all about timing. For instance, I might catch a large company's marketing director as she's planning a huge campaign. We've been fortunate to make a call like that at the right time. Or it may be a matter of keeping in touch with current clients so that I know what they have coming down the pike and can pitch then for jobs.

At an agency, you pitch in and do what's needed to make the client happy. I work with local clients in the industrial sector and service industry, as well as healthcare and higher education clients. I am the face of the agency for new ad business. We do everything: we might do a brochure with general information about a program or we might do a full campaign involving public relations, advertising, social media and other marketing-communications tactics.

2. What are the most important skills and/or qualities for someone in your profession?

Good communication skills are a must. You must write efficiently and get your point across. You'll need some imagination to have a feel for how a campaign might work; you need to be able to work as a team; you need to be organized to keep track of many moving parts.

You also need the confidence to talk to anyone at any level, from a secretary to a CFO to someone on a board of directors. The way to gain confidence is to know your material. Learn as much about an industry as you can before you pitch them. It's like preparing for a job interview.

3. What do you wish you had known going into this profession?

The importance of marketing because it's the basis of all companies. Everyone is selling something.

4. Are there many job opportunities in your profession? In what specific areas?

Advertising sales fall under the marketing-communications umbrella, and this is a growing arena. If you work for an ad agency, you'll deal with many industries and services and will need to learn about all of them. Starting out, it might be easier to be an internal marketing executive for a single company. In addition, you can do special event planning, public relations, sales, graphic design, web design, and, of course, social media.

5. How do you see your profession changing in the next five years, what role will technology play in those changes, and what skills will be required?

Social media plays a huge role, given Facebook, Twitter, Snapchat—all of these apps are used to get information out and new apps will arrive. You need to stay current. We use different platforms here to keep up with the latest technology and understand how our ads and other products work on everything from an old Blackberry to the newest iPhone. We deal in a wide range of demographics, so I don't see email going away. For the same reason, although print will continue to diminish, it will not entirely disappear.

6. What do you enjoy most about your job? What do you enjoy least about your job?

I enjoy the ever-changing nature of my work; I would be bored doing the same thing every day.

I don't mind cold-calling, but it's not something I want to do 9 to 5.

7. Can you suggest a valuable "try this" for students considering a career in your profession?

If your school has a marketing program, see if they have a club that does marketing for the college or local businesses—some do. Also, take that public speaking course! As the generation coming up spends more time communicating on devices, face-to-face time may be challenging for them, but you must have that skill.

An internship with an ad agency or company with an internal marketing department would be great. If you already have a job, see if you can help your company with their website, Twitter or Facebook. I guarantee if they think they're going to get something for free, they'll let you do it!

SELECTED SCHOOLS

Most colleges and universities offer programs related to careers in business, advertising, or sales; a variety of them have more specialized programs. For a list of top schools in sales education, visit the website of the Sales Education Foundation (see below).

MORE INFORMATION

Advertising Age
711 3rd Avenue
New York, NY 10017-4036
212.210.0100
www.adage.com

Advertising Research Foundation
432 Park Avenue South, 6th Floor
New York, NY 10016-8013
212.751.5656
thearf.org

Advertising Women of New York
25 West 45th Street, Suite 403
New York, NY 10036
212.221.7969
www.awny.org

American Advertising Federation
1101 Vermont Avenue, NW, Suite 500
Washington, DC 20005-6306
800.999.2231
www.aaf.org

American Association of Advertising Agencies
405 Lexington Avenue, 18th Floor
New York, NY 10174-1801
212.682.2500
www.aaaa.org

Association for Women in Communications
3337 Duke Street
Alexandria, VA 22314
703.370.7436
www.womcom.org

Association of National Advertisers
708 Third Avenue, 33rd Floor
New York, NY 10017-4270
212.697.5950
www.ana.net

Retail Advertising and Marketing Association
325 7th Street NW, Suite 1100
Washington, DC 20004
202.661.3052
www.rama-nrf.org

Sales Education Foundation
3123 Research Boulevard, Suite 250
Dayton, OH 45420
937.610.4369
www.salesfoundation.org

Susan Williams/Editor

Automobile Salesperson

Snapshot

Career Cluster: Business, Sales & Service

Interests: Automobiles, customer service, sales

Earnings (Yearly Average): $44,232

Employment & Outlook: Average Growth Expected

OVERVIEW

Sphere of Work

Automobile salespeople are responsible for the sale of vehicles, either new or used, to customers. Though some sales may be straightforward, salespeople often need a wide variety of skills and an intimate knowledge of their product in order to complete a sale. Customer-service skills are most important, but an automobile salesperson must also be able to estimate a vehicle's trade-in value, describe complex features to customers with diverse backgrounds and experience, and complete complex financing and sale paperwork.

Work Environment

Automobile salespeople work in new or used automobile dealerships. They may work in a brightly lit, climate-controlled sales floor or in an outdoor lot. Most salespeople spend some time indoors interacting with their customers, and then continue the sales process outdoors, where most sale vehicles are kept. They are often called on to accompany customers on test-drives. Automobile salespeople have periods of time when they must work very quickly; they may also have significant downtime between sales, during which they may be asked to complete other tasks on behalf of the dealership.

Profile

Working Conditions: Work both Indoors and Outdoors
Physical Strength: Light Work
Education Needs: On-The-Job Training, High School Diploma or G.E.D.
Licensure/Certification: Usually Not Required
Opportunities For Experience: Part-Time Work
Holland Interest Score*: ESR

* See Appendix A

Occupation Interest

Individuals drawn to the profession of automobile sales tend to have a strong personal interest in automobiles and an equally strong interest in customer service and sales. They enjoy the process of persuading customers to purchase their product. Since automobile sales can be very lucrative, highly motivated individuals with excellent verbal skills and a focus on customer service tend to be drawn to it.

A Day in the Life—Duties and Responsibilities

The daily duties of an automobile salesperson include greeting customers as they enter the dealership, then assessing the reason for their visit and how they can best be served. Salespeople ascertain the general type and price of vehicle a customer is considering purchasing and whether he or she plans to trade in a vehicle. They typically lead customers through several vehicles, pointing out features and providing performance information about various models.

If the customer shows interest in one or several vehicles, the salesperson may first gather documents to verify the customer's ability to drive a vehicle and then accompany the customer on a test-drive, asking questions to ascertain the suitability of the vehicle to the customer and his or her level of interest. The customer may test-drive several vehicles before one is selected. If the customer chooses not to purchase a vehicle from the facility, the salesperson may gather information about what features or services caused the decision.

If the customer wants to buy an automobile, the salesperson will often offer a slightly discounted price, and then negotiate with the customer to find a mutually agreeable price. Often, service agreements, additional vehicle options, and the value of a trade-in are factored into this final price. Some dealerships have begun responding to customers' desire to avoid negotiating by offering a fixed price for vehicles. When the price has been settled on, the salesperson often becomes a financial advisor as well, offering financing options and payment plans to suit the customer's budget. If there is a separate finance department, the salesperson is expected to deliver the customer there with all of the necessary information. Once a sale has been made, the automobile salesperson will complete all sales orders and paperwork according to local laws and procedures established by the dealership. Automobile salespeople may also be responsible for preparing vehicles for customer pickup and orienting the owner to his or her new vehicle.

Duties and Responsibilities

- Determining what kind of automobile will meet the customer's needs
- Pointing out features of cars or trucks
- Appraising the value of a vehicle to be taken in trade
- Computing the total product sales price, including sales tax, trade-in allowance, license fee and discount
- Preparing the sales contract and obtaining necessary information for completing a credit application

OCCUPATION SPECIALTIES

Automotive-Leasing Sales Representatives

Automotive-Leasing Sales Representatives sell automotive-leasing services to businesses and individuals. They recommend the types and numbers of vehicles that would be needed to do the job satisfactorily and economically.

Automobile Accessories Salespersons

Automobile Accessories Salespersons sell auto supplies and accessories, such as batteries, tires, mufflers, and headlights.

WORK ENVIRONMENT

Relevant Skills and Abilities

Communication Skills
- Persuading others
- Speaking effectively

Interpersonal/Social Skills
- Cooperating with others
- Working as a member of a team

Organization & Management Skills
- Managing time
- Meeting goals and deadlines

Technical Skills
- Applying the technology to a task
- Performing scientific, mathematical and technical work

Physical Environment

Automobile salespeople generally work in new- and used-car dealerships. They often work in indoor areas that are well lit and temperature controlled, though they usually have to spend some time outside in the lot. They must be able to stand for long periods of time and are expected to maintain a professional appearance, though more casual dress has become common at some dealerships. Many large dealerships are open on weekends and in the evening to provide greater customer service, so nontraditional hours may be required.

Human Environment

Automobile salespeople work closely with the public and have many opportunities for interaction during the workday. Advisers interact primarily with customers, but they may also interact with service technicians and other sales personnel throughout the workday. Physical proximity to others is common as well. Excellent verbal skills are required.

Technological Environment

Automobile salespeople deal with a variety of databases that manage inventory, gather and catalog customer information, and provide financial resources. They also must be familiar with advances in automobile technology.

EDUCATION, TRAINING, AND ADVANCEMENT

High School/Secondary

Students interested in a career as an automobile salesperson should have a strong interest in automobiles as a hobby, as well as a solid background in communications, English, and math. Computer skills and marketing classes are also useful.

Suggested High School Subjects
- Auto Service Technology
- Business Math
- English
- Merchandising
- Speech

Famous First

The first car with a body made of plastic laminated fiberglass instead of metal was the 1953 Chevrolet Corvette. The curb weight of the car was 2,900 pounds, considerably less than if the body had been made out of metal. The Corvette was also one of the first cars to include a powerglide automatic transmission as standard equipment. The list price of the car was $3,250 (or about $29,000 in 2015 dollars).

Postsecondary

Though a postsecondary degree is not generally a requirement for employment as an automobile salesperson, there are sales training courses available online and through technical and community colleges.

Related College Majors
- Business
- Business & Personal Services Marketing Operations
- General Retailing & Wholesaling Operations & Skills
- General Selling Skills & Sales Operations
- Vehicle & Petroleum Products Marketing Operations

Adult Job Seekers

Most adult job seekers in this field benefit from on-the-job training. They may move into this position from another job in the automobile industry. Many large dealerships have their own in-house training programs that focus on the particular models that they sell.

Professional Certification and Licensure

A valid driver's license and good driving record is the only nonnegotiable certification required for this position. Training and internal certification generally takes place within the dealership structure.

Additional Requirements

Automobile salespeople must be able to handle demanding customers in a fast-paced environment. They often work more than a standard forty-hour week and are sometimes required to work on weekends and evenings. Excellent verbal and strong writing skills are crucial.

Fun Fact

Cars were almost called "autowain" or "autotruck" until the word "automobile" began appearing regularly after an 1890 New York Times editorial debating what to call the "new fangled" vehicles.

Source: http://autoweek.com/article/car-news/where-did-word-automobile-come and http://jalopnik.com/5972932/the-word-automobile-was-first-used-in-the-new-york-times-114-years-ago-today

EARNINGS AND ADVANCEMENT

Earnings depend on individual ability and experience, geographic location and dealership size. Payments are either by straight commission, salary plus commission, or straight salary. In 2012, the average annual salary for automobile salespersons was $44,232.

Automobile salespersons may receive paid vacations, holidays, and sick days; life and health insurance; and retirement benefits. These are usually paid by the employer. They may also receive a company car and car discounts.

EMPLOYMENT AND OUTLOOK

Retail salespersons, of which automobile salesperson are a part, held about 4.5 million jobs in 2012. Employment of automobile salespersons is expected to grow about as fast as the average for all occupations through the year 2024, which means employment is projected to increase 5 percent to 10 percent. Rising population and personal incomes will lead to increased demand for automobiles. However, this demand may fluctuate from year to year because of changing economic conditions and consumer preferences.

Employment Trend, Projected 2014–24

Parts salespersons: 7%

Retail salespersons: 7%

Total, all occupations: 7%

Sales and related occupations: 5%

Note: "All Occupations" includes all occupations in the U.S. Economy. Source: U.S. Bureau of Labor Statistics, Employment Projections Program

Related Occupations
- Automotive Parts Service Clerk
- Automotive Service Advisor
- Insurance Sales Agent
- Manufacturers Representative
- Real Estate Sales Agent
- Retail Salesperson
- Sales Engineer
- Service Sales Representative
- Technical Sales Representative

Conversation With . . .
RICHARD TRAN

Motoring Advisor, MINI of Peabody
Peabody, Massachusetts
Automobile salesperson, 14 years

1. What was your individual career path in terms of education/training, entry-level job, or other significant opportunity?

I was in college majoring in accounting and found myself in need of a vehicle. I was doing some accounting for a restaurant, but I was so excited about the auto industry that I decided to apply for a sales position. In the many years I've been in this industry, I've worked in different capacities, from sales to customer service to marketing and management. I've found that because of the flexible schedule, a sales position suits my lifestyle and my desire for work/life balance.

2. What are the most important skills and/or qualities for someone in your profession?

Attitude is the most important quality. And what I mean by this is that someone in my profession will be more successful if he/she is driven to succeed and can handle lost opportunities well. Not everyone will want the product or service you are providing. This sometimes can have a negative effect on your self-esteem. But you cannot let this affect your interactions with your clients. The automotive industry is an innovative field. Keeping well informed with regards to new technology and how it will benefit your client is key. And, lastly, communication skills—asking the right questions and knowing when not to speak—are very important to your success.

3. What do you wish you had known going into this profession?

Time management is a skill that I've improved on over the years. Being in sales, you are essentially your own boss. You control the pace of your success. There will be times when you work more than you thought humanly possible. Being organized and setting up realistic expectations will benefit not only you, but also your client.

4. Are there many job opportunities in your profession? In what specific areas?

There are many opportunities to grow within this profession. There are various roles within any car dealership. I work for a Mini Cooper dealer. Within our sales department, we have sales advisors, product knowledge specialists, customer service representatives, assistant managers, finance managers, sales managers, a general sales manager and a general manager.

5. How do you see your profession changing in the next five years? What role will technology play in those changes, and what skills will be required?

These next five years will be very exciting. A lot of research and development goes into what consumers want in their vehicles. With the growing trend of staying connected, my job will require staying in the forefront of integrated technologies, such as migration of smart phones, wearable technologies, and smart home devices. Safety will always be an integral part of vehicles. We are seeing the early stages of vehicle automation. And more importantly than ever, the environmental impact of vehicles will be a huge influence on this industry. Being well-versed in current technologies on top of having great sales skills will benefit you in terms of loyal clients, repeat business and expanding your portfolio.

6. What do you enjoy most about your job? What do you enjoy least about your job?

I'm very fortunate to love the product I sell and the people that I work alongside with and for. Without these components, it would be very difficult for me to enjoy what I do. What I love, though, is making clients happy. Vehicles are not just a mode of transportation. They bring a sense of enjoyment and also are a form of expression. I see big smiles and get to hear great stories about adventures in their vehicles every day from customers and to me, it means the world.

What I don't like about my job is something you can say about many jobs: I work easily 50 to 60 hours a week. Being adaptable to clients' needs and schedule are often needed to get the job done.

7. Can you suggest a valuable "try this" for students considering a career in your profession?

Most of us have experienced car shopping and some of us hate it. There's a huge stigma that car sales is a very deceitful profession, but the fact that information is readily available to anyone willing to do a little research has changed the industry. Part of being a good salesperson is knowing what it's like to shop for vehicles and I encourage you to go along with relatives or friends when they're buying a car or shop for one for yourself. Auto dealers are like any other type of retail business. I would also encourage you to experience a retail environment that has set a standard for quality service. I personally have had amazing service provided to me at The Ritz-Carlton, Disney World, and on a Royal Caribbean cruise. Being in sales, the primary thing that is going to separate you from the rest is the service you provide, because most likely you will be providing a product that can be purchased in many other locations.

SELECTED SCHOOLS

Most colleges and universities offer programs related to careers in business, marketing, or sales; a variety of them have more specialized programs. For a list of schools with sales programs, visit the website of the Sales Education Foundation (see below).

MORE INFORMATION

National Automobile Dealers Association
8400 Westpark Drive
McLean, VA 22102
703.821.7000
www.nada.org

National Independent Automobile Dealers Association
2521 Brown Boulevard
Arlington, TX 76006
800.682.3837
www.niada.com

Sales Education Foundation
3123 Research Boulevard, Suite 250
Dayton, OH 45420
937.610.4369
www.salesfoundation.org

Bethany Groff/Editor

Cashier

Snapshot

Career Cluster(s): Marketing, Sales & Service

Interests: Mathematics, working with money, communicating with others, enjoying a routine

Earnings (Yearly Average): $19,060

Employment & Outlook: Slower than Average Growth Expected

OVERVIEW

Sphere of Work

Cashiers, also known as sales associates or clerks, process money transactions in businesses such as grocery stores, gas stations, department stores, theaters, parking garages, and restaurants. Cashiers greet customers, process product returns, scan product bar codes or Universal Product Codes (UPC), calculate money and taxes owed, make change, accept coupons, issue receipts, bag purchased merchandise, and handle cash, credit card, debit card, and check transactions.

Work Environment

Cashiers work in customer service areas of businesses. Cashiers generally stand throughout their shifts at assigned stations or checkout areas. Cashiers may work as full-time members of retail work teams or as part-time or shift workers. Overtime on weekends and evenings may be required during periods of increased business. Cashiers are at some risk from job-related robberies as well as work-related injuries, such as back strain and repetitive stress injuries.

Profile

Working Conditions: Work Indoors
Education Needs: On-The-Job Training, High School Diploma or G.E.D., High School Diploma with Technical Education
Licensure/Certification: Usually Not Required
Opportunities for Experience: Apprenticeship, Military Service, Part-Time Work
Holland Interest Score*: CES, CSE

* See Appendix A

Occupation Interest

Prospective cashiers tend to be friendly, trustworthy, and competent individuals. Those who excel as cashiers exhibit traits such as patience, honesty, approachability, and efficiency. Cashiers should enjoy customer interaction and be able to stand for long periods. A preference for routines and proficiency with arithmetic are also important. Since there are minimal educational requirements for cashiering, this occupation may be an appealing entry-level position for those who wish to work in retail settings.

A Day in the Life—Duties and Responsibilities

The daily occupational duties and responsibilities of cashiers will be determined by the type of retail environment, the type of products sold, and the geographic location of the business. In general, a cashier is assigned one register or checkout area for the duration of their shift. The cashier is responsible for keeping the station clean and orderly during their work shift. Cashiers greet customers as customers approach the checkout area.

In businesses where customers buy many products and goods, such as grocery stores and department stores, cashiers scan product Universal Product Codes or barcodes, weigh items on scales when appropriate, process product returns, calculate money owed, make change, calculate tax, accept coupons, issue receipts, bag purchased merchandise, and handle cash, check, credit card, food stamp, and debit card check transactions. In businesses where customers self-serve or buy single items, such as movie theater ticket booths or gas stations, cashiers tally the sale, authorize a gas pump or operate ticket issuing machine, tell the customer what they owe, handle monetary transactions, and issue receipts.

Cashiers may also be required to assist customers, stock shelves, price items, resolve customer complaints, explain store policy, clean floors and windows, and prepare bank deposits. At the end of the shift, cashiers are usually responsible for tallying sales and checking their total against the day's credit card receipts and cash tray.

Duties and Responsibilities

- Recording sales and taxes on cash registers
- Clearing, totaling and balancing cash registers
- Accepting payment
- Issuing receipts
- Cashing checks
- Completing credit card charge transactions for customers
- Redeeming coupons
- Checking credit of customers
- Preparing bank deposits
- Answering routine questions
- Weighing and bagging purchases
- Restocking and marking counter items
- Operating office machines

WORK ENVIRONMENT

Physical Environment

Cashiers work in customer service areas of businesses such as grocery stores, gas stations, department stores, theaters, parking garages, and restaurants. Cashiers generally stand throughout their shifts in assigned stations or checkout areas. Their work environments are generally brightly lit, loud, and busy.

Relevant Skills and Abilities

Communication Skills
- Editing written information
- Speaking effectively
- Writing concisely

Interpersonal/Social Skills
- Being sensitive to others
- Cooperating with others

Organization & Management Skills
- Following instructions
- Paying attention to and handling details
- Performing duties which change frequently
- Performing routine work

Research & Planning Skills
- Using logical reasoning

Technical Skills
- Performing scientific, mathematical and technical work
- Working with machines, tools or other objects

Human Environment

Cashiers interact with customers, supervisors, and other store workers, such as supervisors and stock clerks, throughout their shifts. Despite the pace of the work, cashiers should be polite and patient with customers and accept direction from supervisors.

Technological Environment

Cashiers often use automated cash registers, credit card scanners, change-making machines, telephones, barcode scanners, scales, and calculators to complete their work. Some cashiers also need to know how to operate business-specific equipment, such as gas pumps or ticket machines.

EDUCATION, TRAINING, AND ADVANCEMENT

High School/Secondary

High school students interested in becoming a cashier should prepare themselves by building an ease with numbers. Typing, bookkeeping, business, and mathematics classes will provide a strong foundation for work as a cashier. Due to the diversity of cashier responsibilities, interested high school students may benefit from seasonal or part-time work with local retail businesses.

Suggested High School Subjects
- Bookkeeping
- Business & Computer Technology
- Business English
- Business Math
- Merchandising

Famous First

The first cash register was invented in 1879 by James J. Ritty of Dayton, Ohio. Although Ritty's first model was not accurate, in the following year he developed a model that was more reliable. In 1884 Ritty's operation was taken over by the National Cash Register Company (NCR), which has remained one of the dominant players in the industry (although in 2009 NCR moved its operations to Atlanta, Georgia).

Postsecondary

Prospective cashiers are not required to have formal postsecondary training. Since experience is more important than educational attainment, high school graduates can gain potential advantage in their future job searches by securing part-time or seasonal employment with local retail businesses. Some may even find full-time employment as a cashier directly following graduation from high school.

Adult Job Seekers

Adults seeking employment as cashiers should have at least a high school diploma or its equivalent. Most employers offer on-the-job training for newly hired cashiers. Work experience is often the most important qualification for a cashier. Experienced cashiers may be able to find clerical or supervisory positions. Professional retail worker associations can help members with job finding and networking.

Professional Certification and Licensure

Certification and licensure is not required for cashiers. Some employers may require fidelity bonding for their cashiers to ensure against theft.

Additional Requirements

Honesty and professional ethics are required of cashiers who have access to confidential credit card information and large amounts of money. Membership in professional retail unions, such as the United Food and Commercial Workers International Union, can provide job protection measures and benefits.

Fun Fact

The youngest of five brothers, James Ritty of Dayton, Ohio, invented the first cash register in 1878, with the help of one of his brothers, of course.

Source: http://www.ncr.org.uk/page110.html

EARNINGS AND ADVANCEMENT

Earnings range from minimum wage to several times that amount, and depend on the type, size, geographic location, and union affiliation of the employer, and the employee's experience and seniority. Wages tend to be higher in areas where there is intense competition for workers. In 2014, median annual earnings for cashiers were $19,060. The lowest ten percent earned less than $16,610, and the highest ten percent earned more than $28,030.

Cashiers may receive paid vacations, holidays, and sick days; life and health insurance; and retirement benefits. These are usually paid by the employer. Those working in retail establishments often receive discounts on purchases and those in restaurants may receive free or low-cost meals.

Metropolitan Areas with the Highest
Employment Level in this Occupation

Metropolitan area	Employment	Employment per thousand jobs	Annual mean wage
New York-White Plains-Wayne, NY-NJ	104,420	19.37	$22,100
Los Angeles-Long Beach-Glendale, CA	94,180	23.22	$21,820
Chicago-Joliet-Naperville, IL	82,770	22.06	$21,950
Houston-Sugar Land-Baytown, TX	59,730	21.01	$20,190
Atlanta-Sandy Springs-Marietta, GA	52,670	22.06	$19,400
Washington-Arlington-Alexandria, DC-VA-MD-WV	51,270	21.56	$22,070
Philadelphia, PA	44,350	23.82	$21,020
Dallas-Plano-Irving, TX	42,020	18.77	$19,880
Baltimore-Towson, MD	40,120	31.00	$20,610
Phoenix-Mesa-Glendale, AZ	39,150	21.44	$21,330

Source: Bureau of Labor Statistics

EMPLOYMENT AND OUTLOOK

There were approximately 3.4 million cashiers employed nationally in 2014, making it one of the largest occupations in the country. Around one-fourth of all jobs were in grocery stores. Large numbers were also employed by department stores, gasoline service stations, drug stores, restaurants and other retail establishments. Employment of cashiers is expected to grow slower than the average for all occupations through the year 2024, which means employment will increase 0 percent to 5 percent. The rising popularity of purchasing goods online will reduce the employment growth of cashiers, although many customers will always prefer the traditional method of purchasing goods at stores. Also, the growing use of self-service check-out systems, especially at grocery stores, should have a continued negative effect on the employment of cashiers. These self-checkout systems may outnumber checkouts with cashiers in the future in many establishments.

Employment Trend, Projected 2014–24

Total, all occupations: 7%

Retail sales workers: 5%

Cashiers: 2%

Note: "All Occupations" includes all occupations in the U.S. Economy. Source: U.S. Bureau of Labor Statistics, Employment Projections Program

Related Occupations
- Automotive Service Attendant
- Bank Teller
- Billing Clerk
- Bookkeeper & Accounting Clerk
- Counter & Rental Clerk
- Payroll Clerk

Conversation With . . .
SHERRIE SEWELL

Cashier, MOM's Organic Market
Bowie, Maryland
Cashier, 5 years

1. What was your individual career path in terms of education/training, entry-level job, or other significant opportunity?

I was an early education major at Bowie State University, then spent thirty years in public school classrooms in Prince George's County. I taught children from Head Start to third grade. I retired in 2006, and for the first two years had the joy of babysitting my grandchildren. The third year, my mother was terminally ill.

The next year, I thought, "What do I do now?" I started thinking about places I might like to work. I'd always been fascinated with the people who worked the registers; it looked like a fun job. One day when I was in the process of applying for jobs, I looked across a shopping center and saw the MOM's sign, with its big red apple. As I teacher, I thought, "Oh, it's a school supply store." I went home and researched it, and liked that this is a grocery business focused on sustainability and recycling. They stand for something.

The money was a bonus. For me, after thirty years in the classroom with daily structure, having something to do, and interacting with people—I needed that. At the same time, at this stage in my life, I like the flexibility. Working here has made me more aware of trying to eat better, and of spreading the word.

2. What are the most important skills and/or qualities for someone in your profession?

When you're dealing with a variety of people, you have to know how to get along with others. You need to know how to read people, and how to interact with them. I have an old-school philosophy about not being too quick to react. One of my favorite books when I was in the classroom was called "It Could Be Worse."

3. What do you wish you had known going into this profession?

How many changes I would experience. I've encountered and worked with more than 100 people. This is a fluid work environment. People come in and move up, or leave to do other things. It's important to be flexible, to not get too attached to a particular group of people, and to learn to get along with everybody.

4. Are there many job opportunities in your profession? In what specific areas?

I've watched a lot of young people come in and move up to shift manager and into manager-in-training programs. They can cross-train across all aspects of this company. I would think you'd have that opportunity in other grocery or retail companies. If you're interested in running a business, you could take college courses on the fundamentals of running a business while in a job like this, which allows you to see how retail functions and how somebody has created a business model.

5. How do you see your profession changing in the next five years, what role will technology play in those changes, and what skills will be required?

Computer skills will always be required because registers are computerized. Inventory is also computerized; grocery buyers deal with that. Some stores use scanners now at self-checkout lines. Still, I think there will always be a need for the person at the register due to things like price discrepancies that may require human interaction to correct—as well as the inevitable computer malfunction.

6. What do you enjoy most about your job? What do you enjoy least about your job?

I really enjoy the youth and energy of the people I work with. It keeps me tied to my previous profession of seeing young people grow up and move through the ranks.

I least like the inconsistency in my schedule; I might work mornings one week and night shifts the next. But that's part of being flexible, and we receive our schedules two weeks in advance.

7. Can you suggest a valuable "try this" for students considering a career in your profession?

If you're interested in organics, think about working on a farm. Some MOM's workers have taken positions at an organic farm and they really know about the products.

MORE INFORMATION

Association for Convenience and Petroleum Retailing
1600 Duke Street, 7th Floor
Alexandria, VA 22314
703.684.3600
www.nacsonline.com

Food Marketing Institute
2345 Crystal Drive, Suite 800
Arlington, VA 22202
202.452.8444
www.fmi.org

National Grocers Association
1005 North Glebe Road, Suite 250
Arlington, VA 22201-5758
703.516.0700
www.nationalgrocers.org

Service Station Dealers of America & Allied Trades
1532 Pointer Ridge Place, Suite E
Bowie, MD 20716
301.390.4405
www.ssda-at.org

United Food & Commercial Workers International Union
1775 K Street, NW
Washington, DC 20006
202.223.3111
www.ufcw.org

Simone Isadora Flynn/Editor

Customer Service Representative

Snapshot

Career Cluster: Business Administration; Communications & Media; Sales & Marketing

Interests: Talking on the telephone, interacting with people, handling conflict

Earnings (Yearly Average): $30,870

Employment & Outlook: Average Growth Expected

OVERVIEW

Sphere of Work

Customer service representatives provide a wide range of support to customers and serve as the primary point of contact between a company and its customer base. They spend the work day responding accurately to customer questions and inquiries, solving customer problems, and handling customer complaints. Customer service representatives are found in a very broad range of industries and in any context where an organization provides product or service support to its customers. For this reason, customer service representatives are usually well-trained in their company's products and services and

policies and procedures. Many also perform administrative tasks such as placing orders and processing invoices and returns.

Work Environment

Customer service representatives generally work in office environments. Most work in call centers, but many will also work in retail and other commercial environments. Customer service representatives interact constantly with customers. In most cases, this involves phone calls, but it may also involve writing or assisting customers in person. This may include other customer service representatives and supervisors, as well as people from other departments. Customer service representatives engaged in full-time work may expect to work approximately forty hours per week, but work hours may vary significantly depending on the employer and industry. Extended customer service hours usually mean that a customer service representative will work some evening or weekend shifts. Part-time roles are also available.

Profile

Working Conditions: Work Indoors
Physical Strength: Light Work
Education Needs: On-The-Job Training
High School Diploma or G.E.D.
Licensure/Certification: Usually Not
Required
Physical Abilities Not Required: No
Heavy Labor
Opportunities For Experience: Part-
Time Work
Holland Interest Score*: CES

* See Appendix A

Occupation Interest

This occupation suits people who enjoy interacting with other people on a daily basis. Those attracted to customer service roles generally have good communication skills and find satisfaction in interacting with people. They should be able to demonstrate patience and empathy when dealing with customer complaints or questions. In some cases, customer service representatives may also be required to be highly proficient or knowledgeable in a certain technical field (for example, customer service representatives who provide computing helpdesk support).

A Day in the Life—Duties and Responsibilities

TA customer service representative's work involves assisting and supporting customers with their inquiries. This may include answering questions, providing technical help and advice, processing orders, taking payment information, responding to complaints, forwarding customers to supervisors for difficult inquiries, and performing other tasks as needed.

This is a role which requires patience, empathy, and tact, especially when dealing with customer complaints. It also requires the ability to solve problems. In many instances, customer service representatives must be able to deal with a large volume of customer inquiries, especially if they are employed in call centers or similar environments.

Customer interactions may occur in person, on the telephone, and/or via email and instant messaging. In the course of resolving customer inquiries they may be searching for and entering information into databases, preparing letters and emails, and using the Internet.

Customer service representatives may expect to communicate and collaborate with a variety of colleagues and/or third party vendors. Interorganizational coordination may be required among a variety of departments and the customer service representative may be required to attend meetings or regularly liaise with other individuals and groups. They may have to attend periodic training to familiarize themselves with new company products and policies

Duties and Responsibilities

- Taking customer calls
- Informing customers and potential customers of company services
- Demonstrating company goodwill
- Tracing through complicated billing or shipping problems
- Investigating service difficulties and providing solutions
- Solving customer problems

WORK ENVIRONMENT

Physical Environment

Office settings predominate. Many industries employ customer service representatives, and the specific physical environment will be influenced by the size and type of employer. There is a trend among some national and global companies to consolidate their customer support services at a single location. These work environments are often call centers.

Relevant Skills and Abilities

Communication Skills
- Listening attentively
- Speaking effectively

Interpersonal/Social Skills
- Being able to work independently
- Cooperating with others
- Working as a member of a team

Organization & Management Skills
- Managing conflict

Human Environment

Customer service representative roles demand strong communication skills. This job involves almost constant interaction with people, so patience, courtesy, and attention to detail are highly regarded. Some customer service representative roles include face-to-face contact with customers while others may involve only telephone or Internet-mediated contact.

Technological Environment

Daily operations will demand the use of standard office technologies, including telephone, e-mail, photocopiers, and Internet. Customer service representatives are usually also required to use computers and software, including word processing programs, spreadsheets, and specialist databases. Keyboarding skills are an advantage

EDUCATION, TRAINING, AND ADVANCEMENT

High School/Secondary

High school students can best prepare for a career as a customer service representative by taking courses in business and communications. Foreign languages may be advantageous as an increasing number of employers work in cross-cultural contexts and extend into global markets. Studies in mathematics and accounting provide a foundation for the numerical requirements of the role. Likewise, computing and keyboarding would be beneficial. Psychology and cultural studies may help candidates to develop empathetic relationship skills and to gain insight into creative problem solving. Becoming involved in part-time customer service work while still in high school (e.g. afterschool or weekend work in administration, hospitality, or retail) is an excellent way to gain entry-level experience into the customer service profession.

Suggested High School Subjects
- Business & Computer Technology
- English
- Foreign Languages
- Keyboarding
- Mathematics
- Psychology
- Speech

Famous First

The first "truth-in-advertising" law was enacted by New York State in 1898. The law was designed to prevent "misleading and dishonest representations" regarding merchandise for sale. Specifically, it made it a misdemeanor to present any advertisement that had "the appearance of an advantageous offer, which is untrue or calculated to mislead."

Postsecondary

The customer service representative profession generally requires no formal postsecondary educational qualifications, although an associate's or bachelor's degree in psychology, communications, or a related discipline may be attractive to employers. On-the-job experience in customer service support and delivery is usually considered more important than formal qualifications. Many employers will provide extensive induction and on-the-job training to ensure that their customer service representatives become experts in the products and services they represent.

Related College Majors
- Administrative Assistant/Secretarial Science
- General Retailing & Wholesaling Operations & Skills
- General Selling Skills & Sales Operations
- Receptionist Training

Adult Job Seekers

Adults seeking a career transition into or return to a customer service representative position are advised to refresh their skills and update their resume. Entry-level opportunities may exist as part-time, full-time, after-hours or weekend roles, as well as temporary or contract jobs. Aspiring customer service representatives may first obtain experience in the same company at a lower level and then progress to the customer service representative position. Opportunities for career advancement will depend largely on the size and type of organization in which the candidate works and their breadth of experience. Larger organizations may provide a tiered promotional system which ties the customer service representative's position title and wages to their level of experience and/or length of service. Customer service representatives seeking promotion may consider opportunities in supervisory or management roles.

Professional Certification and Licensure

There is no professional certification or licensure required for customer service representatives.

Additional Requirements

High quality customer service is increasingly recognized by business leaders and managers as a major driver of business success, since it helps consumers distinguish between organizations that provide similar goods and services. This is slowly helping to transition the perception of customer service from a basic business support role to a more highly valued profession and career. Those individuals who achieve proficiency in a foreign language may have an advantage over other candidates. Customer service representatives should be skilled at remaining courteous even when conversing with rude customers. Effective, professional conflict resolution is extremely valuable in this position

Fun Facts

A dissatisfied customer will tell between 9-15 people about their experience, and happy customers who get their issue resolved tell about 4-6 people about their experience.
Source: Return on Behavior Magazine, http://returnonbehavior.com/2010/10/50-facts-about-customer-experience-for-2011/.

59% of a company's customers stop doing business with that company due to poor customer service.
Source: https://blog.kissmetrics.com/happy-campers/

A 2011 survey showed that of the 21 percent of complaining customers who did hear back from a business, more than half reacted positively—and 22 percent went on to post a positive comment online.
Source: http://www.slideshare.net/RightNow/2011-customer-experience-impact-report

EARNINGS AND ADVANCEMENT

Advancement may mean becoming head of customer service or, in a small to medium sized firm, becoming an office manager. Median annual earnings of customer service representatives were $30,870 in 2013. The lowest ten percent earned less than $20,000, and the highest ten percent earned more than $50,000.

Customer service representatives may receive paid vacations, holidays, and sick days; life and health insurance; and retirement benefits. These are usually paid by the employer.

Metropolitan Areas with the Highest Employment Level in This Occupation

Metropolitan area	Employment [1]	Employment per thousand jobs	Hourly mean wage
New York-White Plains-Wayne, NY-NJ	82,040	15.65	$19.36
Chicago-Joliet-Naperville, IL	74,600	20.16	$18.06
Atlanta-Sandy Springs-Marietta, GA	60,350	26.15	$17.13
Los Angeles-Long Beach-Glendale, CA	57,910	14.57	$18.28
Dallas-Plano-Irving, TX	52,640	24.49	$16.35
Phoenix-Mesa-Glendale, AZ	51,440	28.88	$15.62
Houston-Sugar Land-Baytown, TX	50,750	18.40	$15.01
Tampa-St. Petersburg-Clearwater, FL	37,490	32.55	$14.90
Minneapolis-St. Paul-Bloomington, MN-WI	37,030	20.67	$18.18
Philadelphia, PA	36,150	19.65	$18.11

[1] Does not include self-employed. Source: Bureau of Labor Statistics

EMPLOYMENT AND OUTLOOK

Customer service representatives held about 2.4 million jobs nationally in 2013. Although they were found in a variety of industries, the largest numbers were employed by call centers (customer contact, or sales solicitation, centers), insurance agencies, retailers, and financial institutions. Employment is expected to grow about as fast as the average for all occupations through the year 2022, which means employment is projected to increase 10 percent to 15 percent. Customer service is critical to the success of any organization that deals with customers, and strong customer service can build sales and visibility as companies try to distinguish themselves from competitors. In many industries, the need to gain a competitive edge and retain customers will become increasingly important over the next decade, and this will result in strong job growth for customer service representatives.

Employment Trend, Projected 2012–22

Customer Service Representatives: 13%

Total, All Occupations: 11%

Office and Administrative Support Occupations: 7%

Note: "All Occupations" includes all occupations in the U.S. Economy. Source: U.S. Bureau of Labor Statistics, Employment Projections Program.

Related Occupations
- Administrative Assistant
- Computer Support Specialist
- Online Merchant
- Receptionist & Information Clerk
- Retail Salesperson
- Secretary

Conversation With . . .
NATALIE SNIDER

Inside Sales and Customer Support for
learning company's online products, 10 years
Isla Mujeres, MX

1. What was your individual career path in terms of education/training, entry-level job, or other significant opportunity?

I was one term short of my nursing degree when a private school contacted me to come work for them. I taught grammar school and middle school for 12 years, and got my undergraduate degree in history through continuing education. I was hired away from teaching by my present employer. They were looking for my teaching experience.

My job is to handle some brief online training. I do webinars for teachers learning to use the product, and I make sure the product works for individual teachers and their students. I also contact people through phone or email to check on how the product is working and to help them with their renewals.

The product is differentiated instruction and diagnostic assessment. So, a student will log on, take an hour-long assessment in reading, and at the end the product will show the student's grade level, why they are where they are, and then give tools to the educator to boost the student's weak skills. We also provide differentiated instruction that aligns with the assessment to provide the student with a virtual one-on-one tutor.

The reason teaching has helped me in this job is that I understand the world of education, how busy teachers' lives are, and what they really need to get started. I can talk to them on an educational level, rather than a technical or business level.

As a practical matter, the thing I do most is walk people through any trouble they are having with their account. I troubleshoot and help them connect with others in our company if I cannot help them. Sometimes it involves taking over their computer and doing remote work for them.

I had this job for two years before my husband and I moved to Isla Mujeres. I talked with my boss about it, and he said, "If you can work remotely and maintain your availability, fine."

2. What are the most important skills and/or qualities for someone in your profession?

You need to be very punctual. You need to keep up with the changing elements of education and our products through continuing education and be self-motivated to do so. You need good conversational skills, and you need to be good at directing people.

3. What do you wish you had known going into this profession?

I wish I had known more small business management terminology that's used within the company. For instance, the first time I heard "IEP" — individualized education program — that term was unfamiliar to me. As an educator in the classroom, I didn't know that acronym

4. Are there many job opportunities in your profession? In what specific areas?

There are probably a lot of opportunities to work remotely. Within this part of the education profession, I don't know. I have a specialized title within my company, and there aren't a lot of people like me.

5. How do you see your profession changing in the next five years, what role will technology play in those changes, and what skills will be required?

You need to stay up on what's new in terms of technology since you need to communicate remotely, as well as to conduct webinars and essentially go into the classroom. Within my company, there are people who to travel but more and more that's changing.

6. What do you like most about your job? What do you like least about your job?

The best thing is that I get to work remotely. I set my own hours for the most part and I like the people I work with.

I least like relying on the internet. If it's down or there's a problem, I have to head off to an internet cafe. Also, working remotely has a downside: I never get a vacation and am almost always available.

7. Can you suggest a valuable "try this" for students considering a career in your profession?

I would suggest taking an online class so that you start connecting yourself with people that way, as well as learning to be accountable for your time.

SELECTED SCHOOLS

For those interested in training beyond high school, most technical and community colleges offer programs in business administration, including sales, marketing, and customer service. Interested students are advised to consult with their school guidance counselor or to research area postsecondary schools and training programs.

MORE INFORMATION

International Customer Management Association
121 South Tejon Street, Suite 1100
Colorado Springs, CO 80903
719.955.8149
www.icmi.com

International Customer Service Association
1110 South Avenue, Suite 50
Staten Island, NY 10314
347.273.1303
www.icsatoday.org

National Customer Service Association
1714 Pfitzer Road
Normal, IL 61761
309.452.8831
www.nationalcsa.com

Kylie Hughes/Editor

E-Commerce Specialist

Snapshot

Career Cluster: Business, Information Technology, Marketing, Sales & Service

Interests: Computers, Internet, advertising, graphic design, sales

Earnings (Yearly Average): $63,490

Employment & Outlook: Faster than Average Growth Expected

OVERVIEW

Sphere of Work

E-commerce (or electronic commerce) specialists help consumers and businesses buy and sell goods and services on the Internet and social media. They focus on three types of transactions: business-to-consumer, in which a business sells directly to individuals; business-to-business, in which a business provides other businesses with necessary services or products, such as office supplies; and consumer-to-consumer, in which a consumer resells products to other consumers, often through online auction sites. E-commerce

specialists assess consumer behavior, analyzing markets and customer preferences. Based on their findings, they research, design, and produce websites and advertisements to market client products and services.

Work Environment

E-commerce specialists work in a wide range of environments, as they only need access to the Internet to conduct business. Some are based in offices, while others may be based out of private residences. Work hours vary and may be erratic, especially when deadlines approach. The physical demands of e-commerce are limited, but the fast pace and financial stakes of the work can be stressful, and there is a risk of back and repetitive motion conditions associated with long periods of computer use.

Profile

Working Conditions: Work Indoors
Physical Strength: Light Work
Education Needs: Bachelor's Degree
Licensure/Certification: Usually Not
  Required
Opportunities For Experience:
  Volunteer Work, Part-Time Work
Holland Interest Score*: ECA

* See Appendix A

Occupation Interest

Individuals attracted to the position of e-commerce specialist are computer savvy and possess an understanding of effective advertising (such as linking consumer behavior to e-commerce strategy). They frequently enter the field with prior experience in an associated industry such as graphic design, marketing, or sales and apply that knowledge to Internet-based commerce. Many specialists are independent consultants, so individuals entering that area of the field must be self-motivated and capable of working independently, while those working on teams must have excellent teamwork and communication skills.

A Day in the Life—Duties and Responsibilities

E-commerce specialists coordinate with clients and web design teams to facilitate online business transactions between a business and consumers, a business and other businesses, or a consumer and other consumers. First, specialists consult with clients to identify client pursuits and needs, as well as to determine the market for the product or service. They then research the market, creating business models, forecasting revenues, analyzing electronic market trends and performance, and monitoring competitors. In order to gain an understanding of consumer behavior in regard to the specific product or service, they analyze search engine patterns, taking into account keywords and phrases that consumers use to find certain services and goods. With this data, specialists tailor a client's website to appear prominently in search engine results for relevant, commonly searched keywords. In addition, specialists assist in customizing the content and functionality of the website so that it will attract and retain customers.

When a client's website is up and running, specialists work to promote it through targeted ad sales and placement, marketing campaigns, sponsorships, and other promotional activities. They monitor the success of their strategies through analysis of website traffic, determining how many individual consumers have viewed the site, what percentage of these visitors made a purchase, in what region the site's visitors live, and other sales and demographic data. Specialists may then modify their marketing strategies or the website itself in order to attract more or different customers.

Depending on their individual roles and employers, e-commerce specialists may also track sales, coordinate procurement and inventory control operations, and update online catalogues. They may generate online transaction security policies and measures, and they may also assist clients in tracking and responding to customer comments and complaints via online and live customer service programs.

Duties and Responsibilities

- Planning and coordinating marketing activities to promote products and services
- Monitoring market trends and developing long-range marketing strategies
- Determining the financial aspects of marketing activities
- Creating content that effectively describes product and service offerings on site
- Completing market research analysis in an effort to increase sales
- Consulting with and supervising marketing, design and technical staff to create design and functionality of site

WORK ENVIRONMENT

Relevant Skills and Abilities

Communication Skills
- Speaking effectively
- Writing concisely
- Listening attentively
- Reading well
- Expressing thoughts and ideas
- Persuading others
- Reporting information
- Editing written information

Interpersonal/Social Skills
- Motivating others
- Cooperating with others
- Working as a member of a team
- Being able to work independently
- Being honest
- Having good judgment

Organization & Management Skills
- Initiating new ideas
- Paying attention to and handling details
- Coordinating tasks
- Managing people/groups
- Managing time
- Managing money
- Managing equipment/materials
- Delegating responsibility
- Demonstrating leadership
- Promoting change
- Selling ideas or products
- Making decisions
- Organizing information or materials
- Meeting goals and deadlines
- Performing duties which change frequently

Physical Environment

E-commerce specialists are typically employed or contracted by corporations, consulting firms, nonprofit organizations, government agencies, and similar groups. Consequently, office settings predominate, although they can range from large spaces in corporations to small home offices.

Human Environment

E-commerce specialists interact and work with a wide range of professionals, private consumers, and clients. These may include salespeople, marketing and advertising executives and professionals, graphic and web designers, webmasters, online editors, warehouse managers, and merchants. Specialists may need to work as part of a team in order to meet client goals, so communication and people skills are essential.

Technological Environment

E-commerce specialists work primarily with computer systems and software. As such, they must be proficient in using hypertext markup language

Research & Planning Skills
- Predicting
- Creating new ideas
- Gathering information
- Identifying problems
- Solving problems
- Setting goals and deadlines
- Defining needs
- Analyzing information
- Developing evaluation strategies

Technical Skills
- Performing scientific, mathematical or technical work
- Working with data or numbers

(HTML), electronic payment systems, spreadsheet programs, and multimedia, graphic design, and computer-aided design (CAD) software.

EDUCATION, TRAINING, AND ADVANCEMENT

High School/Secondary

High school students interested in a career in electronic commerce should study computer science, including business data processing, graphic communications, and other information technology classes that focus on business applications. Business courses themselves are critical, including classes in accounting, economics, and entrepreneurship. Math courses, including algebra and statistics, are also useful. Communications courses such as composition and public speaking help build a student's interpersonal and business presentation skills, while courses in social studies and sociology provide a foundation for the aspiring e-commerce specialist's understanding of consumer behavior.

Suggested High School Subjects
- Accounting
- Algebra
- Applied Communication
- Applied Math

- Arts
- Bookkeeping
- Business
- Business & Computer Technology
- Business Data Processing
- Business English
- Business Law
- Business Math
- College Preparatory
- Composition
- Computer Science
- Economics
- English
- Entrepreneurship
- Geometry
- Graphic Communications
- Keyboarding
- Mathematics
- Merchandising
- Psychology
- Social Studies
- Sociology
- Speech
- Statistics
- Trigonometry

Famous First

The first federal financial transaction over the Internet was a 1998 payment by a branch of the U.S. Treasury to GTE Corporation, a predecessor of Verizon Communications. The electronic checking system used in the transaction was developed by the nonprofit Financial Services Technology Consortium. The amount of the GTE payment was $32,000.

College/Postsecondary

E-commerce specialists generally have a minimum of a bachelor's degree in a relevant field. Some hold degrees in information technology, software design, and similar technical areas, while others approach the profession from a business or graphic design background. Internships, whether paid or volunteer, may prove helpful in exposing postsecondary students to the field.

Related College Majors
- Business & Personal Services Marketing Operations
- Business Administration & Management, General
- Business Marketing/Marketing Management
- Marketing Management & Research
- Marketing Research

Adult Job Seekers

Qualified individuals may apply directly to corporations, consulting firms, and other organizations that post openings on their websites or at job fairs. Established specialists may also choose to pursue independent consulting. Professional trade associations dedicated to e-commerce may provide job listings, career resources, and valuable networking opportunities.

Professional Certification and Licensure

Although there are no required licensure or certification requirements for e-commerce specialists, some professionals choose to obtain certification in e-commerce, e-marketing, and other relevant fields. As with any voluntary certification process, it is beneficial to consult credible professional associations within the field and follow professional debate as to the relevancy and value of any certification program.

Additional Requirements

E-commerce specialists must demonstrate proficiency in both business and information technology, with a particular ability to understand how business practices are adapted to the Internet. They should also be able to effectively communicate and coordinate with clients, many of whom may not be experienced in web-based commerce. Furthermore, specialists must be creative, flexible, and able to quickly adjust when market forces or client needs shift.

Fun Fact

In 2016, half of all consumers are expected to make online transactions via mobile devices. Mobile sales in 2015 were up 38.7 percent from the prior year, at $104.5 billion.

Source: http://www.entrepreneur.com/article/269933 and
https://www.internetretailer.com/mobile500/#!/

EARNINGS AND ADVANCEMENT

Median annual earnings of e-commerce specialists were $63,490 in 2014. The lowest 10 percent earned less than $33,790, and the highest ten percent earned more than $112,680.

E-commerce specialists may receive paid vacations, holidays and sick days; life and health insurance; and retirement benefits. These are usually paid by the employer.

Metropolitan Areas with the Highest
Employment Level in This Occupation

Metropolitan area	Employment	Employment per thousand jobs	Annual mean wage
New York-White Plains-Wayne, NY-NJ	7,140	1.32	$79,900
Los Angeles-Long Beach-Glendale, CA	4,710	1.16	$69,270
Washington-Arlington-Alexandria, DC-VA-MD-WV	4,580	1.93	$84,990
Seattle-Bellevue-Everett, WA	3,850	2.58	$87,520
San Francisco-San Mateo-Redwood City, CA	3,380	3.11	$95,600
Chicago-Joliet-Naperville, IL	3,290	0.88	$67,150
Dallas-Plano-Irving, TX	3,170	1.42	$71,600
Boston-Cambridge-Quincy, MA	2,790	1.55	$79,140
Minneapolis-St. Paul-Bloomington, MN-WI	2,680	1.47	$67,630
San Jose-Sunnyvale-Santa Clara, CA	2,590	2.66	$106,580

Source: Bureau of Labor Statistics

EMPLOYMENT AND OUTLOOK

E-commerce specialists held about 150,000 jobs nationally in 2014. Employment of e-commerce specialists is expected to grow much faster than the average for all occupations through the year 2024, which means employment is projected to increase 25 percent or more. The large number of businesses that are now communicating with their customers and selling their products and services online will continue to create demand in this field for many years to come.

Employment Trend, Projected 2014–24

E-commerce specialists: 27%

Computer occupations: 12%

Total, all occupations: 7%

Note: "All Occupations" includes all occupations in the U.S. Economy. Source: U.S. Bureau of Labor Statistics, Employment Projections Program.

Related Occupations

- Advertising & Marketing Manager
- Advertising Sales Agent
- Copywriter
- Graphic Designer
- Market Research Analyst
- Online Merchant
- Public Relations Specialist
- Statistician
- Web Administrator
- Web Developer
- Writer & Editor

Conversation With . . .
BRENT DURHAM

COO & Founding Partner, iFrog Digital Marketing
Preston, Maryland
E-Commerce specialist, 6 years

1. What was your individual career path in terms of education/training, entry-level job, or other significant opportunity?

Growing up, my good friend's father owned a large car dealership, Preston Automotive Group. Since everybody is going to need a car at some point in life, I picked that as an industry to go into because it covers retail, service, and other skills I could use if automotive didn't work out.

Right out of high school I went to Northwood University in Florida and focused on automotive marketing and business management. I earned a bachelor's in business administration, gained experience working in dealerships, and then went back to Maryland to work at Preston Automotive as an Internet marketing manager.

Digital marketing was new. After developing the company's online marketing, Internet sales was added to my duties and I became Internet Director. After a year, I decided to get an MBA and moved to Virginia to get my degree from Old Dominion University. My focus was digital marketing with a concentration in global marketing.

I returned to Preston after graduating, and at that point had the knowledge to be an entrepreneur. So, I partnered with Preston's owner, Dave Wilson, and we created a spinoff company—iFrog—to handle Internet sales and marketing for our dealership, as well as for non-competing dealerships. Currently, we work with client car dealerships in Cincinnati and the Baltimore-Washington, D.C. area, and we're working our way into Virginia. We also have twenty-two clients (so far) in other types of businesses here in our region.

Everything we do relates to Internet commerce and marketing: ads, page searches, social media, and search engine optimization. We manage metadata, content, advertising for mobile devices, and reputation management. We train clients in social media selling. Auto dealership clients like to deal with people who are born and bred in the automotive sales industry and those are the people I've hired for my team.

2. What are the most important skills and/or qualities for someone in your profession?

The ability to continually learn is huge. The minute you think you know everything is the minute you get left behind. With the Internet, every device constantly changes; we get data from our online traffic and every week we get new data or a new format to advertise to someone. For example, as smart phones became popular, we adapted the way websites, web pages, and displays were viewed by making them "mobile friendly." If you learn code, that will take you far; it's a big portion of this growing field.

Also, you need leadership ability. In high school I actively participated in sports, was student council president, and learned to work with people or a team to accomplish a goal. When we bring on new clients, we are working with a new team. You need to network, too. It doesn't matter what you do in life, there's always somebody who can help you out or give you a leg up.

3. What do you wish you had known going into this profession?

HTML!

4. Are there many job opportunities in your profession? In what specific areas?

As we grow as a company, I'm noticing a diverse number of job opportunities: video animation, HTML, graphic design, and content writing to optimize Google searches. Social media and marketing are huge and not going anywhere.

You need to analyze data to tell whether a certain advertisement is working, or tweak it to get more return on investment. At iFrog, account managers work with their data analysis team and the graphic design team to develop better calls-to-action—which is ad copy that prompts a viewer to take action, such as "Click Here," or "Shop Now"—design layouts, and advertisement targeting. Also, sales jobs are always growing.

5. How do you see your profession changing in the next five years, what role will technology play in those changes, and what skills will be required?

The Internet and widespread connectivity is only going to grow. It gives you different advertising channels. Think about how we went from flip phones to smartphones, and now people like bigger screens so that gives me more opportunity to post an ad.

The amount of data we are able to collect on people will grow. Right now, Google and Facebook have the most data, but that will spread to other avenues and spawn new tactics. I see getting to the point where we can basically identify the person who uses a particular IP address and target tailored advertising to them.

6. What do you enjoy most about your job? What do you enjoy least about your job?

I most like working with my whole team to accomplish a goal. It's nice to see a plan come together and get executed. I least like the long hours. My job means I always have to be connected via my smartphone; hopefully I can eventually disconnect for a day or two.

7. Can you suggest a valuable "try this" for students considering a career in your profession?

Use social media to promote something, maybe a change of lifestyle for yourself, like a new workout routine or an event for an organization like a charity. See how big a following you can grow or how many attendees you can draw to your event.

SELECTED SCHOOLS

Many online, technical, and community colleges offer programs leading to either certification (one year) or an associate's degree (two years) in web development. Interested students are advised to consult with a school guidance counselor or research area postsecondary schools. For those interested in pursuing a bachelor's degree in marketing and/or e-commerce, there are numerous business schools from which to choose.

MORE INFORMATION

eCommerce Merchants Trade Association
917.388.1698
www.ecmta.org

eMarketing Association
243 Post Road, Suite #129
Westerly, RI 02891
401.315.2194
www.emarketingassociation.com

Women in Ecommerce
P.O. Box 550856
Fort Lauderdale, FL 33355-0856
954.625.6606
www.wecai.org

Michael Auerbach/Editor

Financial Analyst

Snapshot

Career Cluster: Business, Finance

Interests: Mathematics, risk assessment, financial trends, data analysis

Earnings (Yearly Average): $78,620

Employment & Outlook: Faster than Average Growth Expected

OVERVIEW

Sphere of Work

Financial analysts, also referred to as investment analysts, financial planners, financial officers, and financial managers, are responsible for the financial investments of businesses, corporations, nonprofit organizations, and government entities. Financial analysts provide diverse financial analysis services, which may include reviewing financial statements and advising organizations about the best investment options, such as stocks, bonds, and commodities. Financial analysts generally work within or alongside management and accounting departments. While most businesses employ a single

financial analyst to oversee investments, financial institutions such as commercial banks, insurance companies, securities firms, mortgage companies, pension funds, and savings and loan associations employ multiple financial analysts to direct their internal investments and those of clients, investors, and customers.

Work Environment

Financial analysts work in offices and are often required to travel to attend annual meetings and stockholder meetings. Depending on employer and particular job description, a financial analyst may telecommute from a home office, visit client offices, or work on a full-time basis in an employer's office. A financial analyst may work as a full-time member of a finance team or as a term-of-project consultant. A financial analyst's work environment is filled with technology, including computers and accounting software programs.

Profile

Working Conditions: Work Indoors
Education Needs: Bachelor's Degree, Master's Degree
Licensure/Certification: Required
Opportunities For Experience: Internship, Part-Time Work
Holland Interest Score*: CIE

* See Appendix A

Occupation Interest

Individuals attracted to the financial analysis profession tend to be ambitious, organized, persuasive, decisive, and detail-oriented people who find satisfaction in tracking financial trends and assessing risks. Those individuals who excel as financial analysts possess financial and mathematical acumen, intense focus, responsibility and ethics, and effective time management. Financial analysts should enjoy finance and informed risk-taking and have a background in risk assessment.

A Day in the Life—Duties and Responsibilities

The daily duties and responsibilities of financial analysts vary by job specialty and employer. Areas of financial analysis job specialization include buy side financial analysts, sell side financial analysts, risk analysts, portfolio managers, fund managers, and ratings analysts. Buy side analysts assist mutual funds, hedge funds, insurance companies, and endowed organizations with developing investment strategies and implementing investment decisions. Sell side financial analysts assist banks and securities dealers with promoting and selling stocks, bonds, and other investment vehicles. Risk analysts assess the risks associated with investment decisions and work to reduce losses by diversifying the portfolio and selling stocks and bonds as needed. Portfolio managers oversee financial teams and the health of financial investments. Fund managers oversee hedge funds and mutual funds and communicate investment decisions and strategies to investors. Ratings analysts assess the likelihood that businesses will pay their debts. Based on these assessments, ratings analysts forecast the default risk. In addition to job specialization, all financial analysts specialize in particular geographic regions or industries.

Regardless of geography or industry specialization, financial analysts use spreadsheets to track financial data, analyze financial data to make investment decisions, and track trends in technology and politics that may affect the finance industry. They recommend investment options, create investment portfolios for individuals and businesses, set securities prices, prepare investment reports for business owners and investors, and advise clients or employers about when to best hold, sell, or trade securities.

In addition to the tasks described above, organizations may also require financial analysts to select, implement, and troubleshoot financial software systems. They must stay up to date with regulatory and ethical issues and news in finance by reading finance industry journals and participating in industry associations. Financial analysts employed by learning organizations also participate in ongoing discussions of work teams, workflows, dynamics, and best practices.

Duties and Responsibilities

- Analyzing financial information to assist an organization in making investment decisions
- Recommending both the type and timing of investments to an organization to create the potential for successful investing
- Presenting oral and written presentations regarding business, industry and economic trends
- Evaluating and comparing the quality of different investment possibilities in any industry
- Staying up to date with the latest developments in the financial industry

OCCUPATION SPECIALTIES

Portfolio Managers

Portfolio Managers supervise a team of financial analysts and help guide companies in building their investment portfolios.

Fund Managers

Fund Managers manage mutual funds or hedge funds for their clients.

Risk Managers

Risk Managers analyze the investment decisions of their clients and determine how to grow profits through diversifying and hedging.

Ratings Analysts

Ratings Analysts determine the ability of companies that issue bonds to repay their debts.

WORK ENVIRONMENT

Relevant Skills and Abilities

Communication Skills
- Speaking effectively
- Writing concisely
- Listening attentively
- Reading well
- Persuading others

Interpersonal/Social Skills
- Being sensitive to others
- Cooperating with others
- Respecting others' opinions
- Representing others

Physical Environment

Financial analysts generally work in office environments. The work of a financial analyst requires sitting at a desk and using computers and phones for long periods each day.

Human Environment

Financial analysts interact with financial teams, business owners, employees, clients,

- Being able to work independently
- Working as a member of a team
- Being honest
- Having good judgment
- Being objective

Organization & Management Skills
- Coordinating tasks
- Making decisions
- Managing money
- Managing time (SCANS Workplace Competency Resources)
- Paying attention to and handling details
- Promoting change
- Organizing information or materials

Research & Planning Skills
- Using logical reasoning
- Analyzing information
- Developing evaluation strategies
- Predicting
- Gathering information
- Defining needs

Technical Skills
- Performing scientific, mathematical and technical work
- Working with data or numbers

and stockholders. Financial analysts should be comfortable attending meetings, giving frequent speeches, persuading clients, listening to client concerns and opinions, and supervising and directing employees.

Technological Environment

Financial analysts communicate by telephone and Internet. They use computers, financial analysis software, and spreadsheets to research, monitor, analyze, and present financial data.

EDUCATION, TRAINING, AND ADVANCEMENT

High School/Secondary

High school students interested in pursuing a career as a financial analyst should prepare themselves by building good study habits as well as an ease with numbers and mathematical functions. High school-level study of bookkeeping and mathematics will provide a strong foundation for college-level study of finance. Due to the diversity of financial analyst responsibilities and given that employers in this field tend to value practical experience, high school students interested in this career path may benefit from seeking internships or part-time work with financial organizations.

Suggested High School Subjects

- Accounting
- Algebra
- Applied Communication
- Applied Math
- Bookkeeping
- Business
- Business & Computer Technology
- Business Law
- Business Math
- College Preparatory
- Computer Science
- Economics
- English
- Government
- Keyboarding
- Mathematics
- Merchandising
- Political Science
- Psychology
- Social Studies
- Sociology
- Speech
- Statistics

Famous First

The first financial news agency was the Kiernan Financial News Agency, established in 1869 by John J. Kiernan at 21 Wall Street, New York City. In 1882, the coverage of the service was expanded to include the results of sports competitions, arrivals of steamships, foreign commodity prices, and other information.

College/Postsecondary

Postsecondary students interested in becoming financial analysts should complete a bachelor's degree in economics, finance, statistics, mathematics, or accounting. Courses in computer science, political science, psychology, and ethics may also prove useful in their future work. Postsecondary students can gain work experience and potential advantage in their future job searches by securing internships or part-time employment with local businesses or financial organizations.

Related College Majors
- Accounting
- Business
- Business Administration & Management, General
- Business/Managerial Economics
- Economics, General
- Finance, General
- International Economics
- Mathematical Statistics

Adult Job Seekers

Adults seeking financial analyst jobs have generally earned a bachelor's degree and, in some cases, a master's of business administration (MBA). Adult job seekers may benefit from joining professional finance or accounting associations as a means of professional networking. Professional finance and accounting associations, such as the Association for Investment Management and Research and the Society of Financial Service Professionals, generally maintain job lists advertising open accounting positions.

Professional Certification and Licensure

Certification and licensure is not legally required for financial analysts but may be required as a condition of employment or promotion. Options for voluntary financial analyst certification include the CFA Institute's Chartered Financial Analyst (CFA) and Certificate in Investment Performance Measurement (CIPM) designations, and the American Academy of Financial Management's (AAFM) Financial Analyst, Risk Management, and Financial Planning designations. These voluntary certifications require education, experience, testing, employer sponsorship, recertification, and continuing education. Those interested in becoming certified should be aware that the Financial Industry Regulatory Authority (FINRA), which is the licensing agency of the securities and finance industry, does not approve or endorse any particular professional financial certification or designation. Certification must be sponsored by one's employer, so when a financial analyst moves to a new company, he or she must go through a recertification process.

Additional Requirements

Individuals who find satisfaction, success, and job security as financial analysts will be knowledgeable about the profession's requirements, responsibilities, and opportunities. They should be able to stay focused on the same project for several hours at a time in order to make informed decisions. They should also be detail-oriented, organized, analytical, and sensitive to their clients' needs and opinions. Financial analysts must exhibit integrity and professional ethics as professionals in this role have access to confidential financial information and influence the financial health of individuals and businesses. Membership in professional finance associations is encouraged among all financial analysts as a means of building professional community.

Fun Fact

Until the U.S. Federal Reserve was created in 1908, individual banks could create their own money.
Source: http://www.slideshare.net/FirmexVirtualDataRoom/10-weird-finance-facts/3

EARNINGS AND ADVANCEMENT

Median annual earnings of financial analysts were $78,620 in 2014. The lowest ten percent earned less than $48,150, and the highest ten percent earned more than $154,680. Financial analysts can also receive bonuses that can be a large part of their total earnings. These bonuses are usually determined by how close their predictions match the actual performance of an investment.

Financial analysts may receive paid vacations, holidays and sick days; life and health insurance; and retirement benefits. These are usually paid by the employer.

Metropolitan Areas with the Highest Employment Level in This Occupation

Metropolitan area	Employment	Employment per thousand jobs	Annual mean wage
New York-White Plains-Wayne, NY-NJ	35,170	6.52	$124,080
Boston-Cambridge-Quincy, MA	13,450	7.49	$105,710
Washington-Arlington-Alexandria, DC-VA-MD-WV	10,230	4.30	$99,430
Chicago-Joliet-Naperville, IL	9,830	2.62	$89,660
Los Angeles-Long Beach-Glendale, CA	7,390	1.82	$97,320
Dallas-Plano-Irving, TX	7,230	3.23	$92,250
San Francisco-San Mateo-Redwood City, CA	6,820	6.28	$130,250
Houston-Sugar Land-Baytown, TX	6,350	2.23	$94,820
Philadelphia, PA	5,950	3.19	$83,690
Atlanta-Sandy Springs-Marietta, GA	5,790	2.43	$80,300

Source: Bureau of Labor Statistics

EMPLOYMENT AND OUTLOOK

Financial analysts held about 278,000 jobs nationally in 2014. Employment of financial analysts is expected to grow faster than the average for all occupations through the year 2024, which means employment is projected to increase 10 percent to 15 percent. This demand for financial analysts is based on very high growth in the industry and the increasing complex nature of investing.

Employment Trend, Projected 2014–24

Financial analysts: 12%

Financial specialists: 10%

Total, all occupations: 7%

Note: "All Occupations" includes all occupations in the U.S. Economy. Source: U.S. Bureau of Labor Statistics, Employment Projections Program.

Related Occupations

- Accountant
- Actuary
- Auditor
- Budget Analyst
- Economist
- Financial Manager
- Insurance Sales Agent
- Insurance Underwriter
- Personal Financial Advisor
- Real Estate Sales Agent
- Securities Sales Agent

Related Military Occupations

- Finance & Accounting Manager

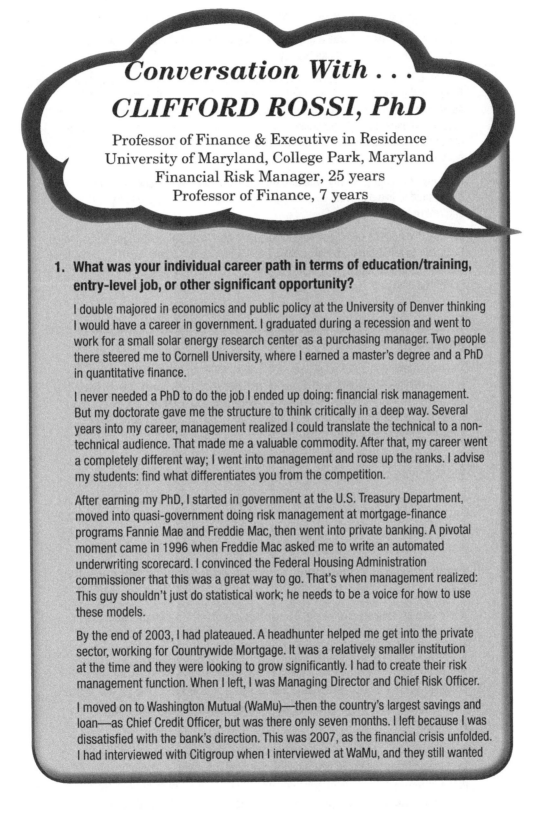

Conversation With . . .
CLIFFORD ROSSI, PhD

Professor of Finance & Executive in Residence
University of Maryland, College Park, Maryland
Financial Risk Manager, 25 years
Professor of Finance, 7 years

1. What was your individual career path in terms of education/training, entry-level job, or other significant opportunity?

I double majored in economics and public policy at the University of Denver thinking I would have a career in government. I graduated during a recession and went to work for a small solar energy research center as a purchasing manager. Two people there steered me to Cornell University, where I earned a master's degree and a PhD in quantitative finance.

I never needed a PhD to do the job I ended up doing: financial risk management. But my doctorate gave me the structure to think critically in a deep way. Several years into my career, management realized I could translate the technical to a non-technical audience. That made me a valuable commodity. After that, my career went a completely different way; I went into management and rose up the ranks. I advise my students: find what differentiates you from the competition.

After earning my PhD, I started in government at the U.S. Treasury Department, moved into quasi-government doing risk management at mortgage-finance programs Fannie Mae and Freddie Mac, then went into private banking. A pivotal moment came in 1996 when Freddie Mac asked me to write an automated underwriting scorecard. I convinced the Federal Housing Administration commissioner that this was a great way to go. That's when management realized: This guy shouldn't just do statistical work; he needs to be a voice for how to use these models.

By the end of 2003, I had plateaued. A headhunter helped me get into the private sector, working for Countrywide Mortgage. It was a relatively smaller institution at the time and they were looking to grow significantly. I had to create their risk management function. When I left, I was Managing Director and Chief Risk Officer.

I moved on to Washington Mutual (WaMu)—then the country's largest savings and loan—as Chief Credit Officer, but was there only seven months. I left because I was dissatisfied with the bank's direction. This was 2007, as the financial crisis unfolded. I had interviewed with Citigroup when I interviewed at WaMu, and they still wanted me to work for them. It was a good move. Soon after, WaMu suffered the largest failure in the nation's financial history.

I became Managing Director and Chief Risk Officer for Citi's Consumer Lending Group. It was the best job I ever had, overseeing 700 people at a prestigious institution. I came on under a new CEO who embraced risk management as he guided the bank through the crisis and its aftermath. I stayed two years, working out of the headquarters in New York. This was a highly stressful time. My job also became more global and demanded extensive travel.

My banking career gave my wife and me the earnings and flexibility to decide how we wanted to live our lives, so when an interesting opportunity arose to shift gears and return home, I took it.

In 2009, I joined the faculty of the University of Maryland's Robert H. Smith School of Business as a full-time professor. Now, I teach graduate students part-time and have become Chief Economist for Radian Guarantee, a large mortgage insurance company in Philadelphia.

2. **What are the most important skills and/or qualities for someone in your profession?**

You need some degree of analytical skill, critical thinking skills, and financial software skills—the ability to mine or extract data and manipulate and analyze it. You have to be able to communicate effectively and you need to be a team player. Risk management is an art and a science, though, so you've also got to have intuition, knowledge and judgment.

3. **What do you wish you had known going into this profession?**

I wish I had known that risk management wasn't viewed as an equal partner in the banking profession at the time I was there. It's become more of a focus for banks since the crisis.

4. **Are there many job opportunities in your profession? In what specific areas?**

If any area of banking is growing, it's risk management. It's a great career. It's at the vortex of everything a bank is about: strategy, analytics, consumers, wealth management—you can work in any part of the business.

5. **How do you see your profession changing in the next five years, what role will technology play in those changes, and what skills will be required?**

With the advent of high-end computing software, the risk management function has become highly quantitative and model-based and the profession is more aligned with actuarial science. Technology will continue to make our profession more quantitative.

6. What do you enjoy most about your job? What do you enjoy least about your job?

In my career in private finance, I enjoyed improving our bank's risk profile and infrastructure.

I detested some of the power-play issues that surround high-level management, such as passive-aggressive behavior from peers, or being ignored. I don't suffer fools lightly.

7. Can you suggest a valuable "try this" for students considering a career in your profession?

Attend an event at the local chapter of a professional association for risk management. People are likely to share their stories and help you understand what it is to be a financial risk manager.

SELECTED SCHOOLS

Many colleges and universities, especially those with business schools, offer programs in finance and business administration. The student can also gain initial training through enrollment at a technical or community college. For advanced positions, a master's of business administration (MBA) with a concentration in finance is usually expected. Below are listed some of the more prominent institutions in this field.

Carnegie Mellon University
Tepper School of Business
500 Forbes Avenue
Pittsburgh, PA 15213
412.268.2268
tepper.cmu.edu

Indiana University, Bloomington
Kelley School of Business
1309 E. 10th Street
Bloomington, IN 47405
812.855.8100
kelley.iu.edu

Massachusetts Institute of Technology
Sloan School of Management
50 Memorial Drive
Cambridge, MA 02142
617.253.2659
mitsloan.mit.edu

New York University
Stern School of Business
665 Broadway, 11th Floor
New York, NY 10012
212.998.4500
www.stern.nyu.edu

University of California, Berkeley
Haas School of Business
S450 Student Services Building #1900
Berkeley, CA 94720
510.642.1421
haas.berkeley.edu

University of Michigan, Ann Arbor
Ross School of Business
701 Tappan Avenue
Ann Arbor, MI 48109
734.763.5796
michiganross.umich.edu

University of North Carolina, Chapel Hill
Kenan-Flagler Business School
Campus Box 3490, McColl Building
Chapel Hill, NC 27599
919.962.3235
www.kenan-flagler.unc.edu

University of Pennsylvania
The Wharton School
1 College Hall
Philadelphia, PA 19104
215.898.6376
www.whatron.upenn.edu

University of Texas, Austin
McCombs School of Business
1 University Station, B6000
Austin, TX 78712
512.471.5921
www.mccombs.utexas.edu

University of Virginia
Darden School of Business
PO Box 6550
Charlottseville, VA 22906
434.924.3900
www.darden.virginia.edu

MORE INFORMATION

American Academy of Financial Management
1670-F E. Cheyenne Mountain Blvd.
Box 293
Colorado Springs, CO 80906
504.495.1748
www.aafm.us

CFA Institute
560 Ray C. Hunt Drive
Charlottesville, VA 22903-2981
800.247.8132
www.cfainstitute.org

Financial Industry Regulatory Authority
1735 K Street
Washington, DC 20006
301.590.6500
www.finra.org

Financial Managers Society, Inc.
100 West Monroe Street, Suite 1700
Chicago, IL 60603
800.275.4367
www.fmsinc.org

Society for Risk Analysis
1313 Dolley Madison Boulevard
Suite 402
McLean, VA 22101
703.7901745
www.sra.org

Simone Isadora Flynn/Editor

Insurance Claims Adjuster and Examiner

Snapshot

Career Cluster(s): Business, Finance, Insurance

Interests: Investigation, risk assessment, solving problems, helping others

Earnings (Yearly Average): $62,220

Employment & Outlook: Slower than Average Growth Expected

OVERVIEW

Sphere of Work

Insurance claims adjusters and examiners, also referred to as insurance claims investigators, insurance claims assessors, insurance claims analysts, and liability assessors, are responsible for investigating and settling claims that insurance policyholders have made to their insurance companies. Adjusters visit the scene of an accident, injury, or natural disaster and estimate the cost of the damage done. They write reports recommending whether the claim

should be approved or not. Examiners are very similar to adjusters, although in some companies they may follow up on adjusters' work by checking their reports for accuracy and to ensure that the adjuster has followed the insurance company's procedures properly. Adjusters and examiners may be independent agents or employed by insurance companies.

Work Environment

Insurance claims adjusters and examiners work in offices writing and evaluating claims reports as well as in the field investigating claims and inspecting damaged property. They visit claimants and insurance policyholders at their homes, accident scenes, hospitals and rehabilitation facilities, and automobile repair shops. Insurance claims adjusters and examiners may work a forty-hour week or in an on-call capacity responding to claims as they are made. They may be expected to work overtime during busy times or when responding to emergencies or natural disasters that affect many people at once. When investigating claims in the field, especially in the aftermath of an event like a tornado or a fire, insurance claims adjusters and examiners may be exposed to physical hazards.

Profile

Working Conditions: Work both Indoors and Outdoors
Physical Strength: Light Work
Education Needs: Junior/Technical/Community College, Bachelor's Degree
Licensure/Certification: Required
Opportunities For Experience: Internship, Part-Time Work
Holland Interest Score*: ESC

* See Appendix A

Occupation Interest

Individuals attracted to the insurance claims adjuster and examiner profession tend to be organized, diplomatic, and detail-oriented people who find satisfaction in resolving questions and helping people in times of need. Those individuals who excel as insurance claims adjusters and examiners exhibit traits such as responsibility, time management, composure under pressure, attention to detail, and a desire to help. Insurance claims adjusters and examiners should enjoy insurance work and have a background in investigation and risk assessment.

A Day in the Life—Duties and Responsibilities

The daily duties and responsibilities of insurance claims adjusters and examiners will vary with job specialty and employer. Areas of insurance claims specialization include claims adjusters, appraisers, examiners, and investigators. Insurance claims adjusters and examiners investigate and settle property damage, liability, and bodily injury claims. Insurance companies encourage insurance claims adjusters and examiners to settle claims without legal arbitration whenever possible.

When they receive claims, insurance claims adjusters and examiners may begin work by reviewing insurance policies to determine what type and amount of coverage applies to the claim. They may travel to the site of damaged property and confirm the cause and extent of the damage; they may interview people involved in the incident, including policyholders, witnesses, first responders (police, firemen, and paramedics), and physicians. They gather information and records related to the incident, such as police reports, and work with appraisers, colleagues, and relevant professionals, such as builders or auto mechanics, to determine the extent of the damage. Providing emotional and customer service support to customers is a very important aspect of processing claims, especially since customers may have experienced a personal loss or a significant loss of property due to the event. Claims adjusters and examiners may assist policyholders with various requests, and communicate with them about the process of investigating the claim. If a widespread natural disaster occurs, the adjuster may be sent to assist local residents with the filing of their claims before the evaluation process begins.

When the initial work is complete, insurance claims adjusters and examiners prepare the claim report and attempt to negotiate a monetary settlement with the policyholder. Most of the time this is successful, but if the claimant contests the company's decision regarding a claim, sometimes claims adjusters and examiners must initiate legal proceedings if an out-of-court settlement cannot be reached. The final claims report is submitted by the adjuster or examiner to supervisors at the insurance company. Examiners are also responsible for checking the accuracy of adjusters' reported findings and for confirming that adjusters followed correct procedures while investigating the claim or claims.

All insurance claims adjusters and examiners should stay up to date with regulatory and ethical issues and news in the insurance industry by reading insurance industry journals and participating in insurance industry associations.

Duties and Responsibilities

- Determining the amount of damage
- Determining if the claim is covered by the insurance policy
- Interviewing or corresponding with the person making the claim
- Inspecting property damage or loss
- Consulting police, fire and medical reports and records
- Preparing a detailed report of findings
- Recommending any legal action necessary
- Testifying in court on contested claims
- Preparing and maintaining files on clients' policies
- Making adjustments to existing policies, such as change in type or amount of coverage

WORK ENVIRONMENT

Physical Environment

Insurance claims adjusters and examiners work in office environments as well as in the field investigating claims and visiting damaged property and injured people. Insurance claims adjusters and examiners generally must be physically able to drive as well as walk over potentially rough terrain damaged by flood, winds, earthquakes, and fire.

Human Environment

Insurance claims adjusters and examiners interact with insurance policyholders, lawyers, doctors, automobile repair mechanics,

Relevant Skills and Abilities

Communication Skills
- Persuading others
- Speaking effectively
- Writing concisely

Interpersonal/Social Skills
- Cooperating with others
- Working as a member of a team

Organization & Management Skills
- Making decisions

Research & Planning Skills
- Developing evaluation strategies

Technical Skills
- Performing scientific, mathematical and technical work

business owners, and coworkers and supervisors. Insurance claims adjusters and examiners should be comfortable meeting with policyholders and industry professionals and show good judgment, objectivity, and tact when responding to policyholders.

Technological Environment

Insurance claims adjusters and examiners use computers, telephones, tape measures, cameras, calculators, Internet communication tools, insurance business software programs, and spreadsheets to complete their work.

EDUCATION, TRAINING, AND ADVANCEMENT

High School/Secondary

High school students interested in pursuing a career as an insurance claims adjuster or examiner should prepare by building good study habits. High school–level study of sociology, bookkeeping, and mathematics will provide a strong foundation for work as an insurance claims adjuster and examiner or for college-level study in the field. High school students interested in this career path will benefit from seeking internships or part-time work with insurance businesses or investigators.

Suggested High School Subjects
- Applied Communication
- Bookkeeping
- Business
- Business Law
- Computer Science
- Economics
- English
- Keyboarding
- Mathematics
- Psychology
- Statistics

Famous First

The first title guaranty insurance company was the Real Estate Title Insurance and Trust Company, organized in Philadelphia on March 31, 1876. It offered security against errors in property titles. Prior to the creation of title insurance, buyers bore sole responsibility for ensuring the validity of land titles.

College/Postsecondary

Postsecondary students interested in becoming insurance claims adjusters and examiners should work toward an associate's or bachelor's degree in economics, finance, statistics, or accounting. Coursework in computer science, political science, and ethics may also prove useful in their future work. Postsecondary students can gain work experience and potential advantage in their future job searches by securing internships or part-time employment with local insurance businesses.

Related College Majors
- Banking & Financial Support Services
- Finance, General
- Insurance & Risk Management

Adult Job Seekers

Adults seeking insurance claims adjuster and examiner jobs have generally earned an associate's or bachelor's degree. Some insurance claims adjuster and examiner jobs require extensive experience and on-the-job training. Adult job seekers should educate themselves about the educational and professional requirements of the organizations where they seek employment. Adult job seekers will benefit from joining professional insurance associations as a means of professional networking. Professional insurance associations, such as the National Association of Professional Insurance Agents, the Independent Automotive Damage Appraisers Association, the Insurance Institute of America, and the National Association of Independent Insurance Adjusters, generally maintain job lists advertising open positions in the field.

Professional Certification and Licensure

Certification is not legally required for insurance claims adjusters and examiners but may be required as a condition of employment or promotion. Extensive options for voluntary insurance claims adjuster and examiner certification exist within the insurance industry. These voluntary credentials or designations have education, experience, testing, employer sponsorship, recertification, and continuing education requirements. Licensing requirements for insurance claims adjusters and examiners vary significantly by state. At least sixteen states require insurance claims adjusters to hold a license earned through satisfying an education requirement or passing an examination. Some states award licenses directly to insurance companies or businesses rather than individual insurance adjusters. Insurance claims adjusters and examiners should contact the agency that oversees insurance in their home state for specific licensing requirements.

Additional Requirements

Successful insurance claims adjusters and examiners adhere to strict codes of professional ethics. Professionals in this occupation have access to confidential information and can influence the financial futures of individuals and businesses. Membership in professional insurance associations is encouraged among all insurance claims adjusters and examiners as a means of building professional community.

Fun Fact

Hurricane Katrina caused an estimated $150 billion in damages, making it the most expensive storm in U.S. history.

Source: http://time.com/money/4011414/homeowners-insurance-katrina/

EARNINGS AND ADVANCEMENT

Earnings depend on the individual's experience and level of the job. Median annual earnings of insurance claims adjusters and examiners were $62,220 in 2014. The lowest ten percent earned less than $37,580, and the highest ten percent earned more than $92,620.

Insurance claims adjusters and examiners may receive paid vacations, holidays, and sick days; life and health insurance; and retirement benefits. These are usually paid by the employer. They may also receive a company car or reimbursement for the use of their own cars on company business.

Metropolitan Areas with the Highest

Employment Level in This Occupation

Metropolitan area	Employment	Employment per thousand jobs	Annual mean wage
New York-White Plains-Wayne, NY-NJ	10,340	1.92	$75,140
Chicago-Joliet-Naperville, IL	10,130	2.70	$65,510
Los Angeles-Long Beach-Glendale, CA	7,000	1.73	$66,550
Philadelphia, PA	6,660	3.58	$63,790
Atlanta-Sandy Springs-Marietta, GA	6,490	2.72	$63,490
Dallas-Plano-Irving, TX	6,110	2.73	$65,210
Boston-Cambridge-Quincy, MA	5,860	3.26	$68,860
Tampa-St. Petersburg-Clearwater, FL	5,530	4.68	$57,870
Phoenix-Mesa-Glendale, AZ	5,380	2.95	$59,720
St. Louis, MO-IL	4,530	3.47	$60,760

Source: Bureau of Labor Statistics

EMPLOYMENT AND OUTLOOK

Nationally, insurance claims adjusters and examiners held about 310,000 jobs in 2014. Employment is expected to grow slower than the average for all occupations through the year 2024, which means employment is projected to increase 1 percent to 6 percent. As long as more insurance policies are being sold to accommodate a rising population, there will be a need for these workers. In addition, a growing elderly population, higher healthcare premiums, and insurance companies' attempts to lower costs will create demand for insurance claims adjusters and examiners. Job openings will also result from the need to replace workers who transfer to other occupations or leave the labor force.

Employment Trend, Projected 2014–24

Total, all occupations: 7%

Claims adjusters, examiners, and investigators: 3%

Insurance appraisers, auto damage: -1%

Note: "All Occupations" includes all occupations in the U.S. Economy. Source: U.S. Bureau of Labor Statistics, Employment Projections Program.

Related Occupations
- Insurance Underwriter
- Personal Financial Advisor
- Real Estate Appraiser

Conversation With . . .
MARY ANNE MEDINA

Director of Business Development & Training
One Call Claims, Orlando, Florida
Insurance adjuster, 25-plus years

1. What was your individual career path in terms of education/training, entry-level job, or other significant opportunity?

After I graduated from college, I taught for a year. Several people in my family worked in claims. It was during a time when the industry was under pressure to hire women. I went to work for a large adjusting firm that had its own training facility, so I got a lot of training. It intrigued me to be able to move into a position with so many benefits and a company vehicle and room for promotions and the ability to learn many aspects of the industry: property claims, catastrophe claims, casualty, litigation. I eventually moved to upper management.

Prior to the job that I have now, I was vice president of Vale Training Solutions, which is a training facility for adjusters. My career path was to go out and experience everything in the field, then bring it back and train others. It came full circle.

2. What are the most important skills and/or qualities for someone in your profession?

I think communication is probably the priority. If you're a catastrophe adjuster, you're dealing with someone who's been devastated and lost their home. You need to be able to guide them through the process. Or if you're called to testify, you have to be able to communicate in a courtroom. You have to be able to communicate with different cultural groups. We constantly get calls for what we call "soft skills." The new people coming in aren't used to not sending that instant text and their writing skills to communicate and explain are not there.

And secondly, being organized. Being an adjuster, especially a catastrophe adjuster, can be very demanding— trying to see everyone and return every call and every email and get people back on their feet.

You have to genuinely like people. If you can't deal with confrontation, it's not for you. You have to be empathetic. It may seem like a mild fender bender to you, but to this grandma who's never had an accident in her life, it's major.

3. What do you wish you had known going into this profession?

I wish I had known how physically demanding the job can be. When it's 105 degrees and you're putting a 70-pound ladder up on a roof 10 times a day or you're going through a commercial building that's been burned and you can't breathe because there's soot in your nasal passages, it's tough. When you go to a catastrophe, you're hoping you can find a hotel room; there may be no water or power. And it's emotionally demanding. I've seen things that I'll never forget. I had a claim for a family in Miami where during the height of a storm—and of course, they blamed themselves, they didn't board the windows up—well, a piece of the window came through and hit their 9-year-old across the chest and he bled to death. Things like that really do impact you.

4. Are there many job opportunities in your profession? In what specific areas?

Yes. No matter what happens with the economy, there are still tornadoes and storms and car accidents and people falling down in grocery stores.

5. How do you see your profession changing in the next five years? What role will technology play in those changes, and what skills will be required?

Technology constantly changes and you have to keep up. Drones can fly over and take pictures for adjusting purposes. We already have satellite capability in areas where the roof is too steep or you can't get to the area. You can examine damage, get in your car, dial your cell phone and update a voice-activated diary: 'Went to Mrs. Jones home, she had 6 feet of water' and Mrs. Jones can log into her claim and see what's going on.

Everything is fast, fast, fast, but now customers are saying, "I got this estimate and I don't understand it." I really see a shift in realizing that fast is not always better, that you can't replace human contact.

6. What do you enjoy most about your job? What do you enjoy least about your job?

Meeting people and helping people. It's a tough industry. I've always looked at it as really helping people get their lives back together.

For a while, what I liked least was the travel. I was missing a lot of the joys of life: my kids, my husband. Catastrophe adjusters can be gone for long periods and you can't get that time back.

7. Can you suggest a valuable "try this" for students considering a career in your profession?

There are claims offices located pretty much everywhere. Go in and talk to an adjuster. There's so much out there that you can read, like Claims Magazine and Claims Management Magazine.

SELECTED SCHOOLS

Many colleges and universities, especially those with business schools, offer programs related to a career in insurance. The student can also gain initial training through enrollment at a technical or community college. Below are listed some of the more prominent institutions in this field.

Georgia State University
PO Box 3965
Atlanta, GA 30302
404.413.2000
www.gsu.edu

Florida State University
Tallahassee, FL 32306
850.644.2525
www.fsu.edu

New York University
70 Washington Square S
New York, NY 10012
212.998.1212
www.nyu.edu

St. Joseph's University
5600 City Hall
Philadelphia, PA 19131
610.660.1000
www.sju.edu

Temple University
1801 N. Broad Street
Philadelphia, PA 19122
215.204.7000
www.temple.edu

University of Georgia
Administration Building
Athens, GA 30602
706.542.3000
www.uga.edu

University of Illinois, Urbana, Champaign
601 E. John Street
Champaign, IL 61820
217.333.1000
illinois.edu

University of Pennsylvania
1 College Hall, Rm 100
Philadelphia, PA 19104
215.898.5000
www.upenn.edu

University of Texas, Austin
1 University Station
Austin, TX 78712
512.471.3434
www.utexas.edu

University of Wisconsin, Madison
500 Lincoln Drive
Madison, WI 53706
608.262.1234
www.wisc.edu

MORE INFORMATION

American College
270 S. Bryn Mawr Avenue
Bryn Mawr, PA 19010
888.263.7265
www.theamericancollege.edu

**Independent Insurance Agents
and Brokers of America**
127 S. Peyton Street
Alexandria, VA 22314
800.221.7917
www.iiaa.org

**Independent Automotive
Damage Appraisers Association**
P.O. Box 12291
Columbus, GA 31917–2291
800.369.4232
www.iada.org

Insurance Institute of America
720 Providence Road, Suite 100
Malvern, PA 19335-0716
800.644.2101
www.aicpcu.org

**National Association of
Independent Insurance
Adjusters**
P.O. Box 807
Geneva, IL 60134
630.208.5002
www.naiia.com

**National Association of
Insurance and Financial
Advisors**
2901 Telestar Court
Falls Church, VA 22042-1205
877.866.2432
www.naifa.org

**National Association of
Professional Insurance Agents**
400 N. Washington Street
Alexandria, VA 22314
703.836.9340
www.pianet.com

Simone Isadora Flynn/Editor

Insurance Sales Agent

Snapshot

Career Cluster(s): Business, Finance, Human Services, Sales & Service

Interests: Sales work, helping others, communicating with others, solving problems

Earnings (Yearly Average): $47,860

Employment & Outlook: Faster than Average Growth Expected

OVERVIEW

Sphere of Work

Insurance sales agents, including independent insurance brokers, are responsible for selling insurance policies to individuals and groups. In general, insurance agents work directly for an insurance company, whereas insurance brokers are independent middlemen arranging sales between customers and any of a number of insurance companies. Insurance sales agents work in collaboration with the underwriters who approve insurance applicants and develop insurance policies to

cover risks. Insurance sales agents tend to specialize in one or more categories of insurance, such as health, life, homeowner's, property and casualty, or business insurance.

Work Environment

Insurance sales agents work as full-time salaried and contract employees in insurance companies or as independent brokers. Insurance sales agents report to sales managers or supervisors. The insurance sales profession tends to require long hours and a high level of commitment to clients. Insurance sales agents generally work forty-hour weeks but may be required to work overtime during periods of increased business, or to work in the evenings to meet customer or client needs. Some may have to travel for work. Employment in this field is not expected to be negatively affected by online sales, as most customers prefer to meet with an agent and develop a relationship with him or her, partly due to the complexity of insurance transactions, and also because buying insurance involves discussing how to plan for the future and protect one's financial interests.

Profile

Working Conditions: Work Indoors
Physical Strength: Light Work
Education Needs: On-The-Job Training, Junior/Technical/Community College, Bachelor's Degree
Licensure/Certification: Required
Opportunities For Experience: Internship, Part-Time Work
Holland Interest Score*: ECS

* See Appendix A

Occupation Interest

Individuals attracted to the insurance sales profession tend to be organized and outgoing, with excellent people skills. Those individuals who excel as insurance sales agents exhibit traits such as good time management, likeability, honesty, and salesmanship. Insurance sales agents should enjoy sales work, be able to maintain a positive and enthusiastic attitude, and be motivated to help customers solve problems.

A Day in the Life—Duties and Responsibilities

The daily duties and responsibilities of insurance sales agents vary by insurance specialty and employer. Areas of insurance specialization include health insurance, life insurance, homeowners' insurance, mortgage insurance, liability insurance, property insurance, automobile insurance, construction or building insurance, malpractice insurance, farm or crop insurance, and commercial or business insurance. Most firms specialize in more than one of these areas.

Insurance sales agents must first meet with clients to interview them about their specific needs, and then educate the client about the different types of insurance and the amounts of coverage available. Matching the appropriate amount and type of insurance to each client is extremely important. Much of a sales agent's business is generated through word-of-mouth referrals from current customers, so it is vital for the customers to be satisfied with the service the agent has provided. The insurance sales agent must meet with policyholders on a regular or as-needed basis to review and reevaluate policy details, record policy changes, and explain additional services as clients experience life-changing events such as the birth of a child or the purchase of a home.

Insurance sales agents may also advise clients about the place of insurance in the financial planning process; network and advertise to attract new customers; and keep thorough records of all sales, premium amounts, renewals, and types of coverage. In addition, all insurance sales agents should stay up to date with regulatory and ethical issues in the insurance industry by reading insurance industry journals and maintaining active membership in insurance industry associations.

Duties and Responsibilities

- **Compiling lists of prospective clients**
- **Advising clients on financial planning**
- **Assisting clients with benefit claims**
- **Computing and collecting premiums**
- **Explaining features of policies**
- **Keeping records of policies**
- **Maintaining regular contact with clients**
- **Selling securities, such as mutual fund shares or annuities**
- **Preparing reports and maintaining records**

WORK ENVIRONMENT

Physical Environment

Insurance sales agents generally work in office environments. Sometimes they are required to travel to interview potential customers or existing policyholders as well as to inspect insured properties and construction sites.

Relevant Skills and Abilities

Communication Skills
- Persuading others
- Speaking effectively
- Writing concisely

Interpersonal/Social Skills
- Cooperating with others
- Working as a member of a team

Organization & Management Skills
- Coordinating tasks
- Making decisions
- Managing people/groups

Research & Planning Skills
- Gathering information

Technical Skills
- Performing scientific, mathematical and technical work
- Working with data or numbers

Unclassified Skills
- Maintaining good public relations

Human Environment

Insurance sales agents interact with clients, policyholders, actuaries, insurance underwriters, insurance adjusters, lawyers, other sales agents, and supervisors.

Technological Environment

Insurance sales agents use computers, actuarial tables, insurance rate and code books, telephones, cameras, calculators, Internet communication tools, and spreadsheets to complete their work.

EDUCATION, TRAINING, AND ADVANCEMENT

High School/Secondary

High school students interested in pursuing a career as an insurance sales agent should focus on mathematics classes, as bookkeeping, accounting, and business skills will provide a strong foundation for work as an insurance sales agent. Because on-the-job experience is highly valued in this profession, high school students interested in this career path will benefit from seeking internships or part-time work with insurance businesses. High school graduates may be able to attain work as insurance customer representatives directly out of high school and work their way up to insurance sales agents through hard work and promotion.

Suggested High School Subjects
- Accounting
- Applied Communication
- Bookkeeping
- Business Law
- Business Math
- College Preparatory
- Computer Science
- Economics
- English
- Keyboarding
- Mathematics
- Merchandising
- Psychology
- Social Studies
- Sociology
- Speech

Famous First

The first accident insurance company was Travelers Insurance Company of Hartford, Conn, started in 1863. The initial type of coverage was for travel accidents only. The first policy was issued to a Hartford resident who paid a small premium for a $1,000 policy covering any accidents occurring while walking between his house and the local post office.

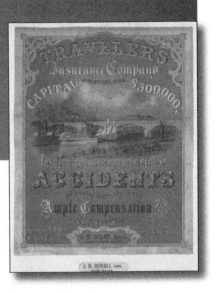

College/Postsecondary

Postsecondary students interested in becoming insurance sales agents should work toward an associate's or bachelor's degree in insurance, business law, business administration, economics, finance, statistics, or accounting. Coursework in computer science, political science, psychology, sociology, and ethics may also prove useful in their future work. Postsecondary students can gain work experience and potential advantage in their future job searches through internships or part-time employment with local insurance businesses.

Related College Majors
- Business
- Finance, General
- Insurance & Risk Management

Adult Job Seekers

Adults seeking insurance sales agent jobs have generally earned an associate's or bachelor's degree, often in business, accounting, or economics. Some insurance sales agent jobs require extensive on-the-job training, but most offer entry-level seasonal and part-time employment. Adult job seekers should educate themselves about the educational and professional requirements of the organizations where they seek employment. Adult job seekers will benefit from joining professional insurance associations as a means of professional networking. Professional insurance associations, such as the National

Association of Professional Insurance Agents and the Insurance Institute of America, generally maintain job lists advertising open sales positions.

Professional Certification and Licensure

Certification is required in all fifty states for insurance sales agents. There are also several options for additional voluntary insurance sales agent certification, including the Chartered Financial Consultant (ChFC), the Life Underwriter Training Council Fellow (LUTCF), and the Chartered Life Underwriter (CLU) designations awarded by American College, and the Chartered Property Casualty Underwriter (CPCU) designation awarded by the American Institute for Chartered Property Casualty Underwriters (AICPCU). These voluntary certifications have education, work experience, testing, ethics, employer sponsorship, recertification, and continuing education requirements. Additional licensing is required for insurance sales agents who sell life insurance, health insurance, property insurance, and casualty insurance, and these requirements vary significantly by state. Insurance sales agents should consult their state department of insurance for information on specific licensing requirements.

Additional Requirements

Successful insurance sales agents tend to share traits like being customer-driven, attentive, flexible, enthusiastic, and focused on problem-solving. Professionals in this role have access to confidential information and must adhere to strict ethical standards. Membership in professional insurance associations is encouraged among all insurance sales agents as a means of building professional community.

Fun Fact

Mariah Carey insured her legs for $1 billion. Keith Richards, the Rolling Stones guitarist, insured the middle finger of his left hand—critical for playing guitar—for $1.6 million.

Source: http://www.business-insurers.com/blog/insurance-fun-facts

EARNINGS AND ADVANCEMENT

Many independent insurance sales agents are paid by commission only, whereas those who are employees of an agency or an insurance carrier may be paid in one of three ways salary only, salary plus commission, or salary plus bonus. In general, commissions are the most common form of compensation, especially for experienced insurance sales agents. The amount of the commission depends on the type and amount of insurance sold and on whether the transaction is a new policy or a renewal. Bonuses usually are awarded when insurance sales agents meet their sales goals or when an agency meets its profit goals.

Median annual earnings of salaried insurance sales agents were $47,860 in 2014. The lowest ten percent earned less than $25,710, and the highest ten percent earned more than $119,570. Insurance sales agents generally pay their own travel expenses. Those who own and operate independent businesses must pay office rent, clerical salaries and other operating expenses.

Full-time insurance sales agents may receive paid vacations, holidays, and sick days; life and health insurance; and retirement benefits. These are usually paid by the employer. Some companies offer a profit-sharing plan, others also pay bonuses based on sales.

Metropolitan Areas with the Highest
Employment Level in This Occupation

Metropolitan area	Employment	Employment per thousand jobs	Annual mean wage
New York-White Plains-Wayne, NY-NJ	13,020	2.42	$81,360
Chicago-Joliet-Naperville, IL	12,360	3.29	$75,430
Los Angeles-Long Beach-Glendale, CA	10,120	2.50	$60,580
Dallas-Plano-Irving, TX	8,370	3.74	$59,140
Atlanta-Sandy Springs-Marietta, GA	6,750	2.83	$75,950
Philadelphia, PA	6,620	3.56	$75,350
Houston-Sugar Land-Baytown, TX	6,570	2.31	$63,490
Nassau-Suffolk, NY	5,480	4.35	$83,470
San Antonio-New Braunfels, TX	5,200	5.69	$53,250
Denver-Aurora-Broomfield, CO	4,790	3.61	$55,300

Source: Bureau of Labor Statistics

EMPLOYMENT AND OUTLOOK

Nationally, there were approximately 466,000 insurance sales agents employed in 2014. About one-fourth of insurance sales agents were self-employed. Employment is expected to grow faster than the average for all occupations through the year 2024, which means employment is projected to increase 6 percent to 12 percent. Job opportunities will be good for those who have developed expertise in a wide range of insurance and financial services. While sales of life insurance are down, rising incomes, as well as a concern for financial security during retirement, may stimulate the sales of mutual funds, variable annuities and other financial products and services. Sales of health and long-term care insurance are expected to rise sharply as the population ages and as the law provides more people with access to health insurance.

Employment Trend, Projected 2014–24

Insurance sales agents: 9%

Sales representatives, services: 7%

Total, all occupations: 7%

Note: "All Occupations" includes all occupations in the U.S. Economy. Source: U.S. Bureau of Labor Statistics, Employment Projections Program.

Related Occupations

- Automobile Salesperson
- Financial Analyst
- Insurance Underwriter
- Manufacturers Representative
- Personal Financial Advisor
- Pharmaceutical Sales Representative
- Real Estate Sales Agent
- Retail Salesperson
- Sales Engineer
- Securities Sales Agent
- Services Sales Representative
- Technical Sales Representative
- Wholesale Sales Representative

Conversation With . . .
RON BLOUNT

Owner/Agent, Ron Blount Insurance Agency LLC
Bowie, Maryland
Insurance business, 4 years

1. What was your individual career path in terms of education/training, entry-level job, or other significant opportunity?

College wasn't in my initial plan, because I was burnt out by the time I graduated from high school. I joined the U.S. Navy two weeks after graduation and went from my hometown of St. Louis, Mo., to boot camp in Great Lakes, Ill., to my ship's home port of Norfolk, Va. I worked on missile launchers as a gunner's mate. I spent two of the three years I was in the Navy on the ship. I travelled to a lot of places that I had previously only dreamed of.

Once I got out, I relocated to the Washington, D.C. area. I started looking for a professional job in electronics—which I had learned in the Navy—but this was before desktop computers and I didn't have enough time in the Navy to qualify for professional-level jobs. I took a minimum-wage job as an office clerk and quickly realized that $3.90 an hour wasn't going to take me very far. So I went to trade school, got a job fixing computers, and moved up to network engineer, then manager of a group of network engineers. At that point, a guy that I had trained, who had a degree, got promoted over me. I asked my manager how that had happened. He explained that they promoted based on a point system, and, unfortunately for me, a college degree carried more weight than my experience.

So I went to college part-time and graduated with a bachelor's in information systems management from the University of Maryland University College at age thirty-five, then went on to get an MBA at age thirty-eight.

After graduation, I moved from the engineering side to the sales side. I sold large computer systems, primarily to the federal government. As time moved on, I wanted to do something else with my career. I saw a billboard for State Farm Insurance and wondered about selling insurance. After doing my research, I felt State Farm offered the best option because they gave me a year's worth of training and a book of existing clients. I know of another insurance company that sells you the book.

There was a learning curve, but State Farm offers a lot of support. I only sell State Farm products, but I don't work for them; I am an independent contractor. I have two employees now, I'm probably going to hire another, and my book is growing every year. I wish I had learned about this opportunity 10 years sooner.

2. What are the most important skills and/or qualities for someone in your profession?

You need business acumen, because you're running a business. You also have to be willing to talk to people. I have to understand you as a client because if I insure you and don't give you coverage to protect what you own, you could be in a bad situation.

3. What do you wish you had known going into this profession?

I didn't realize that you have to continuously educate yourself about the things people need in order to be secure with their retirement or liability coverage. Also, I wish I'd known more about running a business.

4. Are there many job opportunities in your profession? In what specific areas?

Absolutely. You can go into an agency like mine, or you can work at the corporate level, where you could be a sales leader, or go into administrative or executive jobs. The industry is vast and opportunities exist in life insurance, specialty insurances, or even the financial services side of insurance companies. You must be licensed by the state to work in insurance.

5. How do you see your profession changing in the next five years, what role will technology play in those changes, and what skills will be required?

Having enough liability insurance will continue to be important, given the amount of litigation that goes on. From a technology standpoint, more and different apps are available, and online options for consumers to manage their insurance will continue to grow.

That said, most people aren't educated about what they need. That's when you need an agent.

6. What do you enjoy most about your job? What do you enjoy least about your job?

I realized a lot of people in the community aren't being properly served, and I like helping them. They might be their family's first generation to earn a decent wage. As my clients age, they amass assets they need to protect. If you're underinsured and someone sues you, the other guy can come after your paycheck or the equity in your home. People want to create a legacy for their family or to retire comfortably.

I least like the many regulations that sometimes tie my hands and don't allow me to help people as much as I'd like, even though I understand regulations are there for a reason.

7. Can you suggest a valuable "try this" for students considering a career in your profession?

Some agents hire high school kids or interns, which would allow you to see how an insurance office works. Or look for a summer job at one of the corporations; some do that for business majors. This can be a very lucrative career.

SELECTED SCHOOLS

Most colleges and universities offer programs related to careers in business, sales, or insurance; the student may also get started in a technical or community college. For a list of some of the more prominent schools in this field, see the chapter "Insurance Claims Adjuster and Examiner" in the present volume.

MORE INFORMATION

American College
270 S. Bryn Mawr Avenue
Bryn Mawr, PA 19010
888.263.7265
www.theamericancollege.edu

American Institute for CPCU
720 Providence Road
P.O. Box 3016
Malvern, PA 19355-0716
800.644.2101
www.aicpcu.org

Chartered Property and Casualty Underwriters Society
Kahler Hall
720 Providence Road
Malvern, PA 19355-0709
800.932.2728
www.cpcusociety.org

Independent Insurance Agents & Brokers of America, Inc.
127 S. Peyton Street
Alexandria, VA 22314
800.221.7917
www.iiaa.org

Insurance Information Institute
110 William Street
New York, NY 10038
212.346.5500
www.iii.org

Insurance Institute of America
720 Providence Road, Suite 100
Malvern, PA 19335-0716
800.644.2101
www.aicpcu.org

International Claim Association
1155 15th Street NW, Suite 500
Washington, DC 20005
202.452.0143
www.claim.org

**National Association of
Insurance & Financial Advisors**
2901 Telestar Court
Falls Church, VA 22042-1205
877.866.2432
www.naifa.org

**National Association of
Professional Insurance Agents**
400 N. Washington Street
Alexandria, VA 22314
703.836.9340
www.pianet.com

**National Association of Public
Insurance Adjusters**
21165 Whitfield Place, Suite 105
Potomac Falls, VA 20165
703.433.9217
www.napia.com

**Society of Financial Service
Professionals**
19 Campus Boulevard, Suite 100
Newtown Square, PA 19073-3239
610.526.2500
www.financialpro.org

Simone Isadora Flynn/Editor

Insurance Underwriter

Snapshot

Career Cluster(s): Business, Finance, Insurance

Interests: Statistics, risk assessment, working with details, helping others

Earnings (Yearly Average): $64,220

Employment & Outlook: Decline Expected

Sphere of Work

Insurance underwriters, also referred to as account underwriters, property underwriters, commercial underwriters, and health underwriters, are responsible for processing, reviewing, and approving or rejecting insurance applications. They use risk assessment software and actuarial data to evaluate insurance applications for individual and group insurance policies. Insurance underwriters are risk assessment experts who use company or business risk guidelines to determine whether or not selling

insurance to an individual or group falls within acceptable risk
parameters.

Work Environment

Although the insurance profession as a whole is expected to experience
long-term economic growth, the insurance underwriting occupation is
in transition due to the increasing use of computer software that can
analyze data and assess risk in significantly less time than it would
take an underwriter. Consequently, employment opportunities for
underwriters are expected to decline rather than grow; however, the
profession experiences a significant rate of employee turnover, so new
applicants are usually welcome.

Insurance underwriters may travel for work. For instance, health
insurance underwriters may travel to businesses to interview
applicants or union representatives for group health insurance
policies, and construction underwriters may travel to job sites
to inspect the progress and risk of building projects. Insurance
underwriters generally work forty-hour weeks but may be required to
work overtime during periods of increased business.

Profile

Working Conditions: Work Indoors
Physical Strength: Light Work
Education Needs: Bachelor's Degree
Licensure/Certification:
  Recommended
Opportunities For Experience:
  Internship, Part-Time Work
Holland Interest Score*: CSE

* See Appendix A

Occupation Interest

Individuals attracted to the
insurance underwriting profession
tend to be organized, analytical,
and detail-oriented people. Those
individuals who excel as insurance
underwriters exhibit traits such
as responsibility, good time
management, and a desire to help.
Insurance underwriters should
enjoy insurance work and have a
background in statistics and risk
assessment.

A Day in the Life—Duties and Responsibilities

The daily duties and responsibilities of insurance underwriters will
vary with job specialty and employer. Areas of insurance underwriting
specialization include health insurance, life insurance, homeowners

insurance, mortgage insurance, liability insurance, property insurance, automobile insurance, construction or building insurance, and commercial or business insurance.

Insurance underwriters interview insurance applicants to gather information about applicants' health, lifestyle, family history, employment history, home value, geographical location, and natural disaster risks. They may assist insurance applicants with insurance forms or request additional information from applicants to make final coverage and premium decisions. Processing individual and group insurance applications may involve using computer software and actuarial tables (which calculate life expectancy) to analyze risk; confirming the value of property listed in insurance applications; reviewing individual and group insurance policies to assess what type and amount of coverage to offer applicants; and determining premium amounts and levels. Other duties include working with actuaries to develop acceptable risk guidelines for businesses, visiting construction sites to assess progress and on-site risks for workers and community, and travel to businesses to interview union representatives for group health insurance policies.

If the underwriter's data indicates that the monies obtained from monthly premium payments are likely to exceed the costs of insuring the client, he or she writes up a policy that covers the risks in question, and the client is notified. In some cases, an underwriter may have to notify insurance applicants that the company has chosen not to approve their application.

Insurance underwriters may also need to participate in industry seminars and conferences to satisfy continuing education requirements for certification. They should also stay up to date with regulatory and ethical issues in the insurance industry by reading insurance industry journals and participating in insurance industry associations. They usually report to a chief underwriter, supervising underwriter, or managing underwriter.

Duties and Responsibilities

- Reviewing insurance applications, inspection reports and medical examination forms to determine the risk of insuring an applicant
- Reviewing company records on the risk of insuring certain groups
- Declining clients where the risk of insuring is too great
- Deciding whether to issue insurance policies
- Outlining terms of contracts
- Corresponding with policy holders, agents and others

OCCUPATION SPECIALTIES

Life Underwriters

Life Underwriters can further specialize in insuring the lives of individuals or groups.

Multiple Line Underwriters

Multiple Line Underwriters specialize in a combination of risks.

Commercial Account Underwriters

Commercial Account Underwriters handle business insurance only.

Automotive Underwriters

Automotive Underwriters specialize in insuring motor vehicles.

Compensation Underwriters

Compensation Underwriters specialize in insuring employees against injury and illness.

Pension and Advanced Underwriting Specialists

Pension and Advanced Underwriting Specialists insure employees with retirement plans.

Special Risks Underwriters

Special Risks Underwriters insure the unusual, such as art objects and celebrities.

Marine Underwriters

Marine Underwriters insure boats and nautical activities.

Fire Underwriters

Fire Underwriters insure property against fire.

WORK ENVIRONMENT

Physical Environment

Insurance underwriters generally work in comfortable office environments. In some cases, insurance underwriters will be required to travel to the field to interview insurance applicants and inspect insured properties and construction sites.

Relevant Skills and Abilities

Communication Skills
- Speaking effectively
- Writing concisely

Organization & Management Skills
- Making decisions
- Paying attention to and handling details

Research & Planning Skills
- Analyzing information
- Creating ideas

Technical Skills
- Working with data or numbers
- Working with machines, tools or other objects

Human Environment

Insurance underwriters interact with insurance applicants, insurance policyholders, actuaries, insurance sales agents, insurance adjusters, lawyers, coworkers, and supervisors.

Technological Environment

Insurance underwriters use computers, actuarial tables, insurance rate and code books, telephones, cameras, calculators, Internet communication tools, automated underwriting systems, and spreadsheets to complete their work.

EDUCATION, TRAINING, AND ADVANCEMENT

High School/Secondary

High school students interested in pursuing a career as an insurance underwriter should prepare by building good study habits. High school–level study of sociology, bookkeeping, and mathematics will provide a strong foundation for work as an insurance underwriter or for college-level study in the field. Part-time or internship opportunities can provide valuable experience.

Suggested High School Subjects
- Accounting
- College Preparatory
- Composition
- Computer Science
- English
- Mathematics
- Social Studies

Famous First

The first insurance rate standardization was put in place in 1866 by the National Board of Fire Underwriters, an organization of 75 fire insurance companies. Prior to that, rates differed according to individual circumstances.

College/Postsecondary

Postsecondary students interested in becoming insurance underwriters should obtain a bachelor's degree in business administration, law, economics, actuarial science, finance, statistics, or accounting. Coursework in computer science, political science, and ethics may also prove useful in their future work. Postsecondary students can gain work experience and potential advantage in their future job searches by securing internships or part-time employment with local insurance businesses.

Related College Majors
- Finance, General
- Insurance & Risk Management

Adult Job Seekers

Adults seeking insurance underwriting jobs have generally earned a bachelor's degree in business administration or a related field. Some insurance underwriting jobs require extensive experience and on-the-job training. Adult job seekers should educate themselves about the educational and professional requirements of the organizations where they seek employment. They may also benefit from joining professional insurance associations as a means of professional networking. Professional insurance associations, such as the Chartered Property Casualty Underwriters Society, the National Association of Professional Insurance Agents and the Insurance Institute of America, generally maintain job lists advertising open underwriting positions.

Professional Certification and Licensure

Certification is not legally required for insurance underwriters but may be required as a condition of employment, salary increase, or promotion. Associate in Personal Insurance and Associate in Commercial Underwriting designations are available through the Insurance Institute of America and both take one to two years to obtain. A more in-depth option for voluntary insurance underwriter certification is the Chartered Property Casualty Underwriter (CPCU), which requires passing eight exams on different insurance-related topics over a four-year period. The voluntary CPCU certification, offered by the American Institute for Chartered Property Casualty

Underwriters (AICPCU), has education, work experience, testing, ethics, employer sponsorship, recertification, and continuing education requirements. Licensing requirements for insurance underwriters vary significantly by state. Insurance underwriters should consult with the insurance department in their home state for specific licensing requirements.

Additional Requirements

Successful insurance underwriters will be knowledgeable about the profession's requirements, responsibilities, and opportunities. Insurance underwriters have access to confidential information about clients, so they must adhere to strict ethical guidelines set by industry organizations. Membership in professional insurance associations is encouraged among all insurance underwriters as a means of building professional community.

EARNINGS AND ADVANCEMENT

Median annual earnings of insurance underwriters were $64,220 in 2014. The lowest ten percent earned less than $39,260, and the highest ten percent earned more than $113,010.

Insurance underwriters may receive paid vacations, holidays, and sick days; life and health insurance; and retirement benefits. These are usually paid by the employer.

Fun Fact

The first known insurance policy was carved on a Babylonian monument with the Hammurabi Code. It excused a debtor from paying loans if a catastrophe like flooding, disability or death made it impossible to do so.

Source: www.investopedia.com/articles/08/history-of-insurance.asp

Metropolitan Areas with the Highest Employment Level in This Occupation

Metropolitan area	Employment	Employment per thousand jobs	Annual mean wage
Atlanta-Sandy Springs-Marietta, GA	4,540	1.90	$71,120
Chicago-Joliet-Naperville, IL	4,430	1.18	$66,910
New York-White Plains-Wayne, NY-NJ	4,300	0.80	$100,290
Philadelphia, PA	3,090	1.66	$78,630
Boston-Cambridge-Quincy, MA	2,920	1.62	$76,990
Hartford-West Hartford-East Hartford, CT	2,850	5.06	$91,630
Dallas-Plano-Irving, TX	2,300	1.03	$73,160
Los Angeles-Long Beach-Glendale, CA	1,880	0.46	$72,340
Minneapolis-St. Paul-Bloomington, MN-WI	1,750	0.96	$62,850
Seattle-Bellevue-Everett, WA	1,420	0.95	$80,070

Source: Bureau of Labor Statistics

EMPLOYMENT AND OUTLOOK

Insurance underwriters held about 103,000 jobs nationally in 2014. Employment of insurance underwriters is expected to decline somewhat through the year 2024, which means employment is projected to go down by as much as 11 percent. Computer software that helps insurance underwriters analyze policies more quickly and accurately has made workers more productive and their numbers lower; however, economic and population growth will still result in increased insurance needs by businesses and individuals. Most job openings will result from the need to replace workers who join other occupations or retire, especially since turnover in this field is high.

Employment Trend, Projected 2014–24

Financial specialists: 10%

Total, all occupations: 7%

Insurance underwriters: -11%

Note: "All Occupations" includes all occupations in the U.S. Economy. Source: U.S. Bureau of Labor Statistics, Employment Projections Program.

Related Occupations

- Actuary
- Auditor
- Financial Analyst
- Insurance Claims Adjuster and Examiner
- Insurance Sales Agent
- Personal Financial Advisor
- Statistician

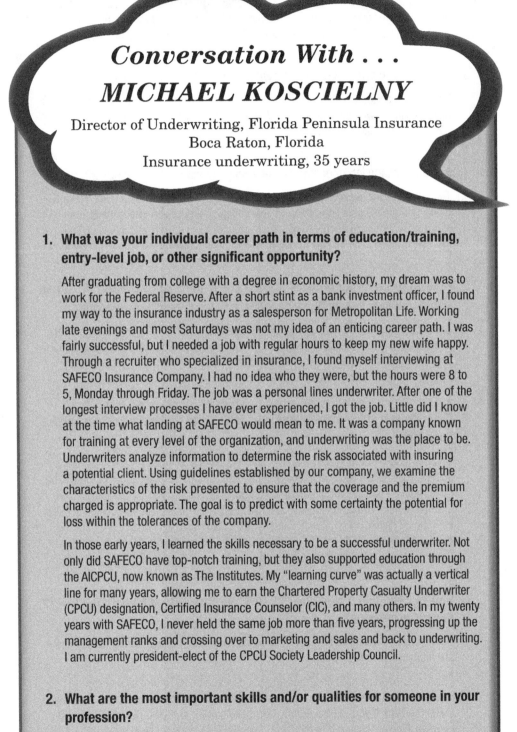

Conversation With . . .
MICHAEL KOSCIELNY

Director of Underwriting, Florida Peninsula Insurance
Boca Raton, Florida
Insurance underwriting, 35 years

1. What was your individual career path in terms of education/training, entry-level job, or other significant opportunity?

After graduating from college with a degree in economic history, my dream was to work for the Federal Reserve. After a short stint as a bank investment officer, I found my way to the insurance industry as a salesperson for Metropolitan Life. Working late evenings and most Saturdays was not my idea of an enticing career path. I was fairly successful, but I needed a job with regular hours to keep my new wife happy. Through a recruiter who specialized in insurance, I found myself interviewing at SAFECO Insurance Company. I had no idea who they were, but the hours were 8 to 5, Monday through Friday. The job was a personal lines underwriter. After one of the longest interview processes I have ever experienced, I got the job. Little did I know at the time what landing at SAFECO would mean to me. It was a company known for training at every level of the organization, and underwriting was the place to be. Underwriters analyze information to determine the risk associated with insuring a potential client. Using guidelines established by our company, we examine the characteristics of the risk presented to ensure that the coverage and the premium charged is appropriate. The goal is to predict with some certainty the potential for loss within the tolerances of the company.

In those early years, I learned the skills necessary to be a successful underwriter. Not only did SAFECO have top-notch training, but they also supported education through the AICPCU, now known as The Institutes. My "learning curve" was actually a vertical line for many years, allowing me to earn the Chartered Property Casualty Underwriter (CPCU) designation, Certified Insurance Counselor (CIC), and many others. In my twenty years with SAFECO, I never held the same job more than five years, progressing up the management ranks and crossing over to marketing and sales and back to underwriting. I am currently president-elect of the CPCU Society Leadership Council.

2. What are the most important skills and/or qualities for someone in your profession?

I would sum up the skills necessary to be a great underwriter with two words: intellectual curiosity. Of course you have to have good communication skills, time-management skills, analytical skills, decisiveness, good judgment and be a team player, but intellectual curiosity is the key. You have to be nosey and question things that just don't make sense. If you love to solve problems, underwriting is the place to be.

3. What do you wish you had known going into this profession?

I wish I had understood while I was in college that insurance includes many careers beyond sales. I wouldn't have wasted two years of my life in the banking industry if someone had shared with me the opportunities in insurance.

4. Are there many job opportunities in your profession? In what specific areas?

The opportunities over the next ten years are huge. One third of the 3 million people working in the insurance industry will retire in the next decade. That means great opportunity for young people to find their way into this industry and succeed. There will be opportunities in all facets of insurance company operations, not just underwriting.

5. How do you see your profession changing in the next five years? What role will technology play in those changes, and what skills will be required?

Technology has removed the mundane from underwriters' work, allowing them to focus on more complex decisions. Routine risk assessments are done by computers, providing potential clients with faster decisions. Risks that cannot be processed electronically are steered to an underwriter. It's a very rewarding job today.

6. What do you enjoy most about your job? What do you enjoy least about your job?

Underwriting—or the systematic evaluation of risks and how I might mitigate, accept or avoid the consequences of those risks—has become a way of life for me. It's a routine I use in every facet of what I do, professionally and personally. I love that every risk I evaluate is a new story with unique twists. I can honestly say there is nothing I dislike about my job. I guess what I like least are those things that do not challenge me. With any job, there are routine things that make it a "job," like paperwork. Not interesting, but necessary.

7. Can you suggest a valuable "try this" for students considering a career in your profession?

Get involved in a degree program at a school with risk management courses. There are many across the country.

Check out insuremypath.org. You can get connected with internships at top insurance companies. There's nothing like taking a career for a test drive before you make the leap. If you're researching colleges, look for one with risk management courses. Finally, reach out to the CPCU Society. They have more than 22,000 members across the country who are more than willing to spend time with students interested in this great industry.

SELECTED SCHOOLS

Most colleges and universities offer programs related to careers in business, sales, or insurance; the student may also get started in a technical or community college. For a list of some of the more prominent schools in this field, see the chapter "Insurance Claims Adjuster and Examiner" in the present volume.

MORE INFORMATION

American College
270 S. Bryn Mawr Avenue
Bryn Mawr, PA 19010
888.263.7265
www.theamericancollege.edu

American Institute for CPCU
720 Providence Road
P.O. Box 3016
Malvern, PA 19355-0716
800.644.2101
www.aicpcu.org

Chartered Property and Casualty Underwriters Society
Kahler Hall
720 Providence Road
Malvern, PA 19355-0709
800.932.2728
www.cpcusociety.org

Independent Insurance Agents and Brokers of America
127 S. Peyton Street
Alexandria, VA 22314
800.221.7917
www.iiaa.org

Insurance Institute of America
720 Providence Road, Suite 100
Malvern, PA 19335-0716
800.644.2101
www.aicpcu.org

National Association of Insurance & Financial Advisors
2901 Telestar Court
Falls Church, VA 22042-1205
877.866.2432
www.naifa.org

National Association of Professional Insurance Agents
400 N. Washington Street
Alexandria, VA 22314
703.836.9340
www.pianet.com

Simone Isadora Flynn/Editor

Manufacturers' Representative

Snapshot

Career Cluster(s): Agriculture, Business, Manufacturing, Sales & Service

Interests: Customer service, communicating with others

Earnings (Yearly Average): $55,020

Employment & Outlook: Average Growth Expected

OVERVIEW

Sphere of Work

Manufacturers' representatives, also called manufacturing sales representatives or manufacturers' agents, sell the goods of a particular manufacturer to businesses or other organizations. These goods might include mechanical and agricultural equipment, computers, or pharmaceuticals. Representatives serve as the face of a manufacturer, interacting with customers on a daily basis. They tell customers about their products, answer questions, and negotiate prices and deals.

Most manufacturers' representatives are self-employed,

which means that they are contracted to different manufacturing companies at different times. Other agents are employed directly by one manufacturer. Manufacturers' representatives work on commission; that is, they are paid per sale, as opposed to being paid on a salary. Earning commissions can be stressful, as can the quotas that some manufacturers set for their representatives, though some representatives make a significant amount of money. Many representatives travel regularly for seminars and meetings.

Work Environment

There are generally two types of manufacturers' representatives: inside sales representatives and outside sales representatives. Inside sales reps work in offices, placing telephone calls to businesses and organizations to talk to them about a particular product or answer incoming questions. An outside sales rep does a significant amount of travel, visiting businesses and potential clients directly.

Profile

Working Conditions: Work Indoors
Physical Strength: Light Work
Education Needs: On-The-Job Training, Junior/Technical/Community College, Bachelor's Degree
Licensure/Certification: Recommended
Opportunities For Experience: Part-Time Work
Holland Interest Score*: ESA

* See Appendix A

Occupation Interest

Successful manufacturers' representatives thrive on personal interaction. They are able to speak confidently about a product, describing its attributes and benefits, and they are very persuasive. Communication skills are the most important component of their work.

A Day in the Life—Duties and Responsibilities

The daily life of a manufacturers' representative varies. An inside manufacturers' representative will spend his or her day at an office, placing telephone calls to businesses and organizations. Often these are cold calls, which means that the representatives are contacting an institution or client who is not expecting their call. Because inside manufacturers' representatives do not have the advantage of speaking with clients in person, they must take care to be courteous and friendly while remaining persistent.

Outside manufacturers' representatives spend a significant amount of time traveling, and their hours are often irregular. A representative might be responsible for covering several towns or several states, depending on circumstance. This type of manufacturers' representative has much more interface with clients. They make regular sales calls and presentations, persuading businesses and organizations to buy their products. They also advise existing clients. Many sales agents demonstrate how to operate machinery or use a particular product and advise clients on how to arrange promotional materials or window displays.

Manufacturers' representatives also spend time analyzing sales figures and reports. Administrative tasks such as scheduling appointments, keeping track of sales accounts, filling our paperwork, and making travel arrangements can also take a significant amount of time. Some manufacturers' reps, depending on the product they are selling, travel with a technical expert who explains the details of a product to customers. This arrangement allows the representative to focus on sales work.

Duties and Responsibilities

- Contacting manufacturers and arranging to sell their products
- Preparing lists of prospective customers
- Studying the buyer's needs and suggesting how products can meet these needs
- Calling on regular and prospective customers
- Demonstrating products
- Answering questions about products
- Promoting products at trade shows and conferences
- Forwarding orders to manufacturers
- Advising customers on credit problems and product pricing

WORK ENVIRONMENT

Physical Environment

Some representatives work in an office, while others spend a significant amount of time on the road. A traveling representative will spend time in airplanes, cars, and trains.

Relevant Skills and Abilities

Communication Skills
- Expressing thoughts and ideas
- Persuading others
- Speaking effectively
- Writing concisely

Interpersonal/Social Skills
- Cooperating with others
- Working as a member of a team

Research & Planning Skills
- Using logical reasoning

Technical Skills
- Performing scientific, mathematical and technical work

Human Environment

Manufacturers' representatives have daily contact with clients and customers. They often speak with numerous clients in one day. Additionally, representatives compete with reps from other companies and attend conferences to learn new skills. A manufacturers' representative divides his or her time between solitary work, such as administrative tasks, and public interface with prospective buyers and other representatives.

Technological Environment

Manufacturers' representatives are responsible for knowing everything about the product they are selling, including any improvements that have been made to that product. In addition, they use personal computers in their work.

EDUCATION, TRAINING, AND ADVANCEMENT

High School/Secondary

An aspiring manufacturers' representative should take high school courses in mathematics, business, accounting, English, and public speaking. A salesperson is always performing. Candidates must be comfortable speaking in front of an audience. Classes or extracurricular activities that build confidence in this area, such as acting, theater, or speech and debate, are valuable to aspiring manufacturers' representatives.

Suggested High School Subjects
- Applied Communication
- Bookkeeping
- Business Math
- College Preparatory
- English
- Mathematics
- Merchandising
- Psychology
- Social Studies
- Speech

Famous First

The first major manufacturer's representative in the tech industry was Computer Marketing Group (CMG), founded in 1981 to be Apple Computer's representative in greater New York City. The company later broadened its range to include computer graphics dealers.

College/Postsecondary

Some manufacturers' representative jobs, such as those that involve nontechnical products or goods, do not require a postsecondary degree. Many people can find jobs in the field with a high school diploma or an equivalent certificate. Other manufacturers' rep jobs require a bachelor's degree in the sciences or engineering or a degree related to the product a candidate is seeking to sell.

Some companies offer their own training courses for employees. These courses can last up to two years and include classroom instruction and field training alongside more experienced personnel. Regardless of a company's policies in terms of employee training, most manufacturers' representatives do not start out making phone calls or personal sales calls alone. Most people who are new to the job will spend a specified amount of time, sometimes up to one year, working alongside an experienced representative.

Related College Majors
- Apparel & Accessories Marketing Management
- General Retailing & Wholesaling Operations & Skills
- General Selling Skills & Sales Operations

Adult Job Seekers

Individuals with experience in sales make good candidates for manufacturers' representative positions, even without a related college degree. Employers look for candidates who have a strong and likeable personality to represent their company to clients. An adult job seeker should acquire certification as a manufacturers' rep to increase his or her employability.

Professional Certification and Licensure

Though official certification is not required for all manufacturers' representatives, seeking certification through the Manufacturers' Representatives Educational Research Foundation (MRERF) is a wise career move for any rep. MRERF offers a program to become a certified professional manufacturers' representative (CPMR). The program offers courses in business and sales as well as courses specific to different industries. Candidates for certification complete the classes over the course of three years. Each year, reps spend one week attending classes that correspond with their level in the program. These include classes in business ethics, financial management, human resources, negotiation, and social media. After a rep has become certified through MRERF, he or she maintains this certification by participating in ten hours of relevant education courses annually.

Additional Requirements

A career as a manufacturers' representative can be competitive, and good reps are driven and goal-oriented people. They are equally comfortable working as a part of a team or working alone. They are good at forming relationships with customers and maintaining those relationships over a long period. Successful reps work well under pressure and are always willing to learn new skills to do their job better.

Fun Fact

It costs six to seven times as much to attract a new customer as it does to hold on to an existing one.

Source: https://www.salesforce.com/blog/2013/08/customer-service-stats.html

EARNINGS AND ADVANCEMENT

Earnings depend on the geographic location of the employer, the type and quality of the product sold, demand for the product, economic conditions and the employee's skills. Most employers use a combination of salary and commissions or bonuses to pay workers. Commissions are usually based on the amount of sales, whereas bonuses may depend on individual performance, on the performance of all sales workers in the group or district or on the company's performance.

Median annual earnings of manufacturers' representatives, working in nontechnical areas, were $55,020 in 2014. The lowest ten percent earned less than $26,790, and the highest ten percent earned more than $116,230.

Manufacturers' representatives may receive paid vacations, holidays, and sick days; life and health insurance; and retirement benefits. These are usually paid by the employer. Manufacturers' representatives are usually reimbursed for their travel and entertainment expenses. Some companies offer free trips or gifts to outstanding workers.

Metropolitan Areas with the Highest Employment Level in This Occupation

Metropolitan area	Employment	Employment per thousand jobs	Annual mean wage
New York-White Plains-Wayne, NY-NJ	60,740	11.27	$78,770
Chicago-Joliet-Naperville, IL	47,750	12.73	$71,200
Los Angeles-Long Beach-Glendale, CA	46,110	11.37	$62,830
Houston-Sugar Land-Baytown, TX	36,370	12.79	$77,040
Atlanta-Sandy Springs-Marietta, GA	36,130	15.13	$62,880
Dallas-Plano-Irving, TX	32,020	14.30	$76,110
Philadelphia, PA	23,710	12.73	$68,870
Minneapolis-St. Paul-Bloomington, MN-WI	23,470	12.86	$76,750
Seattle-Bellevue-Everett, WA	21,570	14.45	$73,380
Denver-Aurora-Broomfield, CO	20,100	15.16	$71,860

Source: Bureau of Labor Statistics

EMPLOYMENT AND OUTLOOK

There were about 1.5 million manufacturers' representatives employed nationally in 2014. Employment is expected to grow about as fast as the average for all occupations through the year 2024, which means employment is projected to increase 5 percent to 10 percent. This continued job growth is due to the increasing variety and number of goods to be sold. Job openings will also occur because of the need to replace workers who transfer to other occupations or retire.

Employment Trend, Projected 2014–24

Sales representatives, wholesale and manufacturing, technical and scientific products: 7%

Wholesale and manufacturing sales representatives: 7%

Total, all occupations: 7%

Sales representatives, wholesale and manufacturing, except technical and scientific products: 6%

Sales and related occupations: 5%

Note: "All Occupations" includes all occupations in the U.S. Economy. Source: U.S. Bureau of Labor Statistics, Employment Projections Program.

Related Occupations

- Automobile Salesperson
- Insurance Sales Agent
- Real Estate Sales Agent
- Retail Salesperson
- Retail Store Sales Manager
- Sales Engineer
- Services Sales Representative
- Technical Sales Representative
- Wholesale Sales Representative

Conversation With . . .
MICHAEL BERRY

President, IES Technical Sales
Danvers, Massachusetts
Manufacturing Sales Representative, 30 years

1. What was your individual career path in terms of education/training, entry-level job, or other significant opportunity?

I thought I wanted to go into marketing/advertising after I earned a bachelor's degree in communications at the University of Massachusetts/Amherst. I was working for a start-up advertising agency in San Diego, barely making ends meet, when I got a call from a friend who was in the high technology measurement and control instrumentation business with his father. They had started a company and offered me an inside sales job. The company, Vacuum General, Inc., used sales reps, and IES Technical Sales was one of those sales rep companies. I ended up managing the rep force and got to know them pretty well. IES was looking to expand. It presented my wife and me an opportunity to move back East. So, I went to work for IES. We do sales and distribution for twelve companies that make products used in high-tech vacuum, thin film/plasma, temperature, flow/pressure, and metrology applications.

2. What are the most important skills and/or qualities for someone in your profession?

Most important is a burning desire to win, but only if your customers win with you. To succeed long-term, you must look out for your customers' best interests. Otherwise, your career as a manufacturer's rep will be very short. You must have the ability to work independently, outside the traditional corporate environment. You must be willing to work hard, both on your product knowledge and on your overall skills. No one will push you to do it. You need excellent communication and listening skills, and must be fast and reliable in your follow-through. We can't know all the answers, but we have to be good at facilitating answers and, eventually, solutions.

3. What do you wish you had known going into this profession?

How to be both an independent salesperson and a company leader at the same time. It's quite challenging to do both well. They're two very different things. Most high-performing salespeople are not high-performing managers. Salespeople focus solely on themselves and their customers, whereas managers need to focus on leadership, coaching, mentoring, and teamwork.

4. Are there many job opportunities in your profession? In what specific areas?

There are tremendous opportunities in the outsourced sales and distribution fields, in all types of markets, not just high tech. We use the term "outsourced sales and distribution" because it gives people a better idea of what we do. Manufacturer's reps are the outside sales department for a company. Good reps have a long history of being an effective way to bring products and services to the market. Reps can bring instant access to a geographical area because they're already calling on most, if not all, of the target customers due to the synergy with their other product lines.

5. How do you see your profession changing in the next five years? What role will technology play in those changes, and what skills will be required?

I see a positive future for the outsourced sales/distribution business, but products and services that are difficult to differentiate due to intense competition will become more challenging to sell. Online transactions, which are efficient and low cost, will continue to pull market share away. But for complex products and services, there will still be a strong demand for effective outside sales talent. The Internet has opened up the world to anyone who wants to reach in and pull out information; thus most companies expect more from their employees.

6. What do you enjoy most about your job? What do you enjoy least about your job?

The two things I enjoy most are face-to-face time with customers—earning their trust and helping them solve problems and meet challenges—and marketing. What I like least is what I call non-value-added work such as accounting/finance and compliance work. When I say "non-value-added," I mean there's no value added to the customer. But it must be done to keep the business going.

7. Can you suggest a valuable "try this" for students considering a career in your profession?

Present yourself to the owner of an outsourced sales or distribution company and offer to work as an intern for a week to a month at no charge. In return, ask to sit in on as many meetings and discussions as possible to learn how the business works. Ask for a positive recommendation on LinkedIn and/or a letter of reference. You might be running errands, filing, entering data, searching for new contacts online, researching competitors' websites, or even making a few calls to dormant clients. It will teach you things you cannot learn in school, and who knows, it might be a gateway to a good job. Spend time on websites such as MANAonline.org or ERA.org, which have resources explaining the nature of the business from both the sales and the manufacturing sides.

SELECTED SCHOOLS

Most colleges and universities offer programs related to careers in business, marketing, or sales; the student may also get started in a technical or community college. For a list of top schools with programs in sales, visit the website of the Sales Education Foundation (see below).

MORE INFORMATION

American Supply Association
1200 N. Arlington Heights Road
Suite 150
Itsaca, IL 60143
630.467.0000
www.asa.net

Manufacturers' Agents National Association
16-A Journey, Suite 200
Aliso Viejo, CA 92656
877.626.2776
www.manaonline.org

Manufacturers' Representatives Educational Research Foundation
8329 Cole Street
Arvada, CO 80005
303.463.1801
www.mrerf.org

National Electrical Manufacturers Representatives Association
28 Deer Street, Suite 302
Portsmouth, NH 03801
800.446.3672
www.nemra.org

Sales & Marketing Executives International
P.O. Box 1390
Sumas, WA 98295-1390
312.893.0751
www.smei.org

Sales Education Foundation
3123 Research Boulevard, Suite 250
Dayton, OH 45420
937.610.4369
www.salesfoundation.org

Molly Hagan/Editor

Online Merchant

Snapshot

Career Cluster(s): Business, Information Technology, Marketing, Sales & Service

Interests: Managing projects, organizing information, customer service, communicating with others

Earnings (Yearly Average): $65,951

Employment & Outlook: Faster than Average Growth Expected

OVERVIEW

Sphere of Work

Online merchants offer goods for sale online. Professionals employed as online merchants, or as staff members of online-only retailers, conduct all of the day-to-day duties of traditional "brick and mortar" retailers but often at a larger scale and without the use of traditional storefronts to display their wares. Online merchants range from specialized small businesses to large corporations offering a variety of products to customers all over the world.

Work Environment

Depending on their particular professional role, online merchants work out of both administrative settings such as offices and call centers as well as in warehouses and other facilities that house goods and inventory. Large online merchants employ a comprehensive array of staff, each designated with a particular set of responsibilities from database administrators, financial experts, and online marketing specialists to warehouse workers, shipment clerks, and order processors. Work in large online merchant corporations requires extensive interaction with coworkers. Small or niche online merchants may be run by single individuals who bear responsibility for entire operations.

Profile

Working Conditions: Work Indoors
Physical Strength: Light Work
Education Needs: On-The-Job Training, Junior/Technical/Community College, Bachelor's Degree
Licensure/Certification: Usually Not Required
Opportunities For Experience: Volunteer Work
Holland Interest Score*: N/A

* See Appendix A

Occupation Interest

Online retailing attracts a diverse array of professionals. Many small-scale, niche online merchants are hobbyists, crafts makers, or artists who have harnessed the power of the Internet to market their goods to the world. These self-starting professionals enjoy the independence and freedom that comes with a career in online retailing. Successful online merchants are also organized, independent, punctual, and skilled communicators who can lead several different projects simultaneously.

A Day in the Life—Duties and Responsibilities

The everyday duties and responsibilities of online retailers can be divided into inventory control, online business marketing, financial tracking, and customer service.

Managing inventory is crucial for online merchants of every scope and size. Online merchants of all sizes track their diverse inventories with financial accounting or spreadsheet software. Warehousing facilities also often conduct quarterly counts of all in-house merchandise as loss-management prevention and to make sure actual on-hand supplies mirror images reflected in computer databases.

Marketing initiatives, particularly digital promotion, are what online merchants employ to attract potential clients to their online point of sale. Online merchants spend a large majority of their time identifying potential avenues from which to recruit their target market. As with many online businesses, there is an increasing trend of online merchants utilizing social media websites to attract site visits and potential customers. Photography of all the merchandise available for sale online is a key facet of the marketing strategy of online merchants.

Managing the sale and purchase of goods is an arena of online merchandising requiring an efficient knowledge of financial management. Merchants have to keep pace with which of their products are generating the most profits and to revaluate the availability or continued sale of struggling portions of their inventory.

Maintaining high functioning customer service is also crucial for online merchants to be successful. While large online retailers can employ large customer service staffs to monitor the questions and concerns of shoppers on a near-constant basis, individual online merchants must complete this task in concert with marketing and financial management responsibilities.

Duties and Responsibilities

- Developing marketing plans
- Designing and maintaining functionality of site
- Writing site content
- Creating advertising
- Buying merchandise
- Working with clients and vendors
- Managing inventory
- Shipping orders
- Handling financial concerns, such as budgets, expenditures and payroll
- Consulting with and supervising staff

WORK ENVIRONMENT

Relevant Skills and Abilities

Communication Skills
- Speaking effectively
- Writing concisely
- Listening attentively
- Reading well
- Expressing thoughts and ideas
- Negotiating with others
- Persuading others

Interpersonal/Social Skills
- Motivating others
- Cooperating with others
- Asserting oneself
- Working as a member of a team
- Being able to work independently
- Being honest
- Having good judgment

Organization & Management Skills
- Initiating new ideas
- Paying attention to and handling details
- Coordinating tasks
- Managing time
- Managing money
- Managing equipment/materials
- Delegating responsibility
- Demonstrating leadership
- Promoting change
- Selling ideas or products
- Making decisions
- Meeting goals and deadlines
- Organizing information or materials
- Performing duties which change frequently
- Managing people/groups

Physical Environment

Warehouse and office settings predominate. Much of the administrative, marketing, and financial tasks of online merchants are conducted in traditional office settings, while storage of goods, packaging, and shipping are usually conducted from warehouse facilities.

Online retailers operate from a diverse array of locations. Large online retail companies are usually housed in industrial-park complexes or business parks.

Human Environment

Much of the work of specialty online merchants who operate their own small businesses is done independently under their own supervision. Large online merchants traditionally have standard corporate hierarchies in which extensive collaboration with fellow staff members and customers is required on a day-to-day basis.

Technological Environment

Online merchants utilize common administrative technologies including telephones, e-mail, web

Research & Planning Skills

- Predicting
- Creating ideas
- Identifying problems
- Solving problems
- Setting goals & deadlines
- Defining needs
- Analyzing information
- Developing evaluation strategies

Technical Skills

- Performing scientific, mathematical or technical work
- Working with data or numbers

conferencing, computer-design software, inventory databases, and shipping software.

EDUCATION, TRAINING, AND ADVANCEMENT

High School/Secondary

High school students can best prepare for a career in the online retail industry with courses in basic math, communications, public speaking, and computer science. High school level business and financial planning courses also help lay important groundwork for future small business owners. English composition course work is effective in building communication and problem-solving skills, and exposure to one or more foreign languages can also assist clients interested in working across a diverse array of markets.

Suggested High School Subjects

- Accounting
- Algebra
- Applied Communication
- Applied Math
- Arts
- Bookkeeping
- Business
- Business & Computer Technology
- Business Data Processing

- Business English
- Business Law
- Business Math
- College Preparatory
- Composition
- Computer Science
- Economics
- English
- Entrepreneurship
- Geometry
- Graphic Communications
- Keyboarding
- Mathematics
- Merchandising
- Psychology
- Social Studies
- Sociology
- Speech
- Statistics
- Trigonometry

Famous First

The first online merchant to accept bitcoin, the digital currency, was Overstock.com, a Utah-based retailer of surplus and new goods. The company started accepting bitcoin on January 9, 2014. On the first day, it achieved sales of over $125,000 in bitcoin, a small percentage of normal cash intake but still notable in the world of e-commerce. By the end of the year Overstock was averaging $300,000 per month in bitcoin sales.

College/Postsecondary

While postsecondary education is not a steadfast requirement for a career as an online merchant, it can be extremely beneficial to have successfully completed associate or bachelor level coursework in one of the many facets related to the profession.

College-level coursework in small-business management, marketing, finance, or database administration can be particularly helpful. Computer proficiency is a skill shared by many successful online merchants, who are adept at creating, maintaining, and editing large websites; graphic design; and online mercantile exchanges.

Related College Majors
- Business
- Business Administration & Management, General
- Enterprise Management & Operation
- Entrepreneurship
- General Retailing & Wholesaling Operations & Skills

Adult Job Seekers

Online merchandising is a popular transitional field for both independent-minded professionals with small-business savvy and hobbyists who abandon established careers to immerse themselves in their specialty interests.

Professional Certification and Licensure

No specific certification or licensure is required.

Additional Requirements

Niche online merchants are disciplined professionals who are willing to risk both time and money to supply a market need where none previously existed. A pioneer spirit and ability to battle through adversity while multitasking is crucial for any niche online merchant to succeed and remain competitive.

Fun Fact

Cyber Monday has caught on in a big way. In 2013, $2.29 billion in sales clicked through on that day.

Source: http://www.cmo.com/articles/2014/5/6/Mind_Blowing_Stats_Online_Shopping.html

EARNINGS AND ADVANCEMENT

Earnings of online merchants depend on many factors, including the type and size of the organization, the demand for the product or service being sold, how well the organization is managed, and the overall economy. Some online merchants may earn only a few thousand dollars a year, while others could earn millions. Median annual earnings of online merchants were $65,951 in 2012.

Online merchants may receive paid vacations, holidays, and sick days; life and health insurance; and retirement benefits. These are usually paid by the employer. However, many online merchants are self-employed and must arrange for their own health insurance and retirement programs.

EMPLOYMENT AND OUTLOOK

Employment of online merchants is expected to grow faster than the average for all occupations through the year 2022, which means employment is projected to increase as much as 20 percent. Consumers enjoy the ease and convenience of online shopping, and this trend will continue to create demand in this field for many years to come.

Related Occupations
- Advertising Director
- Advertising Sales Agent
- Customer Service Representative
- Electronic Commerce Specialist
- Financial Manager
- General Manager & Top Executive
- Graphic Designer

- Market Research Analyst
- Public Relations Specialist
- Purchasing Agent
- Retail Salesperson
- Retail Store Sales Manager
- Sales Engineer
- Services Sales Representative
- Web Administrator
- Web Developer
- Wholesale & Retail Buyer
- Wholesale Sales Representative
- Writer & Editor

Conversation With . . .
CHRIS CHRISTIAN

Owner, OKAIYA
Berlin, MD
Online fishing equipment sales, 6 years

1. What was your individual career path in terms of education/training, entry-level job, or other significant opportunity?

I received my undergraduate degree in marketing from Salisbury University, and ended up in car sales because I wanted to pay for my MBA, which I earned from the same school. I stayed in car sales because, frankly, it became too lucrative not to. I still enjoy it, and have built a huge clientele.

Cars are a passion of mine, but so is fishing. Most of us have heard we should get into something we really have a passion for. So, honestly, I started OKAIYA because I wanted to get a deal on my own fishing equipment. I started making my own poles, then found someone who could mass produce them. I had to buy 15 to get a good deal. I figured I'd sell the rest and they sold very well. I literally saw an ad on the Super Bowl for GoDaddy and made my own website. It worked. That was in 2010. We specialize in offshore equipment and our niche is a quality product that the average person can afford. It's hard to find equipment that's affordable. Our customers are from all over the world, although predominantly in the U.S.

I had my website built and a company manages the website, but I do most of the changes to the website and also do my online marketing. My wife and I operate the business. We bid out a line we want and once someone gives us the quality and price we're looking for, we license them and let them know what quantity we want. We bring the product to our warehouse and ship it from there. We do a lot of trade shows.

The only problem is, I don't have time to fish anymore!

2. What are the most important skills and/or qualities for someone in your profession?

You need to have persistence and drive to stay in front of the market. A good marketer tries to make a good product that has a niche that people are looking for. Online, you have to be on top of everything or it's going to be very difficult. I'm constantly having to change and evolve because the Internet continues to evolve. That's what keeps me successful.

3. What do you wish you had known going into this profession?

We did our research, but still ended up not knowing there's a 10 percent federal excise tax on all fishing equipment. Who knew? That was hard on us. Do your research, because you've got to incorporate that kind of information into your business plan.

4. Are there many job opportunities in your profession? In what specific areas?

There are plenty of sales jobs in general. Everything is moving online such as car sales. The big thing is to get into driving sales to websites. The methods to do that keep changing; it used to be that you'd use certain keywords. Now that's not so valuable anymore. This area is something I think is going to be bigger and bigger.

5. How do you see your profession changing in the next five years, what role will technology play in those changes, and what skills will be required?

To some degree you're going to need a sales person but, as I mentioned, everything is moving online. Of the apps available for sharing information, we find that Facebook drives a lot of our business.

6. What do you enjoy most about your job? What do you enjoy least about your job?

I most enjoy the sales side. I least enjoy accounting or administrative jobs like managing inventory.

7. Can you suggest a valuable "try this" for students considering a career in your profession?

Get a job with a website builder. There are plenty of jobs and it's a way to see if it's something you like.

SELECTED SCHOOLS

Most colleges and universities offer programs related to careers in business, marketing, or sales; a variety of them also have specialized programs in e-commerce. Interested students are advised to consult with a school guidance counselor or research area postsecondary schools.

MORE INFORMATION

ECT News Network, Inc.
P.O. Box 18500
Encino, CA 91416-8500
www.ectnews.com

National Alliance of Online Merchants
40169 Truckee Tahoe Airport Road
Suite 203
Truckee, CA 96161
800.579.6369
naomonline.com

National Institute for Public Procurement
151 Spring Street
Herndon, VA 20170-5223
800.367.6447
www.nigp.org

John Pritchard/Editor

Personal Financial Advisor

Snapshot

Career Cluster(s): Finance, Human Services

Interests: Financial planning, finance, stocks and bonds, commodities and securities, tax law, banking

Earnings (Yearly Average): $81,060

Employment & Outlook: Faster than Average Growth Expected

OVERVIEW

Sphere of Work

Personal financial advisors help direct, plan, and manage the financial investments of individuals. They are also sometimes referred to as wealth managers, private or personal bankers, personal investment analysts, personal financial planners, or personal financial managers. Personal financial advisors review financial statements and advising individuals about the best investment options, such as stocks, bonds, and commodities. In addition, personal financial advisors provide guidance and direction for their clients on matters of insurance, retirement,

education financing, and tax law. Personal financial advisors may be self-employed or employed by financial institutions, such as commercial banks, insurance companies, securities firms, mortgage companies, pension funds, and savings and loan associations.

Work Environment

Personal financial advisors work in offices and are often required to travel for work. Depending on clients, employer, and particular job description, a personal financial advisor may telecommute from a home office, visit client offices as a contractor, or work on a full-time basis in an employer's office. A personal financial advisor may work as a full-time member of a financial services team or a term-of-project consultant. Personal financial advisors use technology constantly throughout the workday, including computers, the Internet, and accounting software programs.

Profile

Working Conditions: Work Indoors
Physical Strength: Light Work
Education Needs: Bachelor's Degree
Licensure/Certification:
  Recommended
Opportunities For Experience: Part-
  Time Work
Holland Interest Score*: ECS

* See Appendix A

Occupation Interest

Individuals attracted to the personal financial advisor profession tend to be ambitious, organized, outgoing, and detail-oriented people who find satisfaction in tracking financial trends and assessing risks. Those who excel as personal financial advisors exhibit traits such as financial and mathematical acumen, focus, analytical thought, honesty, responsibility, effective time management, and a sense of ethics. They should enjoy finance and possess good judgment and risk assessment skills.

A Day in the Life—Duties and Responsibilities

The daily duties and responsibilities of personal financial advisors vary with job specialty and employer. Areas of personal financial advisor job specialization include tax law, retirement, education financing, insurance, and investments.

During a typical workday, personal financial advisors may market and promote financial services to clients, travel to meet with prospective clients, assess clients' attitude toward financial risk, and advise clients on investment options. Some of the most important work done by personal financial advisors is to assess the health of a client's financial holdings or portfolio, help clients plan for their dependents' education costs, advise clients on matters of retirement and estate planning (wills and trusts), and advise clients about when to best hold, sell, or trade assets and securities. Personal financial advisors also work with clients to determine insurance needs and purchase appropriate amounts and types of insurance to cover eventualities and help them choose appropriate financial teams that include accountants and lawyers. In the course of generating recommendations for clients, personal financial advisors use spreadsheets to track financial data, track trends in technology and politics that may affect the finance industry, and analyze those data to make informed investment decisions that take into account a client's short-term versus long-term goals.

Personal financial advisors may periodically attend annual stockholder or shareholder meetings for businesses in which clients own shares. More frequently, they prepare investment reports for business owners and investors.

In addition, all personal financial advisors should stay up to date with regulatory and ethical issues and news in finance by reading finance industry journals and participating in industry associations.

Duties and Responsibilities

- Meeting with clients to gather and analyze their financial information and determine their financial goals
- Preparing financial plans and strategies for clients and reviewing those plans regularly to decide if they need to be updated
- Recruiting new clients and maintaining current clients
- Answering clients' questions about their financial plans and explaining the types of financial services available to them
- Researching potential investment opportunities for clients
- Recommending strategies that clients can use to achieve their financial goals

WORK ENVIRONMENT

Relevant Skills and Abilities

Communication Skills
- Speaking effectively
- Writing concisely
- Listening attentively
- Reading well
- Persuading others

Interpersonal/Social Skills
- Being sensitive to others
- Cooperating with others
- Respecting others' opinions
- Representing others
- Being able to work independently
- Working as a member of a team
- Being honest
- Having good judgment
- Being objective

Organization & Management Skills
- Coordinating tasks
- Making decisions
- Managing money
- Managing time
- Paying attention to and handling details
- Promoting change
- Organizing information or materials

Research & Planning Skills
- Using logical reasoning
- Analyzing information
- Developing evaluation strategies
- Predicting
- Gathering information
- Defining needs

Technical Skills
- Performing scientific, mathematical and technical work
- Working with data or numbers

Physical Environment

Personal financial advisors generally work in office environments. The work of a general financial advisor requires sitting at a desk and using computers and phones for long periods each day.

Human Environment

Personal financial advisors interact with clients, lawyers, banks, accountants, business owners, and stockbrokers. Personal financial advisors should be comfortable leading meetings and consultations with clients.

Technological Environment

Personal financial advisors use computers, telephones, Internet communication tools, financial analysis software, and spreadsheets to complete their work.

EDUCATION, TRAINING, AND ADVANCEMENT

High School/Secondary

High school students interested in pursuing a career as personal financial advisor should prepare themselves by building good study habits and by developing an ease with numbers and mathematical functions. High school classes in bookkeeping and mathematics will provide a strong foundation for college-level study in the field. Due to the diversity of personal financial advisor responsibilities, high school students interested in this career path may benefit from seeking internships or part-time work with financial organizations.

Suggested High School Subjects
- Accounting
- Algebra
- Applied Communication
- Applied Math
- Bookkeeping
- Business
- Business & Computer Technology
- Business Law
- Business Math
- College Preparatory
- Computer Science
- Economics
- English
- Government
- Keyboarding
- Mathematics
- Merchandising
- Political Science
- Psychology
- Social Studies
- Sociology
- Speech
- Statistics

Famous First

The first Wall Street stock index was the Dow Jones Transportation Average, a group of 11 stocks that included railroad companies and Western Union. It was created in 1884 by two New York financial reporters, Charles Dow and Edward Jones, to help investors understand stock market changes. Other indexes followed, including, in 1896, the Dow Jones Industrial Average.

College/Postsecondary

Postsecondary students interested in becoming personal financial advisors should work towards a bachelor's degree in economics, finance, statistics, mathematics, or accounting. Courses in computer science, political science, and ethics may also prove useful in their future work. Postsecondary students can gain work experience and potential advantage in their future job searches through internships or part-time employment with local businesses or financial organizations.

Related College Majors
- Accounting
- Business
- Business Administration & Management, General
- Business/Managerial Economics
- Economics, General
- Finance, General
- International Economics
- Mathematical Statistics

Adult Job Seekers

Adults seeking personal financial advisor jobs have generally earned a bachelor's degree and, in some cases, a master's of business administration (MBA). Adult job seekers may benefit from joining professional finance or accounting associations as a means of professional networking. Professional finance and accounting associations, such as the Financial Planning Association, the Investment Management Consultants Association, and the Society of Financial Service Professionals, generally maintain job lists advertising open accounting positions.

Professional Certification and Licensure

Certification is not legally required for personal financial advisors but may be required as a condition of employment or promotion. Professional organizations, such as the Certified Financial Planner Board of Standards, the CFA Institute, and the American Academy of Financial Management, offer certifications for personal financial advisors. Certification options include Certified Financial Planner (CFP), Chartered Financial Analyst (CFA), Certificate in Investment Performance Measurement (CIPM), Financial Analyst, Risk Management, and Financial Planning credentials. These voluntary credentials or designations have education, experience, testing, employer sponsorship, recertification, and continuing education requirements.

Personal financial advisors who buy or sell stocks and bonds need to be licensed stockbrokers. Individuals can become licensed stockbrokers by passing the General Securities Registered Representatives Examination (commonly referred to as the Series 7 exam) from the Financial Industry Regulatory Authority. Candidates should be aware that the Financial Industry Regulatory Authority, which is the licensing agency of the securities and finance industry, does not rank, promote, or endorse any particular professional financial certification or designation above any other.

Additional Requirements:

Successful financial advisors will be knowledgeable about the profession's requirements, responsibilities, and opportunities. Since personal financial advisors have access to confidential financial information and influence the financial health of individuals and businesses, they must adhere to strict codes of professional ethics. Membership in professional finance associations is encouraged among all personal financial advisors as a means of building professional community.

Fun Fact

Since 1928, the Dow Jones has increased more than 10 percent in one day eight times, and decreased more than 10 percent in one day four times.
Source: http://www.firmex.com/thedealroom/10-weird-finance-facts/#finalslide

EARNINGS AND ADVANCEMENT

Median annual earnings of salaried personal financial advisors were $81,060 in 2014. The lowest ten percent earned less than $35,500, and the highest ten percent earned upwards of $200,000. Self-employed personal financial advisors usually charge an hourly rate for the services they provide. Personal financial advisors usually receive bonuses and also earn commissions and fees for the financial products they sell, such as life insurance.

Personal financial advisors may receive paid vacations, holidays and sick days; life and health insurance; and retirement benefits. These are usually paid by the employer.

Metropolitan Areas with the Highest
Employment Level in This Occupation

Metropolitan area	Employment	Employment per thousand jobs	Annual mean wage
New York-White Plains-Wayne, NY-NJ	23,360	4.33	$139,820
Chicago-Joliet-Naperville, IL	9,500	2.53	$101,230
Los Angeles-Long Beach-Glendale, CA	6,110	1.51	$106,780
Boston-Cambridge-Quincy, MA	5,190	2.89	$137,480
Atlanta-Sandy Springs-Marietta, GA	4,690	1.97	$117,410
San Francisco-San Mateo-Redwood City, CA	4,410	4.06	$135,330
Philadelphia, PA	4,150	2.23	$125,980
Dallas-Plano-Irving, TX	3,860	1.73	$114,820
Santa Ana-Anaheim-Irvine, CA	3,760	2.54	$113,330
Houston-Sugar Land-Baytown, TX	3,720	1.31	$112,730

Source: Bureau of Labor Statistics

EMPLOYMENT AND OUTLOOK

Personal financial advisors held about 250,000 jobs nationally in 2014. Employment of personal financial advisors is expected to grow much faster than the average for all occupations through the year 2024, which means employment is projected to increase 25 percent or more. Millions of workers are expected to retire in the next ten years, and the expertise of personal financial advisors will be in high demand to help them manage and grow their investments.

Employment Trend, Projected 2014–24

Personal financial advisors: 30%

Financial specialists: 10%

Total, all occupations: 7%

Note: "All Occupations" includes all occupations in the U.S. Economy. Source: U.S. Bureau of Labor Statistics, Employment Projections Program.

Related Occupations
- Accountant
- Actuary
- Auditor
- Budget Analyst
- Cost Estimator
- Financial Analyst
- Financial Manager
- Insurance Claims Adjuster and Examiner
- Insurance Sales Agent
- Insurance Underwriter
- Purchasing Agent
- Real Estate Sales Agent
- Stockbroker

Related Military Occupations
- Finance & Accounting Manager

Conversation With . . .
KYLE P. GERMAN, CRPC

Partner, Harbor Financial Group
Annapolis, Maryland
Financial planner, 18 years

1. What was your individual career path in terms of education/training, entry-level job, or other significant opportunity?

I'm a practical person. I've always been interested in finance and the movement of money. This career path has provided me with an opportunity to make a nice living doing something I enjoy. However, I knew I could take an understanding of finance with me into many fields.

So, I took business and finance courses in college, and earned a bachelor's degree from West Virginia University. These classes in no way prepared me for a career as a personal financial advisor. We spent our time studying the theory behind the numbers as opposed to the practical application.

2. What are the most important skills and/or qualities for someone in your profession?

You need to be a people person because you will spend your days meeting with individuals and families, learning about their goals, their concerns, what drives them.

You will not be micromanaged, so you need self-motivation. You need to be creative when prospecting for new clients to set yourself apart from the thousands of other smart young people trying to build a financial planning practice. So, for instance, bring coffee to a business (even if it's a construction company that starts at 5:30) so you can meet people.

Lastly, you must have a thick skin! You will be told "no" thousands of times.

3. What do you wish you had known going into this profession?

I wish had asked for help. My best advice is to offer to help an experienced advisor. This will provide you with an opportunity to learn from someone who's done it and potentially provide you with a future business partner.

4. Are there many job opportunities in your profession? In what specific areas?

Financial advisors are in demand, for two reasons:

First off, baby boomers are retiring and shifting their retirement nest eggs from company 401K savings plans to individual IRAs. This represents the largest transfer of wealth the country has ever seen. And when people retire, they need help managing their money.

Second, this profession has high turnover because it's tough to get started. At my first job, thirty other people started at the same time. Our sole responsibility was to study for the Series 7 Exam, which is basically the stockbroker's exam. We had one month to pass the test. Then we had two weeks to study and complete the Series 66—the state securities law exam—and then we moved on to the Life and Health Exam, which is for insurance. If you failed, you were out. I quickly learned the exams were the easy part. Only two of us were left by the end of the second year. Not all firms have the same exam requirements, but all will expect you to bring in new clients right away.

If you stick with it and get through the years of hard work, it's amazing how lucrative this field can be. Trust me when I say you will work harder than most for less money for ten to fifteen years (depending how successful you are) and then, once you've built your practice, you'll work less than most for more money.

5. How do you see your profession changing in the next five years, what role will technology play in those changes, and what skills will be required?

Clients, especially younger clients, want immediate online access to their statements on their smart phones. They would rather text or email than come in for a meeting. This is all based on efficiency. If you don't adapt to work with them, they'll find someone who will.

That said, in-person meetings build trust. Older clients may be dealing with life's complexities such as illness or death and other matters that have greater consequences than what a young person is typically facing.

6. What do you enjoy most about your job? What do you enjoy least about your job?

I most enjoy the relationships I develop with my clients. A lot of my meetings take place around the dinner table. Clients share every aspect of their lives. This leads to a very close relationship that often lasts a lifetime.

I least like the stress that comes with managing a client's total financial nest egg. When the market drops, or two premier economists have completely opposing viewpoints, managing a portfolio is a big responsibility.

7. Can you suggest a valuable "try this" for students considering a career in your profession?

Pick a company, follow it on the stock market, watch it fluctuate and try to figure out why. I had one college course that really stuck with me and probably the only one that had any practical application to what I do. We bought a hypothetical stock portfolio at the beginning of the semester, explained why we liked the stock, and reported weekly on our transactions. Did we sell it and why? Did we keep it and why? We were graded on the rationale behind our moves.

Also, find a financial advisor you can interview or shadow. Offer to bring coffee or lunch. After all, you need to get used to asking for a meeting!

SELECTED SCHOOLS

Most colleges and universities offer programs related to careers in business and finance. For a list of some of the more prominent schools in this field, see the chapter "Financial Analyst" in the present volume.

MORE INFORMATION

**Certified Financial Planner
Board of Standards**
1425 K Street, NW, Suite 500
Washington, DC 20005
800.487.1497
www.cfp.net

**Financial Industry Regulatory
Authority**
1735 K Street
Washington DC, 20006
301.590.6500
www.finra.org

Financial Managers Society
100 W. Monroe Street, Suite 1700
Chicago, IL 60603
312.578.1300
www.fmsinc.org

Financial Planning Association
7535 E. Hampden Avenue, Suite 600
Denver, CO 80231
800.322.4237
www.fpanet.org

**Investment Management
Consultants Association**
5619 DTC Parkway, Suite 500
Greenwood Village, CO 80111
303.770.3377
www.imca.org

Society for Risk Analysis
1313 Dolley Madison Boulevard
Suite 402
McLean, VA 22101
703.790.1745
www.sra.org

Simone Isadora Flynn/Editor

Pharmaceutical Sales Representative

Snapshot

Career Cluster(s): Business, Management & Administration, Human Services, Marketing, Sales & Service

Interests: Sales, health care, science, business, marketing

Earnings (Yearly Average): $76,644

Employment & Outlook: Average Growth Expected

OVERVIEW

Sphere of Work

Pharmaceutical sales representatives promote legal drugs to doctors, dentists, and other medical professionals. They visit medical professionals at their offices and in hospitals, providing physicians with product samples and information and discussing product benefits in a persuasive, pleasant manner. Pharmaceutical manufacturers hire pharmaceutical sales representatives to persuade medical professionals to begin or continue prescribing their medicines. Pharmaceutical sales representatives also work for

companies that specialize in providing contract sales teams to the pharmaceutical industry.

Work Environment

Pharmaceutical sales representatives visit doctors and other medical professionals at their offices and in hospitals. They may frequently be required to work more than forty hours a week when travel, evening, or weekend activities demand it, but they also usually enjoy the flexibility to set their own schedules. Pharmaceutical sales representatives may work alone or as part of a team in a designated sales territory, travelling extensively to meet with clients. The benefits of this occupation may include a fully maintained vehicle, travel fund, education allowance, and other awards and incentives. Pharmaceutical sales representatives usually derive their income from a combination of salary and sales commissions.

Profile

Working Conditions: Work Indoors
Physical Strength: Light Work
Education Needs: Bachelor's Degree
Licensure/Certification: Usually Not Required
Opportunities For Experience: Part-Time Work
Holland Interest Score*: ESA

* See Appendix A

Occupation Interest

This occupation attracts self-motivated people who enjoy sales and desire a high degree of autonomy and flexible work arrangements. Pharmaceutical sales representatives tend to have outgoing personalities. The ability to cope with rejection is another valuable trait for individuals in this field, since pharmaceutical sales representatives frequently interact with resistant and uncooperative medical professionals and their staff. As this is a highly competitive field in which earnings partly depend on meeting sales goals, those individuals who thrive under pressure have an advantage. An interest in or aptitude for science and health care is essential, although pharmaceutical sales representatives come from a wide range of educational and skill backgrounds.

A Day in the Life—Duties and Responsibilities

A pharmaceutical sales representative usually spends a portion of each day planning for the following day. He or she organizes the next day's schedule, plans travel routes, and prioritizes activities. This process might involve ordering catering for a lunch meeting with an individual doctor or a group of doctors at a hospital or medical practice, replenishing one's stock of medicinal samples and promotional supplies, or estimating travel time between sales calls. By performing these tasks at the end of each day, the pharmaceutical sales representative is ready to begin work immediately the following morning.

Most of each day is spent visiting medical professionals. Sales representatives spend a significant amount of time interacting with "gatekeepers," such as receptionists and nurses. The pharmaceutical sales representative hopes to meet with a doctor for long enough to demonstrate the benefits of their products using data from research papers, clinical trial results, and national prescribing guidelines. However, he or she often has a limited amount of time to speak with doctors, which means communicating the message quickly and succinctly is important.

Scheduling lunch appointments and dinner presentations is one method of ensuring a longer period during which to speak with medical practitioners. Pharmaceutical sales representatives typically arrange presenters, order food, and coordinate other logistics for these events. Therefore, they must have a thorough understanding of the laws and professional and medical ethics that limit the type and cost of these functions, as well as the nature of gifts and incentives that can be offered to medical practitioners.

A significant portion of the pharmaceutical sales representative's day is dedicated to completing paperwork. This includes recording notes from sales calls, keeping records for medical samples that are distributed to doctors and their practices, ordering new supplies, managing a budget, and writing sales reports. To remain current with their paperwork, sales representatives must occasionally put in extra hours.

Duties and Responsibilities

- Giving samples to potential customers
- Traveling to and visiting with prospective buyers and current clients
- Taking orders
- Solving complaints about products
- Obtaining new accounts
- Analyzing sales statistics
- Handling administrative duties

WORK ENVIRONMENT

Physical Environment

Pharmaceutical sales representatives visit medical professionals in their offices and in hospitals. Much time is also spent driving between appointments. Depending on the employer, a pharmaceutical sales representative may be based at their employer's office or from their own home.

Relevant Skills and Abilities

Communication Skills
- Persuading others
- Speaking effectively
- Writing concisely

Interpersonal/Social Skills
- Asserting oneself
- Being able to work independently
- Being patient
- Being persistent
- Cooperating with others
- Working as a member of a team

Research & Planning Skills
- Setting goals and deadlines

Work Environment Skills
- Traveling

Human Environment

Pharmaceutical sales representatives enjoy frequent interaction with medical practitioners and medical support staff. Face-to-face interactions with colleagues and supervisors may be minimal, although daily contact by telephone is expected. Pharmaceutical sales representatives receive intense sales and product training, which demands group work and collaboration.

Technological Environment

Daily operations require the use of standard office technologies, such as a laptop computer, mobile telephone, e-mail, and the Internet. Proficiency in the use of word processing, spreadsheet, and presentation programs is expected. Pharmaceutical sales representatives may also need to use specialized systems, such as sales databases, presentation aids, and enterprise-wide resource platforms.

EDUCATION, TRAINING, AND ADVANCEMENT

High School/Secondary

High school students can best prepare for a career as a pharmaceutical sales representative by studying English and applied communication. Science and health-related subjects, including biology, chemistry, and physical education, are also important. Mathematics, applied mathematics, and business mathematics develop sales-related skills as well. Computer science, psychology, and foreign language classes may also be beneficial. Part-time work at a retail drug store while still in high school may provide some insight into this profession.

Suggested High School Subjects
- Algebra
- Applied Communication
- Business & Computer Technology
- Business Math
- Calculus
- Driver Training
- English
- Mathematics
- Psychology

Famous First

The first pharmaceutical company to operate as a not-for-profit business was OneWorld Health, started in San Francisco in 2000 by Victoria Hale, a scientist formerly with the Food and Drug Administration and, later, Genentech. Working with the Bill & Melinda Gates Foundation and others, OneWorld sought to bring needed drugs and vaccines to developing countries. In 2011 OneWorld merged with another nonprofit health organization, PATH, to develop safe, effective, and affordable drugs for the global market.

College/Postsecondary

An increasing number of employers expect pharmaceutical sales representatives to possess an associate degree as a minimum qualification. However, the competitive nature of employment in the pharmaceutical industry means that many entrants have a bachelor's degree and postgraduate qualifications. Science and health-related disciplines are well regarded, but this does not preclude candidates from pursuing degrees in business, marketing, humanities, social services, or other fields. Extensive training and on-the-job coaching is provided for new pharmaceutical sales representatives.

Opportunities for career advancement depend largely on the size and type of employer and the individual's breadth of experience. Opportunities for advancement may include promotion to supervisory or managerial roles, assignment to desirable territories, and higher compensation.

Related College Majors
- General Selling Skills & Sales Operations
- Pharmacy Technical Assistant Training

Adult Job Seekers

Adults seeking a career transition into a pharmaceutical sales representative role should refresh their skills and update their resume. The candidate should highlight previous clinical, health care, or sales experience. Larger pharmaceutical manufacturers claim to be very liberal in the range of professional backgrounds they will consider among applicants. Networking, job searching, and interviewing are critical. Registering with an employment agency that specializes in pharmaceutical sales roles may also be helpful. Some professional associations also offer job-finding services.

Professional Certification and Licensure

Although many trade associations and education providers claim that their certification programs enhance applicant's job opportunities, no formal certifications or licenses for pharmaceutical sales representatives are required for employment. Employers provide extensive product training and on-the-job coaching for successful candidates. Voluntary certification may be obtained through the Manufacturers Representatives Education Research Foundation.

Additional Requirements

Employers often require a clean driving record.
A criminal background check is also likely to be
mandatory. Pharmaceutical sales representatives
should be aware of the competitive nature of the salary
with commission system, which means earnings are contingent on
meeting sales goals. Individuals who enjoy selling, persuading others,
and working with people will be the most successful in this occupation.

Fun Fact

According to dictionary.com, the root of the word "pharmaceutical" comes from
the Greek *pharmakeutikos*, or "preparer of drugs, poisoner."
Source: http://dictionary.reference.com/browse/pharmaceutical

EARNINGS AND ADVANCEMENT

Advancement for pharmaceutical sales representatives will usually
take the form of an assignment to a larger territory. Experienced
pharmaceutical sales representatives may move into jobs as sales
trainers and possibly on to a sales supervisor or district manager
position.

Most employers use a combination of salary plus commission or salary
plus bonus. Commissions are usually based on the amount of sales,
whereas bonuses may depend on individual performance, on the
performance of all pharmaceutical sales representatives in the group
or district or on the company's performance.

Median annual earnings of pharmaceutical sales representatives were
$78,133 in 2012. The lowest ten percent earned less than $38,944, and
the highest ten percent earned more than $153,085.

Pharmaceutical sales representatives may receive paid vacations, holidays, and sick days; life and health insurance; and retirement benefits. These are usually paid by the employer. Pharmaceutical sales representatives are usually reimbursed for their expenses, such as transportation costs, meals, hotels and entertaining customers. They may also receive the use of a company car and are offered incentives, such as free vacation trips or gifts for outstanding sales performance.

EMPLOYMENT AND OUTLOOK

Manufacturing and wholesale sales representatives, of whom pharmaceutical sales representatives are a part, held about 1.8 million jobs nationally in 2010. Employment is expected to grow about as fast as the average for all occupations through the year 2020, which means employment is projected to increase 10 percent to 19 percent. Continued growth due to the increasing variety and number of prescription drugs to be sold will be tempered by the increased effectiveness and efficiency of sales representatives. Many job openings will result from the need to replace workers who transfer to other occupations or retire.

Related Occupations
- Insurance Sales Agent
- Pharmacy Technician
- Real Estate Sales Agent
- Retail Salesperson
- Retail Store Sales Manager
- Services Sales Representative
- Technical Sales Representative

Conversation With . . .
DOROTHY ROSS

Pharmaceutical Territory Manager
Aqua Pharmaceuticals, LLC, Boston, Massachusetts
Pharmaceutical sales, 18 years

1. What was your individual career path in terms of education/training, entry-level job, or other significant opportunity?

I graduated from college with a bachelor's degree in psychology, but I had no idea what I wanted to be. So I travelled a bit and ended up modeling for a few years. When I moved back home from San Francisco, I got a part-time job at a spa on Newbury Street in Boston, and ended up managing it. After a year, I had made great contacts in the industry, which led to a job selling high-end hair and skincare products for Ales Group.

Entering sales wasn't my plan, but once I started I realized it was a perfect fit for me. At first I was selling to salons, spas and department stores. From there I went to SkinCeuticals, a skincare line sold in spas and doctor's offices. At that point, I realized I enjoyed selling to dermatologists and I loved learning the science of skin and the different disease states of skin. My next jump was to pharmaceutical sales for SkinMedica. My thirst for learning about different medications and skin diseases has kept me motivated in this position. I've been with Aqua Pharmaceuticals for almost three years.

2. What are the most important skills and/or qualities for someone in your profession?

Communication is key. The majority of your job is speaking in front of physicians and other medical professionals. You usually have a short time to get your sales pitch in, so confidence in your communication skills is important. And at the other end of that is listening skills.

You need to be organized because in sales you create your own schedule. Managing your territory is similar to running your own business. You're in charge of everything within that territory, so you need to have everything in order or your business will fail.

A desire to learn as much as you can about all products within your industry—not just the ones you're selling, but the competitors as well—is a must.

3. What do you wish you had known going into this profession?

I wish I had learned the business analytic end of sales earlier in my career. In sales, you're given weekly reports with information on your growth or "negative growth," your competitors' growth, your goals, etc. The reports helps you understand your growth potential, but can be confusing to someone who isn't analytical or has no background in business or even computers. It's important to have strong computer skills and to be able to read spreadsheets.

4. Are there many job opportunities in your profession? In what specific areas?

Yes. For instance, there are several different levels of sales just within the field of dermatology, from over-the-counter products to biologicals. Biologicals, which are usually injectables, are manufactured, extracted from or synthesized from biological sources. They're new to the industry and very big in dermatology right now.

Pharmaceutical reps usually stay in the same field, such as dermatology or cardiology, etc., because you need to maintain your contacts and leads.

5. How do you see your profession changing in the next five years? What role will technology play in those changes, and what skills will be required?

It's a very insurance-driven industry. Doctors have decreased ability to choose prescribing products.

Technology plays a huge role in tracking and providing access to physician data that gives sales representatives a crisp snapshot of whether a physician is prescribing our products. Pharmaceutical companies purchase this data, which gives us numbers on our competitors and generics as well.

6. What do you enjoy most about your job? What do you enjoy least about your job?

I enjoy client relations. It's a great challenge—and a great feeling of success—when you establish strong relations with a difficult account. As a sales person, you want your clients to be happy when you walk in the door. I also enjoy being responsible for my own territory. I enjoy being on the road with a flexible schedule and not being tied down to an office.

I do not enjoy the new restrictions on access to doctors due to Health Insurance Portability and Accountability Act, or "HIPAA," laws and insurance restrictions.

7. Can you suggest a valuable "try this" for students considering a career in your profession?

An entry-level sales job, such as inside sales or direct sales, would be a great start for a summer job or internship. It will give you a good feel for selling over the phone, which is extremely difficult because there's a lot of rejection. You'll get a feel for whether you have that drive for sales!

Pharmaceutical sales normally requires prior sales experience. Companies such as Enterprise Rent-A-Car and FedEx have great sales training programs. Pharmaceutical and high-tech companies love to hire people who have participated in those types of trainings.

When interviewing for a sales position, the hiring manager may ask for a brag book. Be sure to keep a file of all your awards, training or internships that will highlight your hard work and motivation.

SELECTED SCHOOLS

Most colleges and universities offer programs related to careers in business, marketing, or sales; the student may also get started in a community or technical college. For a list of some of top schools in sales education, visit the website of the Sales Education Foundation (see below).

MORE INFORMATION

Manufacturers' Agents National Association
16-A Journey, Suite 200
Aliso Viejo, CA 92656
877.626.2776
www.manaonline.org

Manufacturers' Representatives Educational Research Foundation
8329 Cole Street
Arvada, CO 80005
303.463.1801
www.mrerf.org

National Association of Pharmaceutical Representatives
2020 Pennsylvania Avenue, NW
Suite 5050
Washington, DC 20006-1811
800.284.1060
www.napsronline.org

Sales & Marketing Executives International
P.O. Box 1390
Sumas, WA 98295-1390
312.893.0751
www.smei.org

Sales Education Foundation
3123 Research Boulevard, Suite 250
Dayton, OH 45420
937.610.4369
www.salesfoundation.org

Kylie Hughes/Editor

Property & Real Estate Manager

Snapshot

Career Cluster: Business Administration; Hospitality & Tourism; Sales & Service

Interests: Real estate, business administration, budgeting, finance, marketing

Earnings (Yearly Average): $63,570

Employment & Outlook: Average Growth Expected

OVERVIEW

Sphere of Work

To some real estate professionals, the positions of property manager and real estate manager are interchangeable. To others, a property manager is a type of real estate manager who is in charge of a large property or several properties, whether commercial or residential. In either case, property and real estate managers strive to maintain and maximize the financial value of income-producing properties by marketing the properties to prospective tenants, deciding the amount of rent to charge, minimizing property expenditures, and physically maintaining the properties.

Work Environment

Residential property and real estate managers are responsible for properties in which people live, such as time-share units, apartment complexes, condominiums, and single-family rental houses. They also oversee commercial properties such as shopping centers and marinas. In the case of residential properties they may interact with tenants at any time, day or night, because unlike most commercial properties, residential properties are in use twenty-four hours a day. Some residential property and real estate managers even live in their properties so that they are available in case of emergencies.

Commercial properties house businesses and can run the gamut from office buildings to warehouses to strip malls to tiny kiosks. Each type of commercial property has its unique demands, which property and real estate managers must be able to meet. For instance, a medical office building may need special insurance or maintenance because of the medical equipment it houses, while a bank may require extra security around its facility. Commercial property and real estate managers should have the expertise to handle these situations. Tenant satisfaction is important to all property and real estate managers because satisfied tenants, residential and commercial alike, are more likely to renew their leases.

Profile

Working Conditions: Work Indoors

Physical Strength: Light Work

Education Needs:
Technical/Community College,
Bachelor's Degree

Licensure/Certification: Required

Physical Abilities Not Required: No
Heavy Labor

Opportunities For Experience:
Military Service

Holland Interest Score*: IRE

* See Appendix A

Occupation Interest

Property and real estate management may appeal to people who are already real estate professionals, such as agents or brokers, but desire a slight career change. A background in real estate sales is helpful for property and real estate managers, as knowledge acquired about the real estate market through such work carries over well into the property and real estate management field. Training in other forms of business and/or hospitality management is also useful.

Prospective property and real estate managers must be detail-oriented workers able to multitask, delegate responsibility, and resolve disputes. Because they are the link between property owners and tenants, good communication skills are imperative.

A Day in the Life—Duties and Responsibilities

There are many kinds of property and real estate managers. A manager's property portfolio may consist of only a single property, or it may consist of multiple properties within one geographic region or even throughout several regions. Some managers have on-site offices, while others visit their properties on a regular basis. Because of this variation, responsibilities differ from manager to manager, despite the shared goal of making their properties as profitable as possible.

The workday for on-site property and real estate managers takes place partly in the office. There, they schedule building and security system maintenance, showings of vacant units, and meetings with tenants; make calls; meet with coworkers and clientele; market vacant units; and settle tenant disputes. They also create financial reports tracking property income and expenses for property owners. Other financial responsibilities of property and real estate managers may include collecting rent checks, recording transactions, creating budgets, and determining strategies to increase revenue and decrease expenses.

Property and real estate managers are also responsible for inspecting the landscaping, interior common areas, vacant units, elevators, stairwells, and parking lots of their properties. During these property inspections, managers check for damage, determine what improvements need to be made to increase tenant appeal, and ensure that the properties continue to meet government building codes and relevant lease laws.

Duties and Responsibilities

- Marketing vacant space to prospective tenants
- Establishing rental rates
- Negotiating and preparing lease and rental contracts
- Collecting rents and fees
- Disbursing funds for taxes, mortgages, payroll and insurance
- Ensuring safe use of the property
- Negotiating for maintenance services

WORK ENVIRONMENT

Physical Environment

Property and real estate managers typically work in offices and frequently visit the properties they manage to make sure everything is well kept and in working order. On-site property and real estate managers usually spend most, if not all, of their workdays at their properties and may even live there, as in the case of on-site residential property managers.

Relevant Skills and Abilities

Communication Skills
- Persuading others

Interpersonal/Social Skills
- Being sensitive to others
- Cooperating with others

Organization & Management Skills
- Performing duties that change frequently
- Selling ideas or products

Research & Planning Skills
- Developing evaluation strategies
- Solving problems

Other Skills
- Working with data or numbers as well as with people

Human Environment

Pilots must work with a wide range of people on the ground and on board their planes. Such parties include maintenance crews, security personnel, flight attendants, air traffic controllers, luggage handlers and, of course, the passengers. Pilots must interact directly with many of these individuals, while communicating and coordinating with others on the ground while in flight. Pilots are sometimes responsible for unruly passengers. As part of the Homeland Security Act of 2002, some pilots have been deputized and are federal law enforcement officers, called Federal Flight Deck Officers.

Technological Environment

Property and real estate managers use various software applications to keep tenant records, generate maintenance work orders, create budgets for their properties, and perform other administrative tasks. They also rely on standard office equipment such as fax machines, telephones, copiers, and scanners.

EDUCATION, TRAINING, AND ADVANCEMENT

High School/Secondary

High school students can prepare for careers in property or real estate management with courses in business, English, and social sciences. Part-time work for a property management or real estate company can provide an excellent introduction to the field.

Suggested High School Subjects
- Applied Communication
- Applied Math
- Building & Grounds Maintenance
- Business
- College Preparatory
- English

Postsecondary

A college degree is not always necessary to become a property or real estate manager. However, having completed courses, a degree, or a postsecondary certificate in real estate, finance, or business administration can add to a property or real estate manager's professional capability and provide a competitive edge. Many universities offer undergraduate and graduate degree programs in real estate.

Related College Majors
- Business Administration
- Hospitality Management
- Real Estate

Adult Job Seekers

Employers that hire property and real estate managers include property management companies, full-service and development real estate companies, insurance companies, banks, and government agencies. Adult job seekers can benefit from networking with real estate professionals and joining professional associations such as the

Institute of Real Estate Management (IREM). Networking can alert job seekers to job openings that have not yet been made public, while professional property management associations often post openings on their job boards.

Before pursuing education in real estate or business administration and obtaining the necessary licensure, those interested in property and real estate management may first choose to seek employment in property management support. By working as an assistant to a property or real estate manager or as part of an on-site maintenance team, for example, an aspiring manager can gain valuable on-the-job property management training.

Professional Certification and Licensure

Licensure requirements for property and real estate managers vary from state to state. A real estate license is necessary in most states, and in a few, a separate property management license is as well.

Managers of federally subsidized public housing properties are required to obtain certification, but other real estate and property managers are not. Optional certification offered by professional real estate associations may be beneficial for career advancement. Candidates are typically required to complete a degree program and coursework, pass an exam, and adhere to a code of professional ethics.

Additional Requirements

As property and real estate managers often spend a significant amount of time driving between properties, a driver's license is essential. An interest in both business administration and people or customer service will prove useful as well.

Fun Fact

If you own a haunted house that's scaring you into moving, you may have some explaining to do for potential buyers: 21 states require disclosing "stigmatized property."

Source: http://www.americanbar.org/content/dam/aba/publishing/probate_property_magazine/rppt_mo_premium_rp_publications_magazine_2005_mj_perlin.authcheckdam.pdf

EARNINGS AND ADVANCEMENT

Mean annual earnings of property and real estate managers were $63,570 in 2012. The lowest ten percent earned less than $26,600, and the highest ten percent earned more than $113,400.

Property and real estate managers may receive paid vacations, holidays, and sick days; life and health insurance; and retirement benefits. These are usually paid by the employer. They may also use company cars, and some managers in land development may receive a small share of ownership in projects they develop.

Metropolitan Areas with the Highest Employment Level in this Occupation (Airline Pilot)

Metropolitan area	Employment [1]	Employment per thousand jobs	Hourly mean wage
Los Angeles-Long Beach-Glendale, CA	6,830	1.76	$35.55
Chicago-Joliet-Naperville, IL	4,760	1.31	$28.17
Houston-Sugar Land-Baytown, TX	4,590	1.74	$38.23
Phoenix-Mesa-Glendale, AZ	4,100	2.37	$23.26
Dallas-Plano-Irving, TX	3,920	1.87	$30.05
Santa Ana-Anaheim-Irvine, CA	3,910	2.77	$37.19
New York-White Plains-Wayne, NY-NJ	3,470	0.67	$47.89
San Francisco-San Mateo-Redwood City, CA	3,350	3.35	$43.70

[1]Does not include self-employed. Source: Bureau of Labor Statistics

EMPLOYMENT AND OUTLOOK

Property and real estate managers held about 300,000 jobs nationally in 2012. About one-half were self-employed. Around another one-fourth worked in offices of real estate agents and brokers. Others worked for government agencies that manage public buildings.

Employment is expected to grow about the same as the average for all occupations through the year 2022, which means employment is projected to increase 9 percent to 15 percent. Opportunities are best for those with a college degree in business administration, real estate, or a related field. Growth in the number of apartments and offices should require more property managers. In addition, the number of older people will grow during the next decade, increasing the need for various types of suitable housing, such as assisted-living facilities and retirement communities. There will be demand for property and real estate managers to operate these facilities, especially for those who have a background in the operation and administrative aspects of running a health unit.

Related Occupations
- Building Manager
- Hotel/Motel Manager
- Real Estate Sales Agent

Conversation With . . .
LEIGH LAWSON
Real Estate Manager
26 years in the industry

1. What was your individual career path in terms of education/training, entry-level job, or other significant opportunity?

I always knew I wanted to go into a real estate career and groomed myself toward it early on. My father built spec houses. I gobbled up glamorous real estate books, and studied castles and grounds and interiors. I also studied ballet from age 3 and was in competitions so I traveled a lot, which is the best education when dealing with the hospitality and international real estate industry. The more knowledge and acceptance of another culture you possess, the more successful you can be.

I graduated from the College of William and Mary with a bachelor's degree in business management, then immediately got my real estate license. I then deemed it important to learn the art of financing. If you don't know financing and how it is all entangled and what a buyer is about to embark on for the 30-year length of most mortgages, then you won't be a very good realtor. I got into a loan officer/management training program with First Washington Mortgage in McLean, Va., and did everything. In 1988, I went into real estate full-time in Newport Beach, California. I was "Rookie of the Year" because I did what no other realtor did: figured out how to make a down market work for me and my clients. Nobody wanted to do rentals but I did because nothing was selling. My office was next to the University of California, Irvine and to a number of beach communities. So, I did 122 rentals and made a lot of splash and cash.

At one time I thought I wanted to be a builder/developer, but later found that I'm not that technical. I'm more of a marketing person. That's what I do best.

My company's property management division manages a lot of properties for the government, including U.S. Naval Academy people who get shipped out, or people in the area who own houses and rent them by the week for the academy graduation. We also do a lot for the Baltimore Orioles and the Baltimore Ravens. The baseball players are more transient because they get traded a lot. They spend a lot of money, and they want to be as close to Oriole Park at Camden Yards as possible. Very high end. The Ravens are more stable. They want bigger houses, their wives and girlfriends are more in control, and they're more out in Baltimore County where their training facility is located. We also network with hotels and do vacation rentals. People may stay in the same place every year but as they get elderly they may need a house that is handicapped accessible. Or they want to bring their pets.

2. What are the most important skills and/or qualities for someone in your profession?

Don't have an ego. I see so many realtors who make it all about them. Real estate is and should be about helping buyers and sellers buy and sell their homes, or helping renters find their homes. Homes are peoples' go-to places when they are happy and sad and seek solitude and peace. We are the catalyst and confidant to make dreams a reality, and to keep that dream a reality.

3. What do you wish you had known going into this profession?

To start a 401K retirement account.

4. Are there many job opportunities in your profession? In what specific areas?

Real estate has endless job opportunities. On the property management side, one could manage apartments for resorts, the government (including housing for military, the elderly, and Section 8), hotels and hotel chains, co-ops, cruise lines, or even commercial property management.

You could also pursue real estate with title companies; builders and their representatives; loan companies; architectural firms; retail firms such as Home Depot or Lowes; electrical, plumbing, HVAC/AC; or other related industry associations such as the home builders' associations or the National Association of Realtors or the local realtors' associations.

5. How do you see your profession changing in the next five years? What role will technology play in those changes, and what skills will be required?

The first thing buyers, sellers or renters do is go online. They do their searching before they call a realtor. I have sold homes where I have never met the people. We can do electronic signatures on contracts so we do that, especially with the military and government. But, people will always need someone to value their homes. Realtors bring together a meeting of the minds between buyer and seller. You need to bring a professional into the situation to get the best value for your home. People use property managers when time is of the essence and they don't have time to go place to place and do all the research. If you want to do real estate, know your technology and keep up with any application available.

6. What do you enjoy most about your job? What do you enjoy least?

I love my job of real estating! It's the greatest because of its flexibility. Those who don't like knowing what they will be doing every day won't enjoy this type of job. I also love meeting and talking with new people, and going to functions and events.

7. Can you suggest a valuable "try this" for students considering a career in your profession?

Try working for a real estate office or for a realtor, builder, or loan company before you actually go into the field full-time. Not all are the same and your personality will not always gel with whomever you are working with. It may take a few tries before you say, "This is cool."

SELECTED SCHOOLS

Most colleges and universities have programs in business administration; many also have concentrations in real estate. Training in hospitality management is equally valuable for aspiring property and real estate managers. For some jobs completion of a two-year program at a community college or vocational school may be sufficient. Interested students are advised to consult with a school guidance counselor. Below are listed some of the more prominent institutions in this field.

New York University
School of Continuing and
Professional Studies
7 E. 12th Street, Suite 921
New York, NY 10003
212.918.7100
www.scps.nyu.edu

**University of California,
Berkeley**
Haas School of Business
Baker Faculty Building, F602
Berkeley, CA 94720
510.643.6105
groups.haas.berkeley.edu

University of Connecticut
School of Business
2100 Hillside Road, Unit 1041
Storrs, CT 06269
860.486.3040
www.business.uconn.edu

University of Florida
Heavener School of Business
233 Bryan Hall
PO Box 117160
Gainesville, FL 32611
352.273.0165
catalog.ufl.edu/ugrad/current

University of Georgia
Terry College of Business
Brooks Hall
301 Herty Drive
Athens, GA 30602
706.542.8100
www.terry.uga.edu

**University of Illinois, Urbana
Champaign**
College of Business
1055 Business Instructional Facility
515 E. Gregory Drive
Champaign, IL 61820
217.333.2747
www1.business.illinois.edu

University of Pennsylvania
Wharton School
3620 Locust Walk
Philadelphia, PA 19104
215.898.3030
www.wharton.upenn.edu

**University of Southern
California**
Marshall School of Business
3670 Trousdale Parkway
Los Angeles, CA 90089
213.740.8674
www.marshall.usc.edu

University of Texas, Austin
McCombs School of Business
2110 Speedway, Stop B6000
Austin, TX 78712
512.471.5921
www.mccombs.utexas.edu

University of Wisconsin, Madison
Wisconsin School of Business
975 University Avenue
Madison, WI 53706
608.262.1550
bus.wisc.edu

MORE INFORMATION

Building Owners & Managers Association International
1101 15th Street, NW, Suite 800
Washington, DC 20005
202.408.2662
www.boma.org

Building Owners & Managers Institute International
1 Park Place, Suite 475
Annapolis, MD 21401
800.235.2664
www.bomi.org

Community Associations Institute
6402 Arlington Boulevard
Suite 500
Falls Church, VA 22024
703.970.9220
www.caionline.org

Institute of Real Estate Management
430 N. Michigan Avenue
Chicago, IL 60611-4090
800.837.0706
www.irem.org

National Apartment Association
201 North Union Street, Suite 200
Alexandria, VA 22314
703.518.6141
www.naahq.org

National Association of Residential Property Managers
638 Independence Parkway
Suite 100
Chesapeake, VA 23320
800.782.3452
www.narpm.org

National Property Management Association
4025 Tampa Road, Suite 1203
Oldsmar, FL 34677
813.475.6998
www.npma.org

Property Management Association
7508 Wisconsin Avenue, 4th Floor
Bethesda, MD 20814
301.657.9200
www.narpm.org

Jamie Aronson Tyus/Editor

Real Estate Appraiser

Snapshot

Career Cluster(s): Business, Real Estate, Sales & Service

Interests: Property valuation, construction, commercial development, real estate, architecture, marketing

Earnings (Yearly Average): $52,570

Employment & Outlook: Average Growth Expected

OVERVIEW

Sphere of Work

Real estate appraisers are licensed professionals who estimate the value of real property. Real property includes residences, office buildings, shopping malls, apartment complexes, and many other types of structures, as well as both undeveloped and developed land. Appraisers' services are requested most often when property is sold, so that a lending institution and buyer can settle on a fair mortgage or loan. Real estate appraisers are similar to assessors, but they work for private companies and focus on valuing individual properties. Assessors work for the government and value property for

tax purposes, frequently assessing the value of entire neighborhoods rather than individual properties.

Work Environment

Many real estate appraisers are self-employed, while others are employed by lending institutions, real estate agents, and appraisal management companies. They usually work locally because they need to be familiar with their communities to determine fair market values; however, some appraisers put their expertise to use in regional, national, or even international markets. The amount of interaction between a real estate appraiser and his or her coworkers and staff depends on the size of employer. Most appraisers deal predominantly with clients, realtors, and loan officers. A significant amount of local travel is necessary to appraise properties, with some occasional evening and weekend hours required to complete the work.

Profile

Working Conditions: Work both Indoors and Outdoors
Physical Strength: Light Work
Education Needs: Junior/ Technical/Community College, Bachelor's Degree
Licensure/Certification: Required
Opportunities For Experience: Part-Time Work
Holland Interest Score*: ESC

* See Appendix A

Occupation Interest

People who are attracted to appraising real estate tend to be analytical and have a good sense of judgment. They enjoy gathering and evaluating data and performing mathematical tasks. Their desire to evaluate property and structures usually demonstrates a general interest in architecture or commercial development. Good communication skills are needed to write reports, interact with clients, and defend appraisals. Appraisers must also have a strong sense of ethics and remain unbiased in their appraisals.

A Day in the Life—Duties and Responsibilities

Real estate appraisers may specialize in commercial or residential property valuation or may belong to a company that performs both types of appraisals. When properties are mortgaged, taxed, insured, developed, or sold, appraisers must be hired to determine the current value. Real estate appraisers' expertise is required in a variety of situations, most commonly in conjunction with the sale of a commercial building or residence, but also when a developer needs land appraised or when a municipality needs to issue municipal bonds for a new school, hospital, or other public project. Appraisals are also conducted when property is inherited, when it is taken by eminent domain by a government agency, or when a right of way is requested by a utility company, mass transit company, or other entity.

Appraisers use set procedures to collect a variety of specific data (such as tax assessment figures, local economic statistics, and property size and age) to determine a fair value. They obtain most background information online, but it is necessary to inspect the property in person, paying special attention to any remodeling work, construction additions, or deterioration that may have occurred since the last tax assessment or appraisal. They evaluate the neighborhood, noting the types, conditions, and values of other houses, the proximity of green space or railroad tracks, and other factors that can influence property value. Often, the appraiser takes photographs or video footage to document items or conditions that influence the appraisal process. Because it usually takes longer to collect research and analyze data related to a valuing commercial property, commercial real estate appraisers spend more time in the office than residential appraisers do.

The appraiser also compares the data with recent real estate transactions, or "comps," as well as previous real estate appraisals, before calculating the value of the property. He or she then writes a report detailing the results of the assessment and submits the report to his or her clients and other interested parties. All real estate appraisers must keep accurate, thorough records of each property appraisal process they complete. These records are important not only for documentation and ensuring best practices but may also be used for reference the next time a property is appraised.

Those who are self-employed also handle billing, marketing, and other business management-related tasks.

Duties and Responsibilities

- Inspecting property for construction, condition and functional design
- Interviewing persons involved with the property
- Taking measurements
- Computing depreciation and replacement costs

- **Considering the location and trends or changes that could influence the future value of the property**
- **Researching public records of sales, leases and assessments**
- **Photographing interior and exterior of property**
- **Estimating the value of property**
- **Submitting reports to confirm the estimated value of property**

WORK ENVIRONMENT

Physical Environment

Appraisers spend most of their time working alone in offices and visiting properties. The residences and commercial properties they appraise may sometimes harbor potential health hazards, such as mold, dust, and insect or animal infestations.

Relevant Skills and Abilities

Communication Skills
- Speaking effectively
- Writing concisely

Interpersonal/Social Skills
- Cooperating with others
- Working as a member of a team

Organization & Management Skills
- Following instructions
- Paying attention to and handling details
- Performing duties which change frequently

Research & Planning Skills
- Using logical reasoning

Technical Skills
- Performing scientific, mathematical and technical work

Human Environment

Trainee appraisers work closely with their supervisors. Licensed appraisers might supervise trainees or an assistant or two, while those who work for larger firms or banks report to a director or manager. The interaction between an appraiser and his or her client or realtor can be stressful if an appraisal is significantly higher or lower than the selling price.

Technological Environment

Appraisers use a variety of office equipment, including copiers and fax machines. They rely on financial calculators and computers for the majority of their office work. Digital cameras and video cameras are used occasionally on site.

EDUCATION, TRAINING, AND ADVANCEMENT

High School/Secondary

A college-preparatory program with an emphasis on mathematics and writing provides the best foundation for work in this field. Math courses should include finance, accounting, geometry, and/or statistics. Other relevant courses include English, speech communication, economics, psychology, computer science, business law, and photography.

Suggested High School Subjects
- Applied Communication
- Applied Math
- Blueprint Reading
- Business Law
- Business Math
- College Preparatory
- Economics
- English
- Mathematics
- Photography
- Psychology
- Speech

Famous First

The first year in which the average price of a new house topped $100,000 was 1984. In May of that year, the average price of a new single-family home reached $101,000. By the end of 2015, the average price of a new home had exceeded $374,000.

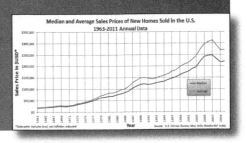

College/Postsecondary

Before undertaking any postsecondary coursework, one should become familiar with the licensing and certification requirements in the desired state(s) of employment. An associate's degree is the minimum recommended requirement for a Certified Residential Real Property Appraiser. Or in lieu of the degree, a minimum of twenty-one semester credit hours must be completed in the following subjects: English composition, economics, finance, statistics, computer science, business or real estate law, and either algebra, geometry, or higher mathematics. A Certified General Real Property Appraiser is required to complete a bachelor's degree or a minimum of thirty semester credit hours that include microeconomics and macroeconomics as well as two additional electives in any of the following subjects: accounting, geography, agricultural economics, business management, or real estate.

In addition to mandatory college coursework, each level of certification requires a specified amount of industry training, known as the Required Core Curriculum. These courses include basic appraisal principles, basic appraisal procedures, and National Uniform Standards of Professional Appraisal Practice (USPAP). The amount of training ranges from fifteen hours for trainees to three hundred hours for Certified General Real Property Appraisers.

Continuing education is necessary to maintain a license or certification. This includes a minimum of fourteen classroom hours annually and a seven-hour National Uniform Standards of Professional Appraisal Practice (USPAP) Update Course every two years.

Related College Majors
- Real Estate

Adult Job Seekers

Adults with a background in real estate sales, economics, finance, or another related discipline have a good foundation for appraising real estate. To update skills or acquire necessary coursework, those with personal obligations might find online courses helpful. Adults who are returning to real estate appraisal should check with their state appraisal boards for regulations concerning time limitations on certification requirements.

Advancement comes with experience and education. Generally, the level of certification is closely tied to an appraiser's compensation; as an appraiser gains additional credentials, he or she can charge higher fees. Experienced appraisers can take on trainees and move into supervisory positions or may establish their own businesses.

Professional Certification and Licensure

The federal government requires that appraisers be certified in their states; however, the specific certification requirements vary from state to state. The Appraiser Qualifications Board (AQB) administers certification exams and makes recommendations for the minimum requirements for Certified Residential Real Property Appraiser and Certified General Real Property Appraiser. Some states have chosen to exceed those requirements.

In addition to state certification, many appraisers obtain additional credentials from national associations, such as the National Association of Independent Fee Appraisers (NAIFA).

Additional Requirements

Real estate appraisers should have excellent analytical and mathematical skills. They should be patient and meticulous and find satisfaction in working with people. Customer service experience is helpful when entering this field, and appraisers should be physically fit enough to travel to multiple properties in one day and evaluate the interior and exterior characteristics of each. Appraisers must comply with the codes of ethics set by the organizations to which they belong. They must also be familiar with the Home Valuation Code of Conduct (HVCC) established by the US Federal Housing Authority (FHA).

Fun Fact

Why do we call it real estate? "Real" is an archaic term for actual or physical things. Real estate means land and buildings "fixed" to the land, as opposed to moveable property like clothes or tools.

Source: http://english.stackexchange.com/questions/66379/whats-the-literal-meaning-of-real-estate

EARNINGS AND ADVANCEMENT

Earnings depend on the real estate appraiser's experience, education and ability and the geographic location of the employer. Real estate appraisers had median annual earnings of $52,570 in 2014. The lowest ten percent earned less than $26,980, and the highest ten percent earned more than $95,020.

Real estate appraisers may receive paid vacations, holidays, and sick days; life and health insurance; and retirement benefits. These are usually paid by the employer. Some employers also provide a company car.

Metropolitan Areas with the Highest Employment Level in This Occupation

Metropolitan area	Employment	Employment per thousand jobs	Annual mean wage
New York-White Plains-Wayne, NY-NJ	1,830	0.34	$64,180
Chicago-Joliet-Naperville, IL	1,400	0.37	$58,700
Minneapolis-St. Paul-Bloomington, MN-WI	1,360	0.74	$69,330
Dallas-Plano-Irving, TX	1,330	0.60	$77,180
Los Angeles-Long Beach-Glendale, CA	1,330	0.33	$79,960
Atlanta-Sandy Springs-Marietta, GA	1,280	0.53	$47,870
Denver-Aurora-Broomfield, CO	1,050	0.79	$62,850
Houston-Sugar Land-Baytown, TX	940	0.33	$73,300
Phoenix-Mesa-Glendale, AZ	880	0.48	$56,450
Miami-Miami Beach-Kendall, FL	850	0.82	$68,880

Source: Bureau of Labor Statistics

EMPLOYMENT AND OUTLOOK

Nationally, there were approximately 86,000 real estate appraisers employed in 2014. Employment is expected to about the same as the average for all occupations through the year 2024, which means employment is projected to increase 6 percent to 11 percent. Job growth will be limited by the increased use of mobile technologies that allow properties to be appraised more quickly. Most job openings will occur to replace those workers who leave the field.

Employment Trend, Projected 2014–24

Financial specialists: 10%

Appraisers and assessors of real estate: 8%

Total, all occupations: 7%

Note: "All Occupations" includes all occupations in the U.S. Economy. Source: U.S. Bureau of Labor Statistics, Employment Projections Program.

Related Occupations
- Construction and Building Inspector
- Insurance Claims Adjuster and Examiner
- Public Administrator

Conversation With . . .
LIZ CLEMENZI

Owner, Commonwealth Appraisal Services
Shrewsbury, Massachusetts
Real estate appraiser, 32 years

1. What was your individual career path in terms of education/training, entry-level job, or other significant opportunity?

I started out in the marketing end of the insurance industry, working in sales promotions for seven years. It wasn't until I became a mother and it came time to put my son in a day care center that I realized I couldn't do it. At that point, I decided I needed a new career. My husband and I were purchasing a home and having an appraisal done. When I opened the door, it was a female appraiser. I knew in an instant that this is what I wanted to do. I put on a pot of coffee and made her tell me everything! I'm very analytical, highly data-driven, and have a passion for real estate. It was a perfect merging of my set of talents. So, I took classes and got my real estate appraiser's license. Appraisers have to apprentice for two years, then take another test to become a full appraiser. I did my apprenticeship under that same female appraiser who came to my door that day. She taught me how to do this job and work around a family. In 1985, two years after I started as an apprentice, I opened my own business.

2. What are the most important skills and/or qualities for someone in your profession?

You have to have really excellent analytical skills. You have to be able to understand real estate, to understand what's going on in a given town and a given neighborhood, and then mathematically scale that information. You need very good math skills! Appraisers need to be able to "sell" our product—to the bank, the underwriters, and to the government-sponsored mortgage finance programs known as Fannie Mae and Freddie Mac. When I write an appraisal, I need to be able to support and defend the value I come up with. Basically, what we're trying to do is recognize trends.

3. What do you wish you had known going into this profession?

I wish I had realized that the significant ups and downs in real estate would result in significant ups and downs in my income. In 1986, we were inundated with a very rapidly expanding real estate market. But by 1988, the market had crashed. We saw the same thing happen in 2005, when there was a real estate feeding frenzy. Then in 2008 and 2009, we were starving for work.

4. Are there many job opportunities in your profession? In what specific areas?

There aren't a lot of young people getting into the industry because it's a difficult industry to break into and a difficult industry to learn. Not that many people can sustain themselves financially during the two-year apprenticeship. And there's a lot to understand: septic systems, conservation restrictions, zoning restrictions.... You have to have knowledge of the market in many different geographic areas. You have to know the difference between how to appraise a "charming 1767 antique" and a "wild contemporary." You need to understand all the banking and underwriting guidelines. Every year, fewer and fewer appraisers renew their licenses. So that creates opportunity; however, is it a field people want to get into?

5. How do you see your profession changing in the next five years? What role will technology play in those changes, and what skills will be required?

Right now, we're adapting to the use of computer tablets, rather than taking a camera and clipboard into the field to appraise a property. Fannie Mae and Freddie Mac and the government have developed systems to take all the data we feed them and come back with a range of value for a given house. So, if you have a credit score of 750 or greater, you may not need to have an appraisal done in coming years. So much of the work that used to be done in the field is now done without leaving the office. I can get on Google Earth and get a feel for a neighborhood. I can pull a field card on a property from a town's website and check a deed online.

6. What do you enjoy most about your job? What do you enjoy least about your job?

I love the flexibility and the freedom. Some days I'm out on the road all day and other days, I'm in the office spending hours writing reports. I could not have designed a better career for my skill set and my personality! What I like least are the ever-changing government regulations. They mostly don't make any sense, honestly, and don't result in a better product.

7. Can you suggest a valuable "try this" for students considering a career in your profession?

I would suggest that you shadow an appraiser. I remember my first time out in the field, I just couldn't wait to take my clipboard and tape measure and go to town!

SELECTED SCHOOLS

Many colleges and universities, especially those with business schools, offer programs related to a career in insurance. The student can also gain initial training through enrollment at a technical or community college. Below are listed some of the more prominent institutions in this field.

Florida State University
Tallahassee, FL 32306
850.644.2525
www.fsu.edu

Marquette University
PO Box 1881
Milwaukee, WI 53201
414.288.7250
www.marquett.edu

New York University
70 Washington Square S
New York, NY 10012
212.998.1212
www.nyu.edu

University of California, Berkeley
110 Sproul Hall
Berkeley, CA 94720
510.642.6000
berkeley.edu

University of Florida
201 Criser Hall
Gainesville, FL 32611
352.392.3261
www.ufl.edu

University of Georgia
Administration Building
Athens, GA 30602
706.542.3000
www.uga.edu

University of Southern California
University Park
Los Angeles, CA 90089
213.740.2311
www.usc.edu

University of Pennsylvania
1 College Hall, Rm 100
Philadelphia, PA 19104
215.898.5000
www.upenn.edu

University of Texas, Austin
1 University Station
Austin, TX 78712
512.471.3434
www.utexas.edu

University of Wisconsin, Madison
500 Lincoln Drive
Madison, WI 53706
608.262.1234
www.wisc.edu

MORE INFORMATION

American Society of Appraisers
11107 Sunset Hills Road, Suite 310
Reston, VA 20190
800.272.8258
www.appraisers.org

**American Society of Farm
Managers and Rural Appraisers**
950 S. Cherry Street, Suite 508
Denver, CO 80246-2664
303.758.3513
www.asfmra.org

Appraisal Foundation
1155 15th Street NW, Suite 1111
Washington, DC 20005
202.347.7722
www.appraisalfoundation.org

Appraisal Institute
550 W. Van Buren Street, Suite 1000
Chicago, IL 60607
888.756.4624
www.appraisalinstitute.org

**National Association of
Independent Fee Appraisers**
401 N. Michigan Avenue, Suite 2200
Chicago, IL 60611
312.321.6830
www.naifa.com

**National Association of Real
Estate Appraisers**
810 N. Farrell Drive
Palm Springs, CA 92262
877.815.4172
www.narea-assoc.org

Real Estate Roundtable
801 Pennsylvania Avenue NW
Suite 720
Washington, DC 20004
202.639.8400
www.rer.org

Sally Driscoll/Editor

Real Estate Sales Agent

Snapshot

Career Cluster(s): Business, Real Estate, Sales & Service
Interests: Sales, real estate, residential and commercial development, marketing, zoning laws, financing
Earnings (Yearly Average): $40,990
Employment & Outlook: Slower than Average Growth Expected

OVERVIEW

Sphere of Work

Real estate sales agents assist clients in the purchasing, selling, and leasing of residential and commercial properties. They possess a comprehensive understanding of the real estate market and related trends, property values, financing options, and local tax and zoning laws for the areas in which they work. Real estate sales agents generally work on a contract basis for a real estate broker who is licensed to run his or her own real estate business. Whether their clients buy or sell property, brokers award real estate sales agents a commission, which is

a fixed percentage of a property's final sale price, once a transaction is complete.

Work Environment

Real estate sales agents primarily show properties to clients, travel between property locations, and meet with potential buyers and sellers. They also spend some time working in a real estate or home office, using the Internet and phone to research, communicate, and negotiate. Real estate sales agents rarely work a standard forty-hour week. As they must accommodate the schedules of clients, they may meet with clients in the evenings and on weekends. They tend to be busier during warmer months.

Profile

Working Conditions: Work Indoors
Physical Strength: Light Work
Education Needs: On-The-Job Training, High School Diploma or GED, Junior/Technical/Community College
Licensure/Certification: Required
Opportunities For Experience: Part-Time Work
Holland Interest Score*: ESR

* See Appendix A

Occupation Interest

Individuals who are interested in becoming real estate sales agents should enjoy working closely with others. Because the field is highly competitive and prospective clients have a choice among real estate agents, candidates should be assertive but polite and maintain a positive attitude. Prospective agents must have a strong interest in real estate as they will spend long hours researching and analyzing the real estate market, as well as gaining a solid understanding of the details of each property they show.

A Day in the Life—Duties and Responsibilities

Real estate sales agents divide their time between property research and meetings with potential buyers and sellers. They continually check current property listings to determine what properties are for sale and how to price new listings appropriately based on the current market value of similar properties. Real estate sales agents also meet with and interview prospective clients to establish a desired price range, solicit listings, show properties, and discuss buying or selling terms and conditions. They often meet with buyers several times in order to discuss location preferences and to show properties that have become newly available. They are also responsible for developing marketing strategies, such as weekend open houses and advertisements, on behalf of sellers.

Real estate sales agents act as the liaison between buyers and sellers. Agents verify property ownership through title searches, negotiate prices and terms on behalf of their clients, and ensure that all contract terms are finalized before the closing of a property. They also make sure that legally required inspections for termites, radon, lead paint, and other potential hazards occur before closing. In many cases, they help buyers research and apply for available mortgage and finance loans.

Most real estate sales agents specialize in residential properties; however, some agents specialize in the sale of commercial, industrial, agricultural, and other nonresidential properties. These agents normally work for larger commercial real estate firms and must have specific knowledge of commercial leasing practices, pricing, and business locations.

Duties and Responsibilities

- Studying property listings to become familiar with properties for sale
- Reviewing trade journals to keep informed of marketing conditions and property values
- Preparing marketing plans
- Interviewing prospective clients to solicit listings
- Accompanying clients to property sites
- Drawing up real estate contracts
- Handling price negotiations between buyer and seller

OCCUPATION SPECIALTIES

Real Estate Brokers

Real Estate Brokers are independent business persons who may own and manage their own real estate firms and engage the services of real estate agents.

WORK ENVIRONMENT

Physical Environment

Real estate sales agents spend some of their time working in clean, comfortable real estate offices or working from home. The rest of their time is spent in and around property locations. In some cases, agents may have to travel and show outdoor properties in inclement weather.

Relevant Skills and Abilities

Communication Skills
- Speaking effectively
- Writing concisely

Interpersonal/Social Skills
- Being persistent
- Cooperating with others
- Working as a member of a team

Unclassified Skills
- Remembering names and faces

Human Environment

Though many real estate sales agents operate independently, they work closely with real estate brokers and clients looking to buy or sell property. Often they communicate with lawyers, appraisers, lenders, inspectors, builders, and other real estate agents.

Technological Environment

Real estate sales agents handle numerous documents and files daily to gather information about properties. They frequently review property listings and advertisements, appraisal files, public records, foreclosure notices, and publications and newsletters. These materials may print materials or information accessed through electronic databases. Real estate sales agents use basic office equipment, such as cell phones, fax machines, photocopiers, computers, and the Internet.

EDUCATION, TRAINING, AND ADVANCEMENT

High School/Secondary

High school students looking to become real estate sales agents should take courses in business, public speaking, mathematics, geography, and social studies. Students are also encouraged to participate in extracurricular activities that allow them to engage with other students. Because selling property involves a high degree of persuasion, students should join clubs like the debate team that will strengthen their oratorical skills. Interested students can start to become familiar with different kinds of properties by visiting local houses listed for sale and studying related details.

Suggested High School Subjects
- Applied Communication
- Applied Math
- Bookkeeping
- Business
- Business Law
- Business Math
- Economics
- English
- Mathematics
- Merchandising
- Psychology
- Social Studies
- Speech

Famous First

The first house to feature a built-in nuclear bomb shelter was shown on May 24, 1959, in Pleasant Hills, Penn. It contained a fully equipped underground shelter to accommodate four persons, with bunks, sanitary facilities, a pantry, refrigerator, a Geiger counter, and other first-aid and emergency equipment. It also had a concrete escape tunnel.

College/Postsecondary

Though real estate sales agents are not required to have an undergraduate degree in order to sell real estate, many find it helpful to take courses in real estate at the postsecondary level. Universities and community colleges commonly offer certificate programs in real estate, and vocational institutions offer associate and bachelor's degrees in the field. These programs cover topics such as salesmanship, appraisal, residential design, principles of real estate, and legal and tax aspects of real estate. Those agents who earn an undergraduate degree find it beneficial to study business administration, economics, and law.

Related College Majors
- Real Estate

Adult Job Seekers

Many new real estate sales agents get their start in the field by shadowing an experienced real estate agent who can train them in the fundamentals of practical real estate sales. Prospective real estate sales agents who want to work for a larger real estate firm can apply directly to the company for an entry-level position, like an office assistant or filing clerk, and then advance to a sales agent position. Qualified adult job seekers may also benefit from the networking opportunities offered by professional real estate associations, such as the National Association of Realtors and National Association of Real Estate Brokers.

Professional Certification and Licensure

Real estate sales agents must obtain professional licensure in their state in order to sell property. Licensure is granted after successful completion of a written examination that typically covers the basic concepts of and laws about real estate. In addition to the written test, most states require completion of thirty to ninety hours of practical instruction in the field. Most real estate sales agents must renew their license every one to two years, depending on their state's regulations. Those who wish to buy or establish their own real estate business must obtain a state broker's license, which usually requires additional formal training and some work experience. Some professional real estate organizations provide voluntary certifications for specialty areas such as residential or commercial sale, sustainable buildings, and housing for the disabled and elderly.

Additional Requirements

To make a living in the highly competitive real estate market, real estate sales agents must anticipate client requests and take advantage of every opportunity by remembering names, faces, prices, and property details. Buyers and sellers are often indecisive, and real estate sales agents must be able to influence a client's opinions and judgments, directing the client toward a fruitful decision. As real estate sales agents have access to clients' confidential financial information, they must demonstrate trustworthiness and professional ethics. Many experienced real estate sales agents belong to the National Association of Realtors, which pledges its members to a code of ethics and professional standards of practice.

Fun Fact

The first Open Houses in real estate, in 1910, were referred to as "Open for Inspection," giving buyers the chance to see inventions like electric lighting. Homes were open daily from 9 a.m. to 9 p.m. until a buyer was found.

Source: /www.realtor.com/news/brief-history-of-the-open-house/

EARNINGS AND ADVANCEMENT

Earnings of real estate sales agents depend on the individual's sales ability and experience and the current economic conditions. Commissions on sales are the main source of earnings of real estate agents. Few are paid a salary. Factors for determining the amount of commission are the city where the property is located, the type of property for sale and its value.

Real estate sales agents had median annual earnings of $40,990 in 2014. The lowest ten percent earned less than $21,540, and the highest ten percent earned more than $105,270.

Some real estate firms furnish life and health insurance. Most real estate sales agents, however, are considered independent contractors and must pay their own social security contribution and other benefits.

Metropolitan Areas with the Highest
Employment Level in This Occupation

Metropolitan area	Employment	Employment per thousand jobs	Annual mean wage
Atlanta-Sandy Springs-Marietta, GA	5,900	2.47	$51,770
Houston-Sugar Land-Baytown, TX	5,700	2.01	$63,700
Orlando-Kissimmee-Sanford, FL	4,850	4.49	$41,300
Chicago-Joliet-Naperville, IL	4,470	1.19	$76,790
Washington-Arlington-Alexandria, DC-VA-MD-WV	4,030	1.69	$63,620
Dallas-Plano-Irving, TX	3,890	1.74	$54,790
Miami-Miami Beach-Kendall, FL	3,710	3.55	$44,660
Los Angeles-Long Beach-Glendale, CA	3,590	0.88	$65,950
Philadelphia, PA	3,170	1.70	$53,350
Santa Ana-Anaheim-Irvine, CA	3,150	2.12	$52,480

Source: Bureau of Labor Statistics

EMPLOYMENT AND OUTLOOK

There were about 420,000 real estate sales agents and brokers employed nationally in 2014. Many worked part-time and over half were self-employed. Employment is expected to grow slower than the average for all occupations through the year 2024, which means employment is projected to increase 0 percent to 5 percent. Prospective customers often can conduct their own searches for properties that meet their criteria by finding real estate information on the internet. However, technology should have only a limited effect on job growth, because most people still want and need the services of real estate sales agents to handle the actual sale.

Employment Trend, Projected 2014–24

Total, all occupations: 7%

Sales and related occupations: 5%

Real estate sales agents: 3%

Real estate brokers and sales agents: 3%

Real estate brokers: 2%

Note: "All Occupations" includes all occupations in the U.S. Economy. Source: U.S. Bureau of Labor Statistics, Employment Projections Program.

Related Occupations

- Advertising Agent
- Automobile Salesperson
- Financial Analyst
- Insurance Agent
- Manufacturers Representative
- Personal Financial Advisor
- Pharmaceutical Sales Representative
- Property and Real Estate Manager
- Retail Salesperson
- Sales Engineer
- Services Sales Representative
- Technical Sales Representative
- Wholesale Sales Representative

Conversation With . . .
MARIBETH LYNCH

Real Estate Broker, Thrive Real Estate Specialists
Shrewsbury, Massachusetts
Real estate agent, 18 years

1. What was your individual career path in terms of education/training, entry-level job, or other significant opportunity?

I majored in criminal justice at King's College in Pennsylvania and worked in the security department at the Park Plaza Hotel in Boston after graduating. Around the same time, my dad had been transferred from Philadelphia to Boston and the whole family went house hunting. The broker was a Texan and larger than life: big hair, big diamonds, big car. Big impression on me!

Real estate started calling, even though I worked at the hotel for two more years. I got my broker's license and went to work for Coldwell Banker Residential Brokerage. It was the late 1980s, a time of double-digit interest rates. Real estate was not exactly humming. But what better way to learn a job than under trying circumstances?

When my kids were small, I left real estate, but eventually returned to it. I was again working at Coldwell Banker when a great opportunity arose to do on-site sales at an over-55 development, so I did that for a few years. But large real estate companies require reams of paperwork—most of it not designed to protect the client—and that wore on me. After toying with the idea for years, I finally struck out on my own in 2014.

2. What are the most important skills and/or qualities for someone in your profession?

It's really important to be able to motivate yourself without a boss making you get to work. You have to be resourceful. You have to be able to problem-solve for your clients. In real estate, if you're doing it the right way, you're doing more listening than talking. You have to be approachable and friendly. You have to dress the part and be able to communicate professionally. I don't feel that salesmanship is a necessary skill. In fact, I hate that people call me a salesperson. You can help homebuyers narrow their choices or maybe help them understand if they have unreasonable expectations, but you can't really "sell" a person a house.

3. What do you wish you had known going into this profession?

There's no way of knowing for sure what your income is going to be. You have to be prepared for a lot of ups and downs. Also, the first year or so can be slow. I tell new agents that they can expect to earn under $10,000 their first year and should expect to spend at least $3,000 on start-up costs. Bottom line, it helps to have a breadwinner at home or large savings to draw from in the beginning.

4. Are there many job opportunities in your profession? In what specific areas?

There's plenty of opportunity. There are a variety of real estate companies out there, but you're either going to succeed in real estate or you're not—the name on the shingle doesn't really matter.

5. How do you see your profession changing in the next five years? What role will technology play in those changes, and what skills will be required?

Technology is huge and it's here. A big percent of real estate shopping, at least initially, is done online. The average real estate broker is in her mid-50s and female and tends not to be very tech-savvy. If you don't adapt and use technology, you'll be left behind.

6. What do you enjoy most about your job? What do you enjoy least about your job?

Probably the flexibility it has afforded me over the years, which is kind of funny because it's also true that when someone calls, you have to jump. But real estate can allow you to live a really good quality life because you have time. You don't have to be an uber-producer; you can be an ordinary salesperson and still do pretty well. Being a broker is like being a social worker and psychologist combined. You're dealing with people's emotions, whether it's an elderly person transitioning from her home to assisted living, or an estate sale where people are selling their parents' home or the home they grew up in, or a bad divorce, or first-time homebuyers.

The thing I don't like is that the barriers to entry are very low, so real estate tends to attract people who don't have the skill set to survive in the business. I'm an advocate for requiring an apprenticeship for two years before you can get your broker's license. Another thing many people don't like about real estate is that you have to work evenings and weekends. I guess because I've done this for so long, it really doesn't bother me—except maybe in the middle of summer!

7. Can you suggest a valuable "try this" for students considering a career in your profession?

Find someone who's willing to mentor you and let you follow them around. Make sure you find someone whose style and personality works for you. Don't just ask your friend's mom who sells real estate.

SELECTED SCHOOLS

Most colleges and universities offer programs related to careers in business, sales, or real estate; the student may also get started in a community or technical college. For a list of some of the more prominent schools in this field, see the chapter "Real Estate Appraiser" in the present volume.

MORE INFORMATION

American Real Estate Society
Member Services
Clemson University
Box 341323
424 Sirrine Hall
Clemson, SC 29634-1323
www.aresnet.org

Association of Energy and Environmental Real Estate Professionals
3082 Evergreen Parkway, Suite H
Evergreen, CO 80439
800.706.4321
www.aeerep.org

National Association of Real Estate Brokers
9831 Greenbelt Road
Lanham, MD 20706
301.552.9340
www.nareb.com

National Association of Realtors
430 N. Michigan Avenue
Chicago, IL 60611-4087
800.874.6500
www.realtor.org

Real Estate Roundtable
801 Pennsylvania Avenue NW
Suite 720
Washington, DC 20004
202.639.8400
www.rer.org

Briana Nadeau/Editor

Retail Salesperson

Snapshot

Career Cluster(s): Business, Retail, Sales & Service
Interests: Sales, customer service, merchandise display, inventory and stocking, merchandise demonstrations, financial transactions
Earnings (Yearly Average): $21,390
Employment & Outlook: Average Growth Expected

OVERVIEW

Sphere of Work

A retail salesperson sells various kinds of commercial merchandise to customers and store patrons and represents the store to the customers by providing reliable, courteous service. In addition to selling products, a retail salesperson is usually responsible for the preparation, arrangement, and maintenance of store merchandise. He or she must also handle financial transactions, open and close the store, maintain a friendly demeanor, and answer questions regarding items for sale. In specialty stores like jewelry or

electronics stores, a retail salesperson is expected to possess in-depth knowledge of the products he or she sells.

Work Environment

Most retail salespersons work in clean, pleasant, and well-lit indoor retail stores. Those who work in larger department stores are on their feet for a majority of the day, walking, bending, and often lifting merchandise. Some retail salespersons work outdoors, selling planting materials, vehicles, or building materials, and sometimes endure extreme temperatures or unpleasant weather. Retail salespersons normally work flexible schedules that often include evenings and weekends and do not follow standard work hours. They work under the supervision of a store manager, supervisor, or owner, and constantly interact with customers and other employees.

Profile

Working Conditions: Work Indoors
Physical Strength: Light Work, Medium Work
Education Needs: On-The-Job Training, High School Diploma or GED, High School Diploma with Technical Education
Licensure/Certification: Usually Not Required
Opportunities For Experience: Internship, Part-Time Work
Holland Interest Score*: ESA, ESR

* See Appendix A

Occupation Interest

Because retail salespersons are in constant communication with store patrons, successful salespersons are expected to be socially outgoing and interested in interacting with others on a regular basis. Prospective retail salespersons should enjoy helping others find what they need quickly, accurately, and effectively. They should also have an interest in the products they sell and should strive to promote a store's merchandise to the best of their ability. They must also possess the customer service skills needed to deal with difficult situations and rude customers.

A Day in the Life—Duties and Responsibilities

Retail salespersons spend the majority of their day conducting financial transactions, interacting with customers, and keeping stores organized. Those who sell apparel or footwear, especially in smaller boutiques, spend a good deal of time fitting and styling customers and aiding them in the selection of clothing or shoes. Their responsibilities may include displaying merchandise in windows or on counters and shelves, recommending and promoting products to store patrons, taking inventory of and stocking merchandise, maintaining sales records, operating the cash register and collecting payments, and packaging purchased items. All retail salespersons must learn, understand, and follow store policies and procedures regarding hours, the handling of money, theft, security risks, customer service, and damaged merchandise.

In larger department stores, retail salespersons often assume numerous responsibilities and must be able to change priorities quickly. In many cases, they must know how to run a variety of stations or departments, which may include layaway, fitting rooms, purchases and returns, price tag adjustment, recovery (the act of cleaning and reorganizing the store upon closing), customer service, and stocking and inventory.

Some of the most experienced retail salespersons take on managerial duties, supervising other store employees and making sure that the store operates properly. Other experienced salespersons are occasionally responsible for making financial deposits at a bank or cash office during the day.

It is customary for patrons to ask salespersons detailed questions related to merchandise as they consider purchases. Therefore, retail salespersons are expected to be able to offer extensive information about the demonstrated function, value, and features of the items they sell.

Duties and Responsibilities

- Interesting customers in merchandise
- Displaying merchandise, sometimes using samples or catalogs
- Demonstrating merchandise emphasizing salable features
- Preparing forms and sales contracts
- Estimating or quoting prices, credit terms and trade-ins
- Advising customers of product servicing and warranty
- Contacting customers
- Receiving cash, check or charge payments
- Making deposits at the cash office

WORK ENVIRONMENT

Physical Environment

Most retail salespersons work inside a small or large retail store that is well ventilated and comfortable. They spend a lot of time on their feet and usually must obtain permission from a supervisor or manager in order to leave the store or take a scheduled break.

Human Environment

Retail salespersons work closely and regularly with retail workers, managers, security guards, and janitorial staff. They also interact with outside vendors, delivery people, and postal workers. They constantly assist and advise store patrons and must be polite and respectful during all interactions, even when they are unable to please a customer.

Relevant Skills and Abilities

Communication Skills
- Persuading others

Interpersonal/Social Skills
- Being patient
- Cooperating with others
- Working as a member of a team

Organization & Management Skills
- Managing conflict
- Managing time
- Meeting goals and deadlines

Research & Planning Skills
- Developing evaluation strategies

Technical Skills
- Performing scientific, mathematical and technical work

Technological Environment

Retail salespersons use numerous tools in their daily activities. Most importantly, they must learn the proper use of a cash register or specialized retail computer for purchases and financial transactions. They also use weight scales, catalogs, calculators, order forms, sales receipts, price tag machines, speaker systems, and telephones in the course of their work. Some may arrange mannequins and other display equipment.

EDUCATION, TRAINING, AND ADVANCEMENT

High School/Secondary

High school students who wish to become retail salespersons can best prepare by studying business, communications, and economics at the secondary level. They should enroll in basic mathematics courses to prepare themselves for the financial aspects of working in retail. Independently, students can visit local retail establishments to become familiar with retail processes and procedures. They can also apply for entry-level retail positions during the summer and holiday seasons, when retail establishments are at their busiest. Those students interested in selling specialty merchandise, like electronics or automobiles, can research products on their own to gain more detailed knowledge of specific merchandise.

Suggested High School Subjects
- Business
- Business & Computer Technology
- Business English
- Business Math
- Economics
- Keyboarding
- Merchandising
- Speech

Famous First

The first retail store to achieve sales of over $1 million in a single day was Macy's in New York City. On December 7, 1944, the store broke the record for one-day sales revenues. It reached sales of $2 million in one day on December 14, 1957; $3 million on December 18, 1965; and $4 million on December 18, 1967.

Postsecondary

Retail salespersons usually earn a high school diploma or its equivalent. Those individuals planning to apply for management positions in the future may find it helpful to have studied aspects of business, marketing, and sales after high school. They can enroll in vocational education or undergraduate programs that teach students about distribution, merchandising, promotion, and management. Such programs often offer work-study opportunities for students, which allows them a method of entry into their desire to field.

Related College Majors
• General Retailing & Wholesaling Operations & Skills

Adult Job Seekers

Prospective retail salespersons should apply directly with retail establishments for entry-level positions in order to gain experience in the industry. It is beneficial for job seekers to apply for retail work during peak seasons (summer months, school vacations, and before and after holidays). Those who accept retail positions in larger department stores often gain valuable knowledge of the various aspects of the job and may learn how to sell a wider range of products than those who work in specialty stores. In contrast, those who sell only a few specific types of items often become virtual experts in their field and usually move up to management positions quickly and easily.

Professional Certification and Licensure

Retail salespersons are not required to receive formal professional certification or licensure in their field. Most small and large retail establishments provide on-the-job training to new retail employees; training usually lasts from a few days up to several weeks depending on the complexities of the job.

Additional Requirements

Because retail salespersons are responsible for handling money and expensive products, they must be trustworthy, sincere, and honest. Employers often look for retail salespersons who will contribute to a store's overall success and who will take personal initiative to help eliminate theft, vandalism, and dishonesty among customers and staff.

Fun Fact

Seventy-two percent of millenials research and shop their options online before they go to a brick-and-mortar store or mall.

Source: A study by The Intelligence Group (TIG) as reported at
http://www.forbes.com/sites/robinlewis/2014/04/30/millennials-double-trouble-for-retail/#473e81724724

EARNINGS AND ADVANCEMENT

Some retail salespersons are paid strictly on a commission basis. Others are paid a salary plus commission. A few retail salespersons are paid a standard salary with no sales commission. Therefore, earnings of most retail salespersons depend on how much merchandise they sell. Factors affecting sales are the selling experience and ability of the employee, the type of merchandise sold and the location of employer.

Median annual earnings of retail salespersons, including commission, were $21,390 in 2014. The lowest ten percent earned less than $17,030, and the highest ten percent earned more than $39,300.

Retail salespersons may receive paid vacations, holidays, and sick days; life and health insurance; and retirement benefits. These are usually paid by the employer. Some retail salespersons may receive additional benefits such as bonuses and merchandise discounts.

Metropolitan Areas with the Highest
Employment Level in This Occupation

Metropolitan area	Employment	Employment per thousand jobs	Annual mean wage
New York-White Plains-Wayne, NY-NJ	183,670	34.07	$26,790
Chicago-Joliet-Naperville, IL	126,350	33.67	$26,030
Los Angeles-Long Beach-Glendale, CA	115,910	28.57	$26,810
Houston-Sugar Land-Baytown, TX	88,320	31.06	$26,320
Atlanta-Sandy Springs-Marietta, GA	82,800	34.67	$25,380
Dallas-Plano-Irving, TX	76,730	34.28	$26,970
Phoenix-Mesa-Glendale, AZ	67,090	36.74	$24,900
Washington-Arlington-Alexandria, DC-VA-MD-WV	66,930	28.14	$25,380
Philadelphia, PA	63,020	33.85	$27,110
Minneapolis-St. Paul-Bloomington, MN-WI	57,670	31.61	$24,100

Source: Bureau of Labor Statistics

EMPLOYMENT AND OUTLOOK

There were approximately 4.6 million retail salespersons employed nationally in 2014. They worked in stores ranging from small specialty shops employing a few workers to giant department stores with hundreds of salespersons. In addition, some were self-employed salespersons of direct-sales companies. The fastest growing employers of retail salespersons are supercenters and warehouse clubs that sell a wide range of merchandise in a single location. Employment of retail salespersons is expected to grow about as fast as the average for all occupations through the year 2024, which means employment is projected to increase 5 percent to 9 percent. This is due to the rising retail purchases of a growing population.

This occupation offers many opportunities for part-time work and is especially appealing to students, retirees and others looking to supplement their income. However, most of those selling "big ticket" items, such as cars, furniture, and electronic equipment, work full-time and have substantial experience. There will continue to be many opportunities for part-time workers, and demand will be strong for temporary workers during peak selling periods, such as the Christmas season.

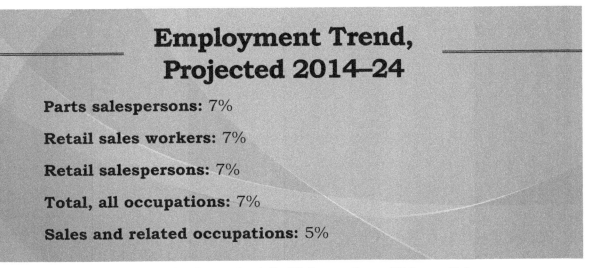

Employment Trend, Projected 2014–24

Parts salespersons: 7%

Retail sales workers: 7%

Retail salespersons: 7%

Total, all occupations: 7%

Sales and related occupations: 5%

Note: "All Occupations" includes all occupations in the U.S. Economy. Source: U.S. Bureau of Labor Statistics, Employment Projections Program.

Related Occupations

- Automobile Salesperson
- Customer Service Representative
- Insurance Sales Agent
- Manufacturers Representative
- Online Merchant
- Pharmaceutical Sales Representative
- Real Estate Sales Agent
- Sales Engineer
- Services Sales Representative
- Technical Sales Representative
- Wholesale and Retail Buyer
- Wholesale Sales Representative

Conversation With . . .
BRAYDEN PLEASANTS

President/Founder, Red Eye Cookie Co.
Richmond, VA
Sales/Customer Service, 12 years
Retail Entrepreneur, 2 years

1. What was your individual career path in terms of education/training, entry-level job, or other significant opportunity?

After high school, I went to a local university, transferred to another, then left to join the Marine Corps in 2005. I originally joined as a reservist with the intent of returning to school after boot camp. Instead, I volunteered to go with my unit to Iraq, and, after training, was deployed for a year as provisional infantry tasked with convoy security and detainee operations.

When I returned, school didn't feel like a fit so I worked landscaping and other manual labor jobs for a couple of years. Then I took a sales and marketing position in 2009 and enrolled at Virginia Commonwealth University. After graduating with a Bachelors' of Science in Business and Marketing, a colleague helped me get a position with a recruiting firm where he worked. It was fast-paced, used my skill set, and was a good opportunity, but I wasn't sure of the path I was on. When I experienced a personal loss six months later, I further questioned the direction of my career. I was building something for someone else. I wanted to build something I could get value from in the future.

A friend was opening a startup and we discussed a partnership. The concept was fun and unique: late night cookie delivery, centered around college markets. We ended up going in different directions, but I saw an opportunity, quit my job, and started Red Eye Cookie Co.

We deliver eleven flavors of cookies—including vegan and gluten-free options—along with ice cream and cold milk. College students still comprise a significant part of our clientele. You can order online and over the phone for delivery or come by the store and pick up. We operate seven days a week and recently extended our hours to include the daytime. Our sales stay fairly evenly split between in-store and online platforms.

As I was developing the concept, a high school friend returned from working abroad in logistics with Doctors Without Borders. After some discussion he came on as a partner and managed Red Eye's operations for our first eight months, helping us get established, before moving on to graduate school.

We've learned and grown a great deal over the last two years and have seen our share of challenges and changes.

2. What are the most important skills and/or qualities for someone in your profession?

I'm a big believer in people focusing on what they do best. I'm a relationship guy, so I fit well on the marketing and business development side. I purposefully surround myself with people who have stronger operational and organizational skills than I do.

3. What do you wish you had known going into this profession?

I sometimes encounter employees or colleagues who may see a particular issue as paralyzing, as I initially did. I wish I knew coming in that, more often than not, problems can be approached as challenges that need to be broken down and dealt with, step-by-step. Many can be opportunities for growth if you can learn to let them.

4. Are there many job opportunities in your profession? In what specific areas?

That's difficult for me to answer since I created my opportunity. So I would say there's always an opportunity to create a position for yourself as an entrepreneur.

5. How do you see your profession changing in the next five years, what role will technology play in those changes, and what skills will be required?

The retail sales environment will continue to grow more competitive, which will only improve the quality of products and experiences brought to consumers. Technology will continue to play a large part of that. We use technology in everything from accepting orders and engaging with customers to scheduling employees and running payroll. Technology helps us work more efficiently at every level so staying abreast of new developments and using them to make our jobs easier and more effective will continue to be a focus.

6. What do you enjoy most about your job? What do you enjoy least about your job?

I enjoy the dynamic and ever-changing nature of what I do. I also find that engaging with customers and seeing the positive experience we leave them with is personally rewarding.

I least enjoy letting people go, and some of the administrative work and red tape that's often a necessary part of the job.

7. Can you suggest a valuable "try this" for students considering a career in your profession?

Talk to people in the field and gain from their experience. Take an entry-level customer service position. Step out of your social comfort zone and talk to different types of people. Sales, at its core, is about the relationships we have with people and the experiences we leave them with.

MORE INFORMATION

American Apparel and Footwear Association
1601 N. Kent Street, 12th Floor
Arlington, VA 22209
800.520.2262
www.apparelandfootwear.org

American Specialty Toy Retailing Association
432 N. Clark Street, Suite 401
Chicago, IL 60654
800.591.0490
www.astratoy.org

National Association of Convenience Stores
1600 Duke Street, 7th Floor
Alexandria, VA 22314
703.684.3600
www.nacsonline.com

National Home Furnishings Association
3910 Tinsley Drive, Suite 101
High Point, NC 27265-3610
800.888.9590
www.nhfa.org

National Retail Federation
325 7th Street NW, Suite 1100
Washington, DC 20004
800.673.4692
www.nrf.com

Retail, Wholesale and Department Store Union
30 East 29th Street
New York, NY 10016
212.684.5300
www.rwdsu.org

United Food and Commercial Workers International Union
Education Office
1775 K Street NW
Washington, DC 20006
202.223.3111
www.ufcw.org

Briana Nadeau/Editor

Sales Engineer

Snapshot

Career Cluster(s): Business, Engineering, Sales & Service
Interests: Sales, engineering, science, negotiations, economics, public speaking
Earnings (Yearly Average): $96,340
Employment & Outlook: Average Growth Expected

OVERVIEW

Sphere of Work

Sales engineers work to build and maintain relationships between manufacturers, distributors, and consumers of scientific and technological products and services. They work in all sectors of industry, including transportation, defense, retail, and information technology. Sales engineers often work in presales, helping potential customers understand how a product functions and helping to introduce innovations to the marketplace. They also serve

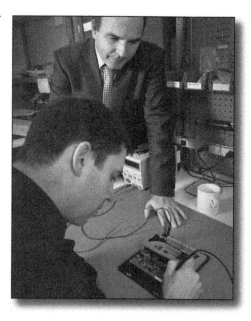

as consultants, helping product designers and engineers develop customer solutions.

Work Environment

Sales engineers spend a lot of their time traveling between meetings with clients. They are often away from home for long periods of time. Company headquarters are typically office environments. At times, a sales engineer may have to enter manufacturing environments or construction and industrial sites.

Profile

Working Conditions: Work both Indoors and Outdoors
Physical Strength: Light Work
Education Needs: Bachelor's Degree
Licensure/Certification: Usually Not Required
Opportunities For Experience: Internship, Part-Time Work
Holland Interest Score*: ERI, ERS, IER

* See Appendix A

Occupation Interest

Sales engineering covers a broad range of knowledge and skills and tends to attract professionals who are excellent communicators and enjoy working with people. Sales engineers excel at explaining what products and services do and why they are worthy of investment. They typically have a strong background in customer service. They are also good listeners who are able to understand the needs of their clients.

A Day in the Life—Duties and Responsibilities

The daily responsibilities of a sales engineer vary depending on the product, service, business, or customer they are working with. They spend a majority of their time traveling to client locations, where they work with sales managers, product representatives, or research-and-development teams. Typically, sales engineers make their own schedules. Since a lot of time is spent traveling and preparing presentations and product reports, sales engineers usually work variable hours.

Before sales engineers meet with potential customers, they prepare presentations detailing the product or service their client is selling. These presentations explain how the product or service will benefit the client and review information concerning costs. While preparing a client presentation, sales engineers will discuss the product or service with other engineers and executives so they are well informed of its unique attributes and advantages.

When a client decides he or she would like to purchase the product or service, the sales engineer negotiates the cost and helps arrange product delivery or distribution. If necessary, a sales engineer will help arrange for product installation. Sales engineers also assist clients in learning how to use a newly acquired service or product.

Duties and Responsibilities

- Interesting retail buyers and purchasing agents in their merchandise
- Calling on customers such as engineers, architects or other professional workers to demonstrate and explain the product or service
- Assisting customers in determining equipment needs
- Preparing cost and operation estimates on equipment
- Recommending new and more efficient ways to use equipment
- Assisting in the development of custom-made machinery
- Providing technical services to clients
- Preparing sales and service contracts

OCCUPATION SPECIALTIES

Mechanical Equipment Sales Engineers

Mechanical Equipment Sales Engineers specialize in the sale and installation of heating equipment.

Electrical Products Sales Engineers

Electrical Products Sales Engineers determine the power requirements of customers who use large amounts of electricity and provide engineering services and technical advice.

Mining-and-Oil-Well Equipment and Services Sales Engineers

Mining-and-Oil-Well Equipment and Services Sales Engineers sell mining and oil well equipment to producers of oil and natural gas and provide technical services.

WORK ENVIRONMENT

Physical Environment

Sales engineers spend a majority of their time traveling, so their work environment can include automobiles, airplanes, and trains. Sales engineers work with a broad range of clients, and their work can take them to a variety of commercial and industrial locations.

Human Environment

Interacting with clients, sales representatives, managers, product designers, and others is essential to the success of sales engineers. They regularly communicate and collaborate with others to help develop and sell products or services.

Relevant Skills and Abilities

Communication Skills
- Speaking effectively
- Writing concisely

Interpersonal/Social Skills
- Being able to work independently
- Cooperating with others
- Teaching others
- Working as a member of a team (SCANS Workplace Competency – Interpersonal)

Organization & Management Skills
- Managing people/groups (SCANS Workplace Competency Resources
- Organizing information or materials
- Paying attention to and handling details
- Performing duties which change frequently

Research & Planning Skills
- Developing evaluation strategies
- Solving problems
- Using logical reasoning

Technical Skills
- Performing scientific, mathematical and technical work

Technological Environment

Sales engineers work with an assortment of technologies that vary from industry to industry. Regardless of industry, a sales engineer commonly works with computers and projectors to make presentations, as well as basic office technology.

EDUCATION, TRAINING, AND ADVANCEMENT

High School/Secondary

Sales engineers are typically required to have a high school diploma or an equivalent degree. There are several standard high school courses that will benefit an individual interested in becoming a sales engineer, including basic mathematics, computer science, public speaking, and writing. Any courses related to science and engineering are also beneficial.

Suggested High School Subjects

- Blueprint Reading
- Calculus
- Chemistry
- College Preparatory
- Composition
- Drafting
- English
- Geometry
- Humanities
- Merchandising
- Physics
- Social Studies

Famous First

The first school for sales engineering was a school established in 1923 in Whiting, Indiana, by Standard Oil Company. The school was designed to train employees and new recruits in the fundamentals of technical sales.

College/Postsecondary

Employers usually require that applicants have a bachelor's degree in a relevant field, such as business or economics. For sales-engineering positions related to computers or manufacturing, an engineering degree is normally required. Engineering programs at colleges and universities commonly last up to four years. Students getting their postsecondary degree should take courses that will give them a strong background in mathematics and computer science. Since being a sales engineer covers a broad range of subjects, students should approach their studies in a multidisciplinary manner.

Most postsecondary programs require a student to select a specialization. Individuals interested in the sales-engineering profession should select a major that provides instruction in electrical, mechanical, or civil engineering. Many technical and vocational schools offer courses and training programs related to the product and service industries in which sales engineers work. These schools are an excellent way for an individual to network with more experienced people in the field, and many offer job-placement programs.

Related College Majors

- Electrical, Electronics & Communications Engineering
- Mechanical Engineering
- Mining & Mineral Engineering
- Systems Engineering

Adult Job Seekers

Adults seeking to transition to sales engineering should seek training in the field from a technical or vocational school. Being a sales engineer requires a lot of traveling, which may necessitate spending long periods away from family. Sales engineers make a majority of their income through commission, so experience in sales and business communication is a plus.

Professional Certification and Licensure

While no certification or licensure is required to become a sales engineer, an individual may be required to go through sales training before being able to work independently. Training can involve accompanying a more experienced sales engineer during a sales trip.

Through working with a more experienced colleague, new hires will learn about business practices, procedures, and clients.

Sales engineers should be open to continuing their education throughout their career. Continued training is essential to keep up with the latest sales trends and technologies. This is especially important for those in the information technology and advanced electronics fields.

Additional Requirements

Sales engineers must have strong interpersonal communication skills. Technological knowledge and skills are also necessary to sell certain services and products and explain their advantages to clients.

Fun Fact

Many sales engineers begin their careers as engineers because they realize they need to understand their field – and the technology use in it – in order to sell it.

Source: http://www.careeroverview.com/sales-engineer-careers.html

EARNINGS AND ADVANCEMENT

Earnings of sales engineers depend on the type of industry, the type of product, volume of sales, amount of commissions and bonuses and the individual's territory size and level of experience. Most employers use a combination of salary plus commission or salary plus bonus. Commissions are usually based on the amount of sales, whereas bonuses may depend on individual performance, on the performance of all sales workers in the group or district, or on the company's performance.

Median annual earnings of sales engineers, including commission, were $96,340 in 2014. The lowest ten percent earned less than $55,850, and the highest ten percent earned more than $160,250.

Sales engineers may receive paid vacations, holidays, and sick days; life and health insurance; and retirement benefits. These are usually paid by the employer. Sales engineers generally are reimbursed for business expenses and are provided a car or mileage allowance.

Metropolitan Areas with the Highest Employment Level in This Occupation

Metropolitan area	Employment	Employment per thousand jobs	Annual mean wage
San Jose-Sunnyvale-Santa Clara, CA	3,340	3.43	$133,060
Los Angeles-Long Beach-Glendale, CA	3,090	0.76	$105,410
Chicago-Joliet-Naperville, IL	2,610	0.69	$104,470
Boston-Cambridge-Quincy, MA	2,350	1.31	$111,110
Houston-Sugar Land-Baytown, TX	2,340	0.82	$94,970
Atlanta-Sandy Springs-Marietta, GA	2,210	0.93	$106,700
Dallas-Plano-Irving, TX	2,130	0.95	$123,810
San Francisco-San Mateo-Redwood City, CA	1,990	1.83	$145,640
Minneapolis-St. Paul-Bloomington, MN-WI	1,660	0.91	$96,700
New York-White Plains-Wayne, NY-NJ	1,630	0.30	$108,720

Source: Bureau of Labor Statistics

EMPLOYMENT AND OUTLOOK

Sales engineers held about 70,000 jobs nationally in 2014. Employment is expected to grow about as fast as the average for all occupations through the year 2024, which means employment is projected to increase 5 percent to 9 percent. There will be continued job growth due to the increasing variety and number of products to be sold. Many job openings will result from the need to replace workers who transfer to other occupations or leave the labor force.

Employment Trend, Projected 2014–24

Sales engineers: 7%

Total, all occupations: 7%

Sales and related occupations: 5%

Note: "All Occupations" includes all occupations in the U.S. Economy. Source: U.S. Bureau of Labor Statistics, Employment Projections Program.

Related Occupations

- Automobile Salesperson
- Cost Estimator
- Insurance Sales Agent
- Manufacturers Representative
- Online Merchant
- Real Estate Sales Agent
- Retail Salesperson
- Services Sales Representative
- Technical Sales Representative
- Wholesale Sales Representative

Conversation With . . .
EVAN MULVIHILL

Sales Engineer, Sweetwater Sound, Inc
Fort Wayne, Indiana
Sales engineer, 3 years

1. What was your individual career path in terms of education/training, entry-level job, or other significant opportunity?

I went to school for music composition at the University of Illinois and for recording arts at Tribeca Flashpoint College, a media, arts, and communications school in Chicago. I'm a musician and play several instruments, but piano is my "forte." (Musician joke!) Throughout school, I gained experience by doing freelance engineering work, such as mixing and recording bands and post-production/location sound for video. I was a boom operator for several feature-length films and helped out with sound at a 40,000-square-foot haunted house called Fear City. When I was hired as a sales engineer by Sweetwater Sound, I had to complete a three-month training and certificate program known as "Sweetwater University" before rolling out onto the sales floor. I liken the program to drinking from a fire hose because the amount of information you're required to absorb is like getting a master's degree in thirteen weeks.

2. What are the most important skills and/or qualities for someone in your profession?

Because a sales engineer is essentially a salesman with expert knowledge in a given technical field, being knowledgeable in your field is obviously important, as is the willingness to learn new information and remain relevant. Being a problem-solver and being a people person are important too. You need to be compassionate when a customer calls with some issue they're struggling with. Even if you don't know the answer or can't solve their problem, if you show them you care, that's the start of a long-term relationship. A quote that's always resonated with me is "Nobody cares how much you know until they know how much you care." But if I had to choose one quality that's a must, it's the ability to strive to improve what you aren't good at and to refine what you are good at.

3. What do you wish you had known going into this profession?

As much as I love studying all the minutia of audio technology, what I've realized over the years is that technical details often don't matter to the customer and rarely, if ever, come up. What's more important is to aid the decision making-process and help them feel that they've made the right choice.

4. Are there many job opportunities in your profession? In what specific areas?

The music industry in general has very limited job opportunities, but it's a different story for the equipment-sales segment of the industry. Because of piracy, making it as a band or finding paid work in recording studios is almost impossible. However, because musicians are now buying equipment for touring or for producing their own music at home, the retail side of the music industry is booming. During the gold rush, a prospector could work all day and never strike gold; however, there was always business for the guy selling him the tools.

5. How do you see your profession changing in the next five years? What role will technology play in those changes, and what skills will be required?

That's hard to say. Music technology is constantly changing, with products being released and discontinued almost every month. It's hard to know what new products are being dreamt up right now. But given how rapidly technology evolves in this industry, all I can say is I'm excited to see what's in store. Of course, the skills that will be required are technological know-how and the willingness to learn how to use and master new products.

6. What do you enjoy most about your job? What do you enjoy least about your job?

I love learning about and having access to cool new products, but I really love the people side of the business, too. I love my customers, many of whom I've worked with for years and consider friends. I also love the people I work with, my co-workers and managers. I love having job flexibility. I feel fortunate to work for a company that goes above and beyond to make sure all of its employees are taken care of and happy.

Most of my customers are really awesome people, but what I like least are the small handful who aren't pleasant to talk to or that you have to tiptoe around because they'll blow up over the smallest thing.

7. Can you suggest a valuable "try this" for students considering a career in your profession?

Being a professional salesperson is all about figuring out what issues the customer is facing and fixing them. Sometimes the solution to their problem is a product you can sell them. Sometimes it's just advice or resources. Try this: The next time you strike up a conversation with someone, find out if they're having difficulty with something and help them fix it. Being successful at sales starts with a genuine interest in helping people.

SELECTED SCHOOLS

Most colleges and universities offer programs related to careers in business, marketing, or sales; the student may also get started in a technical or community college. For a list of top schools with programs in sales, visit the website of the Sales Education Foundation (see below).

MORE INFORMATION

American Association of Engineering Societies
1801 Alexander Bell Drive
Reston, VA 20191
202.296.2237
www.aaes.org

Manufacturers' Agents National Association
16-A Journey, Suite 200
Aliso Viejo, CA 92656
877.626.2776
www.manaonline.org

Manufacturers' Representatives Educational Research Foundation
8329 Cole Street
Arvada, CO 80005
303.463.1801
www.mrerf.org

Sales & Marketing Executives International
P.O. Box 1390
Sumas, WA 98295-1390
312.893.0751
www.smei.org

Sales Education Foundation
3123 Research Boulevard, Suite 250
Dayton, OH 45420
937.610.4369
www.salesfoundation.org

Technical Sales Association
P.O. Box 250355
Atlanta, GA 30325
404.249.9618
www.technicalsalesassociation.org

Patrick Cooper/Editor

Securities Sales Agent

Snapshot

Career Cluster(s): Business, Finance, Sales & Service

Interests: Finance, Securities Analysis, Financial Planning, Financial Counseling, Economics, Advertising

Earnings (Yearly Average): $72,070

Employment & Outlook: Average Growth Expected

OVERVIEW

Sphere of Work

Securities Sales Agents advise individual clients, groups, or businesses on beneficial financial investments. They analyze and assess financial trends, market conditions, and company histories to determine the most profitable potential investments for their clients. Securities Sales Agents buy, sell, and transfer stocks and bonds (types of securities) based on the financial needs of their customers. When a Securities Sales Agent successfully completes a financial transaction, he or she receives a

commission. Securities Sales Agents are responsible for finding and retaining clientele and cultivating strong connections within the financial world.

Work Environment

This field is highly competitive. Securities Sales Agents often need to be persistent and resilient to succeed, especially early in their careers when they are developing a client base. Typically, Securities Sales Agents work for large firms and spend the majority of their time in a fast-paced office environment where they continually receive updated securities information. Many of them work more than forty hours per week and they are expected to accommodate clients during evenings and weekends. New Securities Sales Agents frequently travel to various locations to recruit and meet with prospective clients. Brokerage firms can be highly stressful environments, where successful financial transactions depend upon quick decisions and accurate calculations. An employee's job security is highly dependent on making money for the client and the firm.

Profile

Working Conditions: Work Indoors
Physical Strength: Light Work
Education Needs: Bachelor's Degree
Licensure/Certification: Required
Opportunities For Experience:
  Internship
Holland Interest Score*: ESA

* See Appendix A

Occupation Interest

The environment in which Securities Sales Agents buy, sell, and trade stocks is inherently frenetic; therefore, prospective Securities Sales Agents should be aggressive and thick-skinned. Brokers must deal with demanding clients who expect to see returns on their investments. Brokers should be outgoing and possess excellent interpersonal skills. A strong desire to succeed and a willingness to work overtime to acquire and retain clients are essential. Securities Sales Agents should have a passion for economics and enjoy researching current market trends.

A Day in the Life—Duties and Responsibilities

One of the most important components of a Securities Sales Agent's job is to identify and secure potential clients. To this end, new Securities Sales Agents must develop and manage advertising campaigns, social and professional networking opportunities, and mailing lists. After obtaining a client, Securities Sales Agents consult with him or her to establish investment preferences, financial goals, and assets, and then provide advice on the buying and selling of securities based on the client's needs. Once a client has reviewed and accepted a specific investment opportunity, a Securities Sales Agent transmits the order to the securities exchange floor and notifies the client that the transaction is complete. Securities Sales Agents compile investment portfolios and accurately document investment transactions for clients.

When not actively buying, selling, or trading stocks, Securities Sales Agents generate and implement financial plans for clients, review transactions to ensure their compliance with agency regulations, and report orders to firm trading departments. They also closely monitor market conditions, review financial and business periodicals, evaluate mandatory annual statements (such as Form 10-K reports), and calculate earnings ratios to identify highly profitable stocks.

Securities Sales Agents must continue to recruit new clients while maintaining strong relationships with existing customers. They contact potential clients, often via "cold calling" or e-mails, to describe available services and to introduce suitable investment ideas.

Duties and Responsibilities

- Relaying orders to buy or sell securities to various security exchanges
- Analyzing market conditions and trends to determine when to buy and sell
- Keeping up-to-date on trends that influence stock prices
- Developing a varied group of stocks for clients to own
- Recording transactions accurately and keeping clients informed of those transactions
- Offering financial counseling to customers
- Devising individual financial portfolios for clients

OCCUPATION SPECIALTIES

Securities Traders

Securities Traders buy and sell securities in the trading division of an investment or brokerage house.

WORK ENVIRONMENT

Physical Environment

Securities Sales Agents perform the majority of their work in clean, busy, and pleasant offices. They spend a significant amount of time sitting at a desk and communicating with clients via phone and e-mail. Some Securities Sales Agents work on the floor of a noisy, crowded stock or commodities exchange. Securities Sales Agents frequently travel to client meetings, both during regular work hours and at other times.

Relevant Skills and Abilities

Communication Skills
- Persuading others

Interpersonal/Social Skills
- Asserting oneself
- Cooperating with others
- Working as a member of a team

Organization & Management Skills
- Making decisions
- Managing time
- Meeting goals and deadlines
- Paying attention to and handling details

Research & Planning Skills
- Using logical reasoning

Technical Skills
- Working with data or numbers

Human Environment

Securities Sales Agents interact often with their clients and tend to develop close relationships with individuals and business groups. They commonly work and communicate with other Securities Sales Agents and financial professionals, including financial services sales agents, advisors, investment bankers, brokerage clerks, and administrative personnel.

Technological Environment

Securities Sales Agents typically use computer terminals or quotation boards (which display current market information) as their main point of access into the commodities exchange. In addition, they use telephones, calculators, fax machines, transaction logs, and ratings books. They review financial publications, Form 10-K reports, buy and sell orders from clients, and economic forecasts.

EDUCATION, TRAINING, AND ADVANCEMENT

High School/Secondary

High school students who are interested in becoming Securities Sales Agents can best prepare by taking courses in mathematics, including algebra, geometry, calculus, and trigonometry. They should also study economics, government, communications, ethics, and business. Participation in extracurricular activities that involve public speaking—such as debate team, student government, or drama club—helps to build communication skills. Outside of school, students can become familiar with the stock market by researching, selecting, and following a specific corporation's stock value over a period of time, noting its gains and losses.

Suggested High School Subjects
- Accounting
- Bookkeeping
- College Preparatory
- Computer Science
- Economics
- English
- Mathematics
- Political Science
- Social Studies
- Sociology
- Speech

Famous First

The first stock ticker was installed on December 29, 1867, at the offices of David Groesbeck & Company, a member of the New York Stock Exchange. The ticker was the invention of Edward A. Callahan of the American Telegraph Company. A rental fee of $6 per week was charged for the service, which was operated by famed businessman Daniel Drew.

College/Postsecondary

After graduating from high school, students should plan to earn a bachelor's degree in a subject like business, accounting, or economics. Students who enroll in these programs generally learn about banking and finance, the Federal Reserve System, and financial analysis, among other subjects. Business students should also continue to study mathematics at an advanced level. Because Securities Sales Agents rely primarily on computers and financial software, students should develop computer and software skills, as well as a familiarity with financial industry software and databases.

In their last year of college, many students obtain work as summer interns for large brokerage firms. Such firms may offer a qualified intern a full-time position upon graduation from college.

Advancement within this field is usually contingent upon earning a master's degree in business administration (MBA) at an accredited school, or advanced professional certification through the Financial Industry Regulatory Association (FINRA), which also administers the basic certification required for all Securities Sales Agents. An MBA equips Securities Sales Agents with real-world business skills and practical knowledge of buying, analyzing, and trading stocks.

Related College Majors
- Finance, General

Adult Job Seekers

Employers commonly provide new employees with on-the-job training; some firms offer classroom instruction in effective speaking, securities analysis, and sales strategies. Many job seekers work in sales in other fields, for example real estate or insurance, before entering the securities industry. Though Securities Sales Agents are not required to have a master's degree in order to gain employment, many candidates find it to be beneficial when applying for a job at a brokerage firm. A job candidate who has earned an MBA is likely to be offered a higher starting salary, a larger signing bonus, and more advanced job duties than a candidate without an MBA.

Professional Certification and Licensure

All Securities Sales Agents must be professionally certified in order to begin trading legally. To obtain licensure, they must work for a registered firm for at least four months and pass the General Securities Registered Representative Examination (the Series 7 exam), which is administered through FINRA. Candidates are given six hours to complete a multiple-choice exam, and test takers must receive a score of 70 percent or higher to pass. Once these requirements have been fulfilled, Securities Sales Agents become eligible to register as representatives of their firm with the North American Securities Administrators Association (NASAA). In addition, many states require Securities Sales Agents to complete the Uniform Securities Agent State Law Examination (the Series 63 exam), which covers securities business, record keeping, and customer protection requirements for that particular state.

Additional Requirements

Ultimately, Securities Sales Agents should possess a solid understanding of financial markets and regulations. They should have the ability to process complex mathematical problems quickly and easily. Because they repeatedly handle financial transactions and highly confidential information, they should be trustworthy, loyal, and reliable. Since much of their success relies upon their ability to convince others to make large investments, Securities Sales Agents should be effective communicators. A background in sales or some experience working on commission is desirable.

Fun Fact

The first chairman of the U.S. Securities Exchange Commission, created after Great Depression, Joseph P. Kennedy, President John F. Kennedy's father.

Source: http://www.american-historama.org/1929-1945-depression-ww2-era/securities-and-exchange-commission.htm

EARNINGS AND ADVANCEMENT

Securities sales agents are usually paid a commission based on the amount of stocks, bonds, mutual funds, insurance and other products they sell. Earnings from commissions are likely to be high when there is much buying and selling and low when there is a slump in market activity. Most firms provide securities sales agents with a steady income by paying a "draw against commission" which is a minimum salary based on commissions they can be expected to earn.

Median annual earnings of securities sales agents were $72,070 in 2014. The lowest ten percent earned less than $32,170, and the highest ten percent earned more than $200,000.

Securities sales agents may receive paid vacations, holidays, and sick days; life and health insurance; and retirement benefits. They also usually have stock options and savings plans. These are usually paid by the employer.

Metropolitan Areas with the Highest
Employment Level in This Occupation

Metropolitan area	Employment	Employment per thousand jobs	Annual mean wage
New York-White Plains-Wayne, NY-NJ	52,190	9.68	$159,130
Chicago-Joliet-Naperville, IL	16,730	4.46	$106,660
Los Angeles-Long Beach-Glendale, CA	11,630	2.87	$96,740
Houston-Sugar Land-Baytown, TX	8,330	2.93	$86,830
Boston-Cambridge-Quincy, MA	7,190	4.01	$145,390
Dallas-Plano-Irving, TX	7,010	3.13	$95,130
San Francisco-San Mateo-Redwood City, CA	6,850	6.31	$140,860
Philadelphia, PA	6,090	3.27	$112,730
Minneapolis-St. Paul-Bloomington, MN-WI	5,840	3.20	$94,870
Denver-Aurora-Broomfield, CO	5,810	4.38	$73,060

Source: Bureau of Labor Statistics

EMPLOYMENT AND OUTLOOK

Nationally, there were approximately 342,000 securities sales agents employed in 2014. Employment is expected to grow about as fast as the average for all occupations through the year 2024, which means employment is projected to increase 7 percent to 13 percent. The replacement of traditional pension plans with individual retirement accounts has given more Americans the opportunity to hold stock. About half of all American households now own stock, and the number of new investors grows daily. However, growth in this occupation will be tempered by the use of online stock trading which allows investors to conduct transactions on their own.

Employment Trend, Projected 2014–24

Securities, commodities, and financial services sales agents: 10%

Sales representatives, services: 7%

Total, all occupations: 7%

Note: "All Occupations" includes all occupations in the U.S. Economy. Source: U.S. Bureau of Labor Statistics, Employment Projections Program.

Related Occupations
- Economist
- Financial Analyst
- Insurance Sales Agent
- Personal Financial Advisor

SELECTED SCHOOLS

Most colleges and universities offer programs related to careers in business and finance. For a list of some of the more prominent schools in this field, see the chapter "Financial Analyst" in the present volume.

MORE INFORMATION

Financial Industry Regulatory Authority
1735 K Street
Washington, DC 20006
301.590.6500
www.finra.org

National Association of Securities Sales Agents
12707 High Bluff Drive, Suite 200
San Diego, CA 92130
858.455.7422
www.naSecurities Sales Agents.com

North American Securities Administrators Association
750 1st Street NE, Suite 1140
Washington, DC 20002
202.737.0900
www.nasaa.org

Securities and Exchange Commission Headquarters
100 F Street NE
Washington, DC 20549
202.942.8088
www.sec.gov

Securities Industry and Financial Markets Association
120 Broadway, 35th Floor
New York, NY 10271
212.313.1200
www.sifma.org

Society of Financial Service Professionals
19 Campus Boulevard, Suite 100
Newtown Square, PA 19073-3239
610.526.2500
www.financialpro.org

The NASDAQ Stock Market
1 Liberty Plaza
165 Broadway
New York, NY 10006
212.401.8700
www.nasdaq.com

Briana Nadeau/Editor

Services Sales Representative

Snapshot

Career Cluster: Business Administration; Sales & Service

Interests: Sales, marketing, business, customer relations, communication

Earnings (Yearly Average): $51,030

Employment & Outlook: Average Growth Expected

OVERVIEW

Sphere of Work

Services sales representatives sell their company's services to other companies or individuals. Services sales representatives work across a broad range of industries and offer both technical and nontechnical services. Technical services may include financial services, construction and building services, design, engineering, and software customization. Nontechnical services may include Internet and cable television services, vehicle leasing, outdoor advertising, cleaning, and home or office maintenance. Services sales representatives can be found

in any industry where a company provides a service to businesses, government, or individual consumers.

Work Environment

The work environment for services sales representatives is influenced by their industry, and the type of services they represent. Those who work in technical services tend to be outside service sales representatives. Outside services sales representatives visit prospective clients at their homes, offices, or work sites such as farms, factories, construction sites, or manufacturing facilities. Inside services sales representatives usually work in an office or call center environment and sell their company's services by telephone and the Internet. Services sales representatives, especially outside representatives, may have little face-to-face interaction with their colleagues and supervisors, but they must have excellent interpersonal skills and communicate confidently with people from a wide variety of backgrounds.

Services sales representatives may frequently be required to work more than forty hours a week when travel, evening, or weekend activities demand it, but they also often enjoy the flexibility to set their own schedules. For outside representatives, extensive travel is usually mandatory. Inside representatives may be required to work evenings and weekends, depending on the best time to contact their prospects. The benefits of this occupation may include a fully maintained vehicle. A services sales representative's income may be derived from a combination of salary and commission or from commission only.

Profile

Working Conditions: Work Indoors
Physical Strength: Light Work
Education Needs:
  Technical/Community College,
  Bachelor's Degree
Licensure/Certification: Required
Physical Abilities Not Required: No
  Heavy Labor
Opportunities For Experience: Part-
  Time Work
Holland Interest Score*: ESA

* See Appendix A

Occupation Interest

This occupation attracts self-motivated people who love sales, enjoy autonomy, and desire flexible work arrangements. An outgoing, assertive personality is an advantage. Maintaining a positive attitude and remaining persistent are especially important since sales representatives must frequently deal with resistant and uncooperative prospects.

Services sales representatives should possess good organization skills because they must manage their own time and priorities to meet sales goals and deadlines. They must also be able to respond positively to customer and supervisors' feedback in order to succeed. Those who desire work in a technical field must acquire appropriate knowledge, skills, and qualifications.

A Day in the Life—Duties and Responsibilities

Services sales representatives work in one of two ways: business-to-business, or "B2B," sales describe sales transactions in which the seller and buyer are both businesses while sales that occur between a business and an individual consumer are known as business-to-customer, or "B2C," sales.

A typical services sales representative's day involves a combination of planning, prospecting (looking for potential new customers), presenting, and following up with contacts. The sales process begins with an activity called "lead generation." Some services sales representatives are provided sales leads by their company, while others need to develop their own leads from referrals, networking, and contact lists. Depending on the nature of the services they represent, services sales representatives may contact leads by telephone, while others may drop in on leads at their homes or workplaces. Outside representatives may spend much of the day traveling to meet with prospects.

Services sales representatives are likely to attend sales appointments with prospects and clients. Some appointments may be to initiate new sales, while others may be to manage ongoing relationships or to develop further sales opportunities. The services sales representatives conduct sales presentations in which they explain the features, benefits, and costs of the services they represent. Technical sales (sometimes known as solution sales) may demand an extensive audit, interview, and needs assessment process before presenting a customized solution to the prospect.

A significant portion of a services sales representative's day is dedicated to completing paperwork. This includes recording notes from their sales calls, ordering new supplies, managing a budget, preparing expense claims, and writing sales reports, proposals, presentations, and orders.

Duties and Responsibilities

- Developing client lists
- Looking for new clients in assigned territory
- Contacting prospects to determine needs
- Outlining types and prices of services
- Recommending services
- Writing, phoning or visiting prospective clients or contributors
- Following up with clients

WORK ENVIRONMENT

Relevant Skills and Abilities

Communication Skills
- Persuading others
- Speaking effectively
- Writing concisely

Interpersonal/Social Skills
- Asserting oneself
- Being persistent
- Cooperating with others
- Motivating others
- Providing support to others
- Working as a member of a team

Organization & Management Skills
- Coordinating tasks
- Managing people/groups
- Managing time
- Meeting goals and deadlines

Unclassified Skills
- Keeping a neat appearance
- Using set methods and standards in your work

Physical Environment

The work environment for services sales representatives depends largely on the industry in which they work and the services they represent. Inside representatives usually work in an office or call center environment, while some may also work from home. Outside representatives travel frequently to visit prospects and clients at their homes or workplaces.

Human Environment

Services sales representatives enjoy a high level of interaction with prospects and customers. They must be able speak confidently with new people and with people from a wide variety of backgrounds. Face-to-face interactions with colleagues and supervisors may be minimal, although daily contact by telephone is to be expected.

Technological Environment

Daily operations require the use of standard office technologies, including a laptop computer, mobile telephone, e-mail, and the Internet. Proficiency in the use of word processing, spreadsheet, and presentation programs is expected. Services sales representatives may also need to use specialized systems, such as sales databases, presentation aids, and enterprise-wide resource platforms.

EDUCATION, TRAINING, AND ADVANCEMENT

High School/Secondary

High school students can best prepare for a career as a services sales representative by studying English and applied communication, business, applied mathematics, and economics. Typing and computer science classes may help prepare the student for the technology requirements of the role, while studies in psychology may provide an understanding about human behavior, motivation, and different communication styles. Foreign language proficiency may also be useful. Part-time sales, retail, or customer service employment during high school may provide an opportunity to gain valuable experience and insight into the sales profession.

Suggested High School Subjects
- Business
- College Preparatory
- Composition
- Economics
- English
- Speech

Famous First

The first chamber of commerce was New York's chamber, founded in 1768 by twenty New York City merchants interested in "promoting and encouraging commerce, supporting industry, adjusting disputes relative to trade and navigation, and procuring such laws and regulations as may be found necessary for the benefit of trade in general."

College/Postsecondary

Prior sales experience is often considered more important than formal qualifications in the services sales profession. Nonetheless, the competitive nature of employment in this field means that many employers are seeking candidates who possess an associate's or bachelor's degree in business or another relevant field. Some technical sales positions require a bachelor's degree as minimum requirement, and many employers may prefer a relevant postgraduate degree or professional certification. Examples of technical sales specialties include financial services, technology and software development, engineering, architecture, design and manufacturing services, and medical devices. A relevant degree along with sales experience provides applicants with an advantage over other candidates.

Related College Majors
- Business & Personal Services Marketing Operations
- General Retailing & Wholesaling Operations & Skills
- Hospitality & Recreation Marketing Operations
- Hotel/Motel & Restaurant Management

Adult Job Seekers

Adults seeking a career transition to a services sales representative role are advised to refresh their skills and update their resume. Meeting sales goals is extremely important in this job, so good sales results and any sales awards should be emphasized. Registering with an employment agency that specializes in sales employment or obtaining further education about a specific product or industry may be helpful.

Professional Certification and Licensure

In real estate sales, financial services, insurance, transportation services, and certain other industries or professions, sales representatives are required to hold state certification and licensure. Individuals interested in pursuing employment in these fields should research and fulfill the industry-specific requirements of their home state.

Additional Requirements

A clean driving record is often required by employers. A criminal background check may also be mandatory. Services sales representatives who have a college degree, advanced product knowledge, and an outgoing, persuasive personality will be the most successful

Fun Facts

Consumers are more likely to give a company repeat business after a good service experience (81%) than they are to never do business with a company again after a poor experience (52%).

Source: https://blog.kissmetrics.com/happy-campers/

As long ago as 2012, those who used social media outperformed their peers by a whopping 78 percent.

Source: http://www.forbes.com/sites/markfidelman/2013/05/19/study-78-of-salespeople-using-social-media-outsell-their-peers/#2270c0bc7c32

EARNINGS AND ADVANCEMENT

Earnings of services sales representatives depend primarily on sales performance. Earnings of services sales representatives who sold technical services generally were higher than earnings of those who sold non-technical services. Successful services sales representatives who establish a strong customer base can earn more than managers in their firm. Services sales representatives are paid in a variety of ways. Some receive a straight salary; others are paid solely on a commission basis. Most firms use a combination of salary and commissions.

Median annual earnings of services sales representatives were $51,030 in 2013. The lowest ten percent earned less than $25,000, and the highest ten percent earned more than $110,000.

Services sales representatives may receive paid vacations, holidays, and sick days; life and health insurance; and retirement benefits. These are usually paid by the employer

Metropolitan Areas with the Highest
Employment Level in This Occupation

Metropolitan area	Employment	Employment per thousand jobs	Hourly mean wage
New York-White Plains-Wayne, NY-NJ	36,390	6.94	$38.84
Los Angeles-Long Beach-Glendale, CA	29,690	7.47	$29.70
Houston-Sugar Land-Baytown, TX	22,100	8.02	$30.32
Chicago-Joliet-Naperville, IL	22,010	5.95	$31.29
Dallas-Plano-Irving, TX	20,610	9.59	$30.86
Atlanta-Sandy Springs-Marietta, GA	16,390	7.10	$29.45
Washington-Arlington-Alexandria, DC-VA-MD-WV	16,010	6.76	$36.55
Phoenix-Mesa-Glendale, AZ	15,560	8.73	$26.63
Minneapolis-St. Paul-Bloomington, MN-WI	14,260	7.96	$29.16
Santa Ana-Anaheim-Irvine, CA	13,190	9.08	$32.39

Source: Bureau of Labor Statistics

EMPLOYMENT AND OUTLOOK

Services sales representatives held about 800,000 jobs nationally in 2012. Employment is expected to grow about as fast as the average for all occupations through the year 2022, which means employment is projected to increase 6 percent to 11 percent. Turnover in this field is relatively high, particularly among those services sales representatives who sell non-technical services.

Employment Trend, Projected 2012–22

Total, All Occupations: 11%

Services Sales Representatives: 8%

Sales and Related Occupations (All): 7%

Note: "All Occupations" includes all occupations in the U.S. Economy. Source: U.S. Bureau of Labor Statistics, Employment Projections Program.

Related Occupations

- Advertising Agent
- Automobile Salesperson
- Insurance Sales Agent
- Manufacturers Representative
- Online Merchant
- Pharmaceutical Sales Representative
- Real Estate Sales Agent
- Retail Salesperson
- Sales Engineer
- Technical Sales Representative
- Wholesale Sales Representative

Conversation With . . .
MICHAEL RHIM

Principal and retirement services expert, 6 years
PRM Consulting, Washington, DC
Financial Services field, 20 years

1. What was your individual career path in terms of education/training, entry-level job, or other significant opportunity?

I was a business management major at Howard University in Washington, DC. After my first year, a new insurance program was created and top-level students were encouraged to apply. I entered the program because it offered a scholarship that allowed me to stay at the university and gain summer employment through internships. I was pleasantly surprised by the career opportunities in the insurance industry. My first job was at the Wyatt Co., an actuarial consulting firm, as a technician writing computer programs for actuaries. I later was recruited to TIAA CREF, one of the country's largest financial services companies. I took a job as an institutional consultant – in essence, an account manager. My job was to keep the retirement clients happy, to introduce new services, and to handle any client service needs. I later moved into management and became an assistant vice president in Detroit. There, I managed a team of financial planners and a team of account managers. We worked with institutional clients such as colleges and universities to help them refine and manage their retirement plans. I later moved back to DC, moved up, and my career took off. I stayed at TIAA CREF for 20 years, but got to the point where I had had enough of corporate life. I came to work at PRM, a small minority-owned human resources consulting firm. I liked the firm's entrepreneurial spirit. We provide human resource services across the gamut, from benefits to executive searches to diversity training. I came in as a principal and was put in charge of a growing retirement practice since that is my area of expertise. I evaluate clients' retirement plan designs, look at their investment options, and work with them to hire appropriate financial firms. It's kind of like being a watchdog for the client.

Since I am a principal, my main role is to create revenue for the firm and bring in new clients.

2. What are the most important skills and/or qualities for someone in your profession?

Without people skills, you can't even get to sales. I am talking about the skillset of really being able to understand a client's needs by listening and anticipating, and then being able to address their needs. You also need analytical skills to dissect and evaluate benefits or retirement plans. When people come to us, they want things fixed.

Sometimes, clients may not know they have needs, and I must be astute enough to ask the right questions to find out what they need. I also need technical skills, such as knowledge of legal issues surrounding benefits and labor laws, and awareness of legislation and how that impacts benefits. I need to understand how investments work. Finally, I need compliance skills. For instance, most 401K plans require ongoing discrimination testing. You must be able to articulate to clients why these tests are important; it's because they could be fined significantly if their plans are out of compliance with Internal Revenue Services laws that affect retirement plans.

3. What do you wish you had known going into this profession?

The value of relationship building. We're in the people business and every person I meet is an opportunity.

4. Are there many job opportunities in your profession? In what specific areas?

Yes, although sometimes it's cyclical. In recent years, due to the Affordable Care Act, firms have needed analytical work on health care. Right now, retirement is a growth area as financial services firms are hiring more people to provide services to the retiring Baby Boomer generation. In addition, there are three generations currently in the workplace so institutions are hiring people to provide more online services — such as those for mobile devices — to address each generation's needs. Institutions are also looking to firms like ours to help them manage their retirement plan investment options.

5. How do you see your profession changing in the next five years? What role will technology play in those changes, and what skills will be required?

Institutions are wrestling with how to deliver the different generations' retirement needs. Firms like ours have to be able to assess the best way for institutions to take advantage of technology to manage their retirement programs, or to attract the kind of people they want. And we need to use technology such as social media or blogs to grow our own business and demonstrate our expertise.

You need a license to practice skills such as investment advising. Plus, certifications in various areas of human resources consulting are a must.

6. What do you like most about your job? What do you like least about your job?

When I was a manager in the corporate world, I managed people and I was too far removed from what I enjoy most, which is dealing with clients. That's what I enjoy here - providing solutions. However, it's a constant challenge to find new business.

7. **Can you suggest a valuable "try this" for students considering a career in your profession?**

    Find an internship in a consulting firm and see what goes on. There may be one segment of the business you like, and one you don't. For instance, if you like math, you might enjoy working in the compensation area.

SELECTED SCHOOLS

Most colleges and universities offer programs in business administration, often with a concentration in sales. The student can also gain initial training at a technical or community college. Interested students are advised to consult with their school guidance counselor or to research area postsecondary schools and training programs..

MORE INFORMATION

National Association of Sales Professionals
555 Friendly Street
Bloomington Hills, MI 48341
www.nasp.com

Sales and Marketing Executives International, Inc.
P.O. Box 1390
Sumas, WA 98295
312.893.0751
www.smei.org

Technology Services Industry Association
17065 Camino San Bernardo
Suite 200
San Diego, CA 92127
858.674.5491
www.tsia.com

United States Reps Association
www.usra.info

Kylie Hughes/Editor

Technical Sales Representative

Snapshot

Career Cluster: Business Administration; Manufacturing; Sales & Service

Interests: Sales, marketing, communications

Earnings (Yearly Average): $74,520

Employment & Outlook: Average Growth Expected

OVERVIEW

Sphere of Work

Technical sales representatives sell their company's products or services primarily to other companies and institutions. Most technical sales, sometimes referred to as solution sales, are business-to-business (B2B) sales, in which both the seller and buyer are businesses or institutions. Technical sales representative opportunities exist in a broad range of industries but are likely to be concentrated in fields such as agriculture, manufacturing, engineering, construction, military, science, computing, technology, mining, and education.

Work Environment

The work environment for technical sales representatives depends on the industry in which they work and the type of products or services they represent. Representatives of computer solutions may visit potential customers, or prospects, in their offices, while those who sell agricultural products may visit prospects on farms. Travel across a defined sales territory is generally mandatory. As such, the benefits of this occupation may include a fully maintained vehicle. Technical sales representatives may have little face-to-face interaction with their colleagues and supervisors, but they must be able to initiate contact with new people and confidently communicate with people from a wide variety of backgrounds. They may frequently be required to work more than forty hours a week when traveling, or when evening or weekend activities demand it, but they usually have the flexibility to set their own schedules.

Profile

Working Conditions: Work Indoors
Physical Strength: Light Work
Education Needs: On-The-Job Training, Bachelor's Degree
Licensure/Certification: Usually Required
Physical Abilities Not Required: No Heavy Labor
Opportunities For Experience: Part-Time Work
Holland Interest Score*: ESR

* See Appendix A

Occupation Interest

A career as a technical sales representative suits self-motivated people who enjoy autonomy and flexible work arrangements. A gregarious personality is a further advantage, as this role regularly involves meeting new people. However, it should be balanced with empathy, cooperativeness, and an awareness of different communication styles in order to develop good relationships with a broad range of people. A technical sales representative should have the confidence to interact with new people and the assertiveness to close sales. The ability to cope with rejection is also important, as sales representatives must frequently deal with resistant and uncooperative prospects.

Technical sales representatives should possess good organization and prioritization skills, as well as expert knowledge in their particular field, which may be gained through practical experience or formal training. They must be able to manage their own time and priorities in order to meet deadlines. Despite working independently, they must also possess a positive approach to teamwork, including the ability to receive and act on feedback and coaching from supervisors and trainers.

A Day in the Life—Duties and Responsibilities

A technical sales representative's day will involve a combination of planning, searching for potential new customers, presenting sales proposals, and following up with clients. The sales process begins with an activity called lead generation. Some technical sales representatives will have sales leads provided to them by their company, while others will need to develop their own leads from referrals, networking, and contact lists. Searching for potential customers, or prospecting, can be accomplished in a variety of ways, including contacting prospects via telephone, mail, or e-mail, calling on them in person, or meeting them at conferences, networking events, and other functions. Technical sales representatives may spend a significant proportion of the day driving or traveling.

Technical sales representatives are likely to attend sales appointments with prospects and clients. Some of these appointments may be to initiate new sales, while others may be to manage ongoing relationships or develop further sales opportunities.

The key to technical sales is to develop cost-effective solutions to customers' problems and challenges. This involves researching the problem to gain a thorough understanding of it. Therefore, the sales process may include auditing, interviewing, or conducting a detailed needs assessment before developing a customized solution. Technical sales representatives plan and conduct sales presentations, during which they explain the features, benefits, and cost-effectiveness of the products and services they recommend.

A portion of the technical sales representative's day is dedicated to paperwork. This includes recording notes from sales calls, ordering new supplies, managing budgets, preparing expense claims, and writing sales reports, proposals, presentations, and orders.

Duties and Responsibilities

- Calling on regular customers to obtain orders
- Preparing lists of prospective customers and scheduling appointments
- Presenting samples, pictures or catalogs illustrating products to customers
- Checking inventories of retail stores and ordering needed items
- Assisting retailers in updating inventory and ordering systems
- Advising retailers on pricing, advertising and arranging window and counter displays
- Checking on delivery dates
- Preparing reports
- Entertaining customers

WORK ENVIRONMENT

Physical Environment

The work environment for technical sales representatives depends largely on the industry in which they work and the products and services they represent. Some may spend their time in laboratories, manufacturing plants, or corporate offices, while others visit farms, factories, or military facilities. Extensive travel by car or air may be expected.

Human Environment

Technical sales representatives have a high level of interaction with prospects and customers. They must be able speak confidently with new people from a wide variety of backgrounds. Face-to-face interactions with colleagues and supervisors may be minimal, although daily contact by telephone is to be expected. Teamwork and collaboration skills are important.

Relevant Skills and Abilities

Communication Skills
- Persuading others
- Speaking effectively
- Writing concisely

Interpersonal/Social Skills
- Being able to work independently
- Cooperating with others
- Working as a member of a team

Organization & Management Skills
- Making decisions

Research & Planning Skills
- Developing evaluation strategies

Technical Skills
- Performing scientific, mathematical and technical work

Technological Environment

Daily operations will demand the use of standard office technology, including laptop computers, mobile telephones, e-mail, and the Internet. Proficiency in the use of word processing, spreadsheet, and presentation programs is expected. Technical sales representatives may also need to utilize specialized systems, such as sales databases, presentation aids, and enterprise-wide resource platforms.

EDUCATION, TRAINING, AND ADVANCEMENT

High School/Secondary

High school students can best prepare for a career as a technical sales representative by studying English and applied communication. Subjects such as business, applied mathematics, and economics may also be beneficial. Computing and keyboarding will prepare the student for the technology requirements of the role, while studies in psychology may provide an understanding of human behavior, motivation, and different communication styles. Foreign languages may also be useful. Part-time sales, retail, or customer service work will provide an opportunity to gain valuable experience and insight into the sales profession.

Suggested High School Subjects
- Applied Communication
- Bookkeeping

- Business Math
- English
- Merchandising
- Speech

Famous First

The first shipment of merchandise by airplane occurred in 1910, when five bolts of silk manufactured by the New York firm of Rogers & Thompson were delivered to the Morehouse-Martens Company of Columbus, Ohio. The first leg of the journey, to Dayton, Ohio, was accomplished by conventional land transport. But in Dayton the silk was placed onto a Wright bi-plane and flown to Columbus, 60 miles away. The flight, part of a publicity stunt, took just under one hour.

College/Postsecondary

Prior sales experience is often considered more important than formal qualifications in the sales profession. Nonetheless, the competitive nature of employment in this field means that many employers prefer candidates who possess an associate's or bachelor's degree in a relevant subject. Some employers may also expect a postgraduate degree or professional certification, as well as practical experience in an appropriate industry.

Related College Majors
- Agricultural Supplies Retailing & Wholesaling
- General Retailing & Wholesaling Operations & Skills
- General Selling Skills & Sales Operations
- Industrial/Manufacturing Technology
- Physical Science Technologies

Adult Job Seekers

Many employers prefer candidates for technical sales roles who have extensive experience using their products or services, while others seek candidates with sales experience. Applicants from sales backgrounds should note their experience representing specific companies, products, or services; specify the territories in which they have worked; and highlight outstanding sales results and any awards received. Candidates who come from a non-sales background should emphasize their expertise and experience in their field and may consider undertaking sales training with a private organization or professional association, which can also provide valuable networking opportunities.

Professional Certification and Licensure

In certain industries, sales representatives are required to hold state-based certificates and licenses. Technical sales representatives should consult reputable professional associations in the appropriate technical field to determine whether certification is needed.

Additional Requirements

Technical sales representatives often must have a clean driving record and may need to pass a criminal background check

Fun Facts

Nearly 12.3% of all the jobs in the U.S. are full time sales positions, and over one trillion dollars is spent annually on sales force salaries.

Source: http://www.salesforcetraining.com/sales-training-blog/sales-training-2/friday-fun-facts-interesting-stats-about-sales/

Some of the hardest jobs to fill are those in technical sales, even though it's a rewarding career that doesn't require a college degree.

Source: http://www.hbs.edu/news/releases/Pages/middle-skills-jobs-critical-competitiveness.aspx

EARNINGS AND ADVANCEMENT

Earnings depend on the type of employer, the type of product sold, the assigned sales territory and the employee's experience and ability. Technical sales representatives are paid a combination of salary and commission. Median annual earnings of technical sales representatives were $74,520 in 2013. The lowest ten percent earned less than $38,000, and the highest ten percent earned more than $145,000.

Technical sales representatives may receive paid vacations, holidays, and sick days; life and health insurance; and retirement benefits. These are usually paid by the employer. Most employers provide technical sales representatives with an expense account and a car or mileage allowance

Metropolitan Areas with the Highest Employment Level in This Occupation

Metropolitan area	Employment	Employment per thousand jobs	Hourly mean wage
Chicago-Joliet-Naperville, IL	16,600	4.48	$37.20
Houston-Sugar Land-Baytown, TX	11,590	4.20	$46.06
Los Angeles-Long Beach-Glendale, CA	10,590	2.66	$38.84
New York-White Plains-Wayne, NY-NJ	9,400	1.79	$46.37
Atlanta-Sandy Springs-Marietta, GA	8,800	3.81	$38.95
Boston-Cambridge-Quincy, MA	8,470	4.84	$44.47
San Jose-Sunnyvale-Santa Clara, CA	7,960	8.55	$58.34
Santa Ana-Anaheim-Irvine, CA	7,680	5.28	$40.55
Dallas-Plano-Irving, TX	7,350	3.42	$36.24
Phoenix-Mesa-Glendale, AZ	6,910	3.88	$42.58

Source: Bureau of Labor Statistics

EMPLOYMENT AND OUTLOOK

In 2012, technical sales representatives held about 350,000 jobs nationally. Employment of technical sales representatives is expected to grow about as fast as the average for all occupations through the year 2022, which means employment is projected to increase 6 percent to 12 percent. This is due to the increasing variety and number of goods to be sold. Many job openings will result from the need to replace workers who transfer to other occupations or leave the labor force.

Employment Trend, Projected 2012–22

Total, All Occupations: 11%

Technical Sales Representatives: 9%

Sales and Related Occupations (All): 7%

Note: "All Occupations" includes all occupations in the U.S. Economy. Source: U.S. Bureau of Labor Statistics, Employment Projections Program.

Related Occupations
- Automobile Salesperson
- Insurance Sales Agent
- Manufacturers Representative
- Pharmaceutical Sales Representative
- Real Estate Sales Agent
- Retail Salesperson
- Sales Engineer
- Services Sales Representative
- Wholesale Sales Representative

Conversation With . . .
KAREN BEALE

Business Unit Executive, 21 years
North America Server Sales
IBM

1. What was your individual career path in terms of education/training, entry-level job, or other significant opportunity?

When I was young, I liked puzzles that required logic, such as crosswords, jigsaws and cryptograms. In high school I took AP classes in logic-based subjects. I wasn't sure what direction to take, but knew that math majors scored the highest on the GMAT, LSAT, and MCAT exams. That told me I could be a math major and delay a decision about my career for four years. In my sophomore year at Spelman College in Atlanta, one of my teachers was an IBM employee on loan to teach. He asked if I'd do an internship with IBM. The project I worked on helped me see I could use the logic I'd developed—like finding a pattern through cryptograms—and get paid. I learned to write computer programs and went on to minor in computer science. I was only one of two girls in my computer science class to do so. IBM invited me back, and at the end of that internship said they would hire me after graduation. I hesitated because IBM was the only place I'd worked. John Hancock Insurance offered me an internship in actuarial science, so I did that for six months. I started to write programs to automate some of their tasks. That made me want to go back to programming, so I returned to IBM as a programmer. I went into sales a few years later.

I had flexible hours, could work from home, and could raise my kids—unusual at the time—so I stayed in the sales force until my children were grown. My projects included helping a major retailer get garments to stores in the appropriate season. For example, if Store A in Kansas wasn't selling blue mohair sweaters, while Store B in New York City couldn't keep them on the shelves, how do you know and how do you get the sweaters to stores where they're needed? We helped them streamline their processes and run their stores more efficiently.

In my first management job, I consolidated the jobs of selling hardware and software so we could move to solution sales. I started in the Mid-Atlantic area managing a technical sales team that supported IBM's largest clients, then led a team for the eastern U.S., helping to architect server and solution areas, as well as Linux. Now I manage technical sales teams and managers for the entire U.S.

When I started, the closest person in age was 15 years older—and I was one of only two women in a group of 400 to 500 men. I've typically always been the only person of color. African-American women in this field remain unique.

2. What are the most important skills and/or qualities for someone in your profession?

Knowing what questions to ask and how to listen. You need to get to the root cause of any problem your client wants you to solve.

If your client can't install the coolest widget because their current infrastructure won't support it, their software doesn't integrate, or they have no one to manage it, it doesn't matter if you've made the most architecturally sexy thing ever. You must listen.

3. What do you wish you had known going into this profession?

I wish I'd better known how to step outside my daily responsibilities to see what other people do, and to network. I am surrounded by highly intelligent people and haven't always understood the value that I could bring to other positions. My extensive IBM-certified training honestly probably amounts to a doctorate or two.

4. Are there many job opportunities in your profession? In what specific areas?

Yes. Sales skills are transferable, and being able to translate the complex into something more simple than non-technical people can understand is rare.

5. How do you see your profession changing in the next five years? What role will technology play in those changes, and what skills will be required?

The huge question is this: how do you take advantage of social media without becoming just another voice in the crowd? Also, sensors reside in 90 percent of products being sold today. How do you make something meaningful of it? How do you leverage the global connectivity people have and maintain a competitive advantage?

6. What do you like most about your job? What do you like least about your job?

I enjoy interacting with so many people across so many areas. I have many high-level clients, so I see all types of industries, people, and problems. Their needs are a new puzzle to solve.

I least like the amount of time that I'm sitting – for example, on conference calls. I don't think that's good for my–or anyone's–health.

7. **Can you suggest a valuable "try this" for students considering a career in your profession?**

Seek out internships. Look for online contests and challenges posted by companies that interest you. They may ask you to figure out a cool app that could transform the way somebody does business. Then submit. People are winning money, or even getting internships or jobs this way. It's important exposure.

SELECTED SCHOOLS

Most colleges and universities offer programs in business administration, often with a concentration in sales and marketing. The student can also gain initial training at a technical or community college. Interested students are advised to consult with their school guidance counselor or to research area postsecondary schools and training programs.

MORE INFORMATION

American Supply Association
222 Merchandise Mart Plaza
Suite 1400
Chicago, IL 60654
312.464.0090
www.asa.net

Manufacturers' Agents National Association
16-A Journey, Suite 200
Aliso Viejo, CA 92656
877.626.2776
www.manaonline.org

Manufacturers' Representatives Educational Research Foundation
8329 Cole Street
Arvada, CO 80005
303.463.1801
info@mrerf.org
www.mrerf.org

Sales & Marketing Executives International
P.O. Box 1390
Sumas, WA 98295-1390
312.893.0751
www.smei.org

Kylie Hughes/Editor

Urban and Regional Planner

Snapshot

Career Cluster(s): Architecture & Construction, Government & Public Administration, Real Estate

Interests: Public Policy, Architecture, Geography, Community Services, Public Planning, Community and Urban Infrastructure

Earnings (Yearly Average): $66,940

Employment & Outlook: Average Growth Expected

OVERVIEW

Sphere of Work

Urban and regional planners decide how best to use the land and resources of a certain community or region, then develop the plans to do so. Their work may include establishing guidelines for the preservation of ecologically sensitive areas, formulating a strategy to attract new businesses to the region, or helping to draft legislation that will address environmental and social issues, such as public parks and homeless shelters. Planners study different

elements of a particular area, including population demographics, employment numbers, and aspects of public infrastructure such as highways and sewer lines, in order to determine the best use of land for the community as a whole.

Work Environment

Urban and regional planners generally work in offices in consulting firms or government organizations. They often spend time in the field, inspecting sites intended for development. Planners work at least forty hours per week, plus some evenings and weekends when participating in public meetings.

Profile

Working Conditions: Work Indoors
Physical Strength: Light Work
Education Needs: Bachelor's Degree, Master's Degree
Licensure/Certification: Recommended
Opportunities For Experience: Internship, Volunteer Work, Part-Time Work
Holland Interest Score*: ESI

* See Appendix A

Occupation Interest

Individuals attracted to urban and regional planning tend to find satisfaction in providing services to others and seeing projects through from start to finish. They are spatially oriented and can visualize how various projects will affect local communities. Planners should have an affinity for math and geographic information systems and be able to use statistical data to solve problems.

A Day in the Life—Duties and Responsibilities

Urban and regional planners are responsible for the development of a particular area. On a given day, a planner who works for a government organization may help devise plans and policies that will affect community interests like zoning and public utilities, or make recommendations on how officials should respond to development proposals. Planners in private companies may spend their time negotiating with those same officials, conducting feasibility studies on proposed projects, or collecting and analyzing data on current land use. Urban and regional planners often must attend public hearings to address the questions and concerns of the community. Their responsibilities may also include soliciting and selecting proposals from developers, coordinating building plans with consultants and various construction personnel, or reviewing geographical information system maps to determine what services are needed in what areas, which could be anything from more fire hydrants to greater access to public transportation.

Duties and Responsibilities

- Preparing detailed studies and data showing current use of land for housing, commerce and community purposes
- Conferring with local authorities, civic leaders, social scientists and land planning and development specialists
- Presenting reports indicating the arrangement of streets, highways, water and sewer lines and location of schools, libraries and recreational areas
- Recommending governmental measures affecting the community
- Providing information on industry, population, employment and economic trends in the community
- Preparing reports and materials that show how programs can be carried out and the approximate costs
- Discussing proposals with government officials, civic groups, land developers and the news media

WORK ENVIRONMENT

Immediate Physical Environment

Urban and regional planners prepare and assess data in an office setting, but are usually required to visit various outdoor work sites. While they use computers in their daily activities, they do not spend all day at a desk.

Human Environment

Urban and regional planners interact with the public, government workers, peers, and supervisors in person, by phone, and via e-mail. When conducting field investigations, they may work with people such as land developers, public officials, and community representatives. They must cooperate with and adapt to a variety of personalities in a deadline-oriented environment.

Relevant Skills and Abilities

Communication Skills
- Speaking effectively
- Writing concisely

Interpersonal/Social Skills
- Cooperating with others
- Working as a member of a team

Organization & Management Skills
- Paying attention to and handling details
- Performing duties which change frequently

Research & Planning Skills
- Analyzing information
- Developing evaluation strategies

Technical Skills
- Performing scientific, mathematical and technical work

Technological Environment

An urban planner's technological environment will generally include computers, global positioning system (GPS) devices, and computer-aided design (CAD) software, as well as software for desktop publishing and map creation.

EDUCATION, TRAINING, AND ADVANCEMENT

High School/Secondary

High school students interested in pursuing a career in urban planning should study math and computer science and should also take classes that help to develop strong communication skills. An internship or part-time job in local government will provide valuable experience

Suggested High School Subjects
- Algebra
- Applied Biology/Chemistry
- Applied Communication
- Applied Math
- Audio-Visual
- College Preparatory
- Drafting
- Economics
- English
- Geometry
- Government
- Mechanical Drawing
- Political Science
- Social Studies
- Sociology
- Trigonometry

Famous First

The first urban master plan in the United States was adopted by the city council of Berkeley, Calif., in April 1955. The plan divided the city into 28 neighborhoods and required development of a local plan for each one.

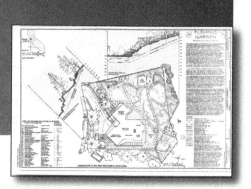

College/Postsecondary

Urban and regional planners should earn their undergraduate degree in economics, political science, geography, environmental design, or a similar subject. They should then pursue postgraduate studies in an accredited planning program or a related field such as geography or urban design; individuals with only a bachelor's degree often stay in entry-level urban planning positions and need a master's degree in order to advance. Coursework should include architecture, law, earth sciences, economics, and statistics. Graduate students usually participate in urban planning seminars, workshops, lab courses, problem-solving activities, and local government internships.

Related College Majors

- City/Urban, Community & Regional Planning
- Urban Studies/Affairs

Adult Job Seekers

Adults looking for urban planning work should have at least a bachelor's degree, and in most cases a master's degree is required. Job seekers can apply directly to local government agencies, private architecture and engineering firms, and technical consultancies for any open positions.

Professional Certification and Licensure

Very few states require licensure. Planners with the required education and professional experience can obtain voluntary certification from the American Institute of Certified Planners, part of the American Planning Association, by passing a written examination.

Additional Requirements

Urban and regional planners need to have good written and oral communication skills, and must be able to use diplomacy when reconciling different points of view. They should also be flexible, decisive, and good listeners, with an affinity for spatial thinking.

Fun Fact

A major point of discussion at America's first planning conference in 1898 centered on ridding New York City streets of incessant manure from horses—the main mode of transportation at the time.

Source: http://www.citylab.com/work/2012/08/brief-history-birth-urban-planning/2365/

EARNINGS AND ADVANCEMENT

Earnings of urban and regional planners depend on the size of the employer, the size and geographic location of the community in which they work and the individual's education and experience. Median annual earnings of urban and regional planners were $66,940 in 2014. The lowest ten percent earned less than $42,220, and the highest ten percent earned more than $99,560.

Urban and regional planners may receive paid vacations, holidays, and sick days; life and health insurance; and retirement benefits. These are usually paid by the employer.

Metropolitan Areas with the Highest
Employment Level in This Occupation

Metropolitan area	Employment	Employment per thousand jobs	Annual mean wage
Los Angeles-Long Beach-Glendale, CA	2,160	0.53	$74,230
Seattle-Bellevue-Everett, WA	1,080	0.72	$83,890
New York-White Plains-Wayne, NY-NJ	860	0.16	$75,480
Boston-Cambridge-Quincy, MA	800	0.44	$72,000
Washington-Arlington-Alexandria, DC-VA-MD-WV	790	0.33	$83,260
Minneapolis-St. Paul-Bloomington, MN-WI	790	0.43	$68,920
San Francisco-San Mateo-Redwood City, CA	720	0.66	$91,790
Philadelphia, PA	680	0.37	$66,900
Sacramento--Arden-Arcade--Roseville, CA	660	0.76	$81,260
Oakland-Fremont-Hayward, CA	640	0.62	$87,600

Source: Bureau of Labor Statistics

EMPLOYMENT AND OUTLOOK

There were approximately 38,000 urban and regional planners employed nationally in 2014. About two-thirds were employed by local governments. Employment is expected to grow about as fast as the average for all occupations through the year 2024, which means employment is projected to increase 4 percent to 8 percent. Most new jobs for urban and regional planners will be in rapidly growing communities. Local governments need urban and regional planners to handle many issues dealing with population growth. For example, new housing developments require roads, sewer systems, fire stations, schools, libraries, and recreation facilities to be planned. Jobs will also occur from the need to replace experienced workers who transfer to other occupations or retire.

Employment Trend, Projected 2014–24

Social scientists and related workers: 12%

Total, all occupations: 7%

Urban and regional planners: 6%

Note: "All Occupations" includes all occupations in the U.S. Economy. Source: U.S. Bureau of Labor Statistics, Employment Projections Program.

Related Occupations

- Architect
- City Manager
- Civil Engineer
- Construction Manager
- Economist
- Landscape Architect
- Market Research Analyst
- Social Scientist

Conversation With . . .
CAROL RHEA, FAICP

Partner, Orion Planning & Design
President, American Planning Association
Huntsville, Alabama
Urban planner, 31 years

1. What was your individual career path in terms of education/training, entry-level job, or other significant opportunity?

Like most planners, I never knew planning existed as a potential career until I was well into college. I earned a bachelor's degree in earth science from the University of North Carolina at Charlotte and went on to earn a master's in geography with a concentration in planning.

My first job was with the Southwest Florida Regional Planning Council, where I worked on regional comprehensive plans as well as community development programs for housing and land use studies, such as the environmental impact of oil and gas leasing on the Outer Continental Shelf. From there, I moved to the North Carolina Division of Community Assistance. We provided consulting services, mainly to governments, but also non-profits, chambers of commerce, or downtown development programs. One of my major projects was helping translate the state's water protection program to local governments.

I went on to become Director of Planning and Development for Monroe, N.C. During this time, I got involved with the North Carolina chapter of the American Planning Association (APA), and became state president. I later was elected to the national board.

After I started my family, I was a consultant for many years. Then one day in 2010 I got an email asking if I'd be interested in joining forces with other talented people who knew each other through APA and creating a firm. Today, Orion Planning + Design has six partners. We work all over the country. I do mostly comprehensive master planning and code work for communities. Codes include zoning codes and subdivision regulations. We often start with a master plan and end with a code plan because codes help implement the plans. We work closely with a community's staff because they need to see this as their plan. We're not just in it for the money; having our plans implemented is the goal.

2. What are the most important skills and/or qualities for someone in your profession?

Number one is the ability to communicate, both orally and written. You need to take large amounts of data and information, determine what's relevant to a community, and convey that to stakeholders such as government staff, residents, and bankers and lawyers. Teamwork is essential. A big part of the job is building bridges and creating avenues of cooperation.

3. What do you wish you had known going into this profession?

I would have gotten a joint planning and law degree. You must gain an understanding of the legal framework involved with codes.

4. Are there many job opportunities in your profession? In what specific areas?

Yes. Historically, planners are in government jobs, but increasingly we're seeing them in non-traditional fields. For example, I know a planner who works with AARP, and helped to create their livability index. We'll see demand in health-related jobs because we now understand that the way we build cities directly impacts health. Transportation planning and environmental planning will grow. The federal government has planners at its facilities—including military—around the world. Planning generalists will always be in demand.

5. How do you see your profession changing in the next five years, what role will technology play in those changes, and what skills will be required?

People will increasingly demand 24/7 access to data and public processes. It won't be enough to have a meeting or two or post information on Facebook or websites.

Until now, we've based plans on the 10-year census and estimates, but that will change dramatically. Real-time data-driven plans will be big.

The so-called "sharing economy," including businesses like Uber and Airbnb, is changing the way communities view transportation and land use. Airbnb doesn't lend itself to a strict zoning policy, for example.

As the housing crisis gets bigger, that will drive new ways to create affordability. In California we're seeing three-hour commutes because people can't afford to live close to their jobs. Maybe parking lots will be converted to housing.

Climate change and globalization also will drive planning. More communities are embracing planning for events such as tornados and earthquakes. Globalization means, for example, that a small town in North Carolina watched its main employer, an Alcoa plant, shut down when Russia started flooding the market with aluminum.

6. What do you enjoy most about your job? What do you enjoy least about your job?

I love the variety. I love the people I work with in my firm and my clients; the people we work with are fun and challenge us and really make our days better. I love that planners are passionate and care about communities and people. I also like that I keep my eye on what's happening at a national and global level, but also what's happening on the street.

I least like dealing with people who are obstructionists for no reason, who don't come to the table with a spirit of cooperation to help their communities.

7. Can you suggest a valuable "try this" for students considering a career in your profession?

Participate in your community's planning process. Go to public meetings. Volunteer. Intern with or shadow a planner so you can see what they do on a daily basis.

SELECTED SCHOOLS

Many colleges and universities offer programs related to a career in urban and regional planning. Below are listed some of the more prominent institutions in this field.

Cornell University
Ithaca, NY 14853
607.254.4636
www.cornell.edu

Harvard University
86 Brattle Street
Cambridge, MA 02138
617.495.1551
www.harvard.edu

Massachusetts Institute of Technology
77 Massachusetts Avenue
Cambridge, MA 02139
617.253.1000
web.mit.edu

Rutgers University
33 Livingston Avenue
New Brunswick, NJ 08901
848.932.5475
www.rutgers.edu

University of California, Berkeley
110 Sproul Hall
Berkeley, CA 94720
510.642.6000
berkeley.edu

University of California, Los Angeles
405 Hilgard Avenue
Los Angeles, CA 90095
310.825.4321
www.ucla.edu

University of Illinois, Urbana, Champaign
601 E. John Street
Champaign, IL 61820
217.333.1000
illinois.edu

University of North Carolina, Chapel Hill
103 South Building cb 9100
Chapel Hill, NC 27599
www.unc.edu

University of Pennsylvania
1 College Hall, Rm 100
Philadelphia, PA 19104
215.898.5000
www.upenn.edu

University of Southern California
University Park
Los Angeles, CA 90089
213.740.2311
www.usc.edu

MORE INFORMATION

American Planning Association
205 N. Michigan Avenue, Suite 1200
Chicago, IL 60601
312.431.9100
www.planning.org

**Association of Collegiate Schools
of Planning**
6311 Mallard Trace
Tallahassee, FL 32312
850.385.2054
www.acsp.org

Urban Land Institute
1025 Thomas Jefferson Street, NW
Suite 500 West
Washington, DC 20007
202.624.7000
www.uli.org

Susan Williams/Editor

Visual Merchandiser

Snapshot

Career Cluster(s): Business, Marketing, Sales & Service
Interests: Advertising, marketing, fashion and design, decorating, construction and assembly, product display
Earnings (Yearly Average): $26,590
Employment & Outlook: Average Growth Expected

OVERVIEW

Sphere of Work

Visual merchandisers, also known as merchandise displayers, display artists, and window dressers, work mostly in retail establishments where they dress mannequins, decorate windows, and create various other visually attractive product displays. Some specialize in a particular product or department, such as home furnishings or clothing fashions. They also create displays for other types of businesses, such as hotels, grocery stores, and travel agencies, and for trade shows and other special events. While their work might be admired for its creativity, the

goal is to increase sales or, in the case of window displays, attract customers.

Work Environment

Visual merchandisers work mostly on site in department stores, boutiques, and other types of retail outlets. Some travel between stores if they are employed by a chain, or from one business to another if they are either self-employed or employed by a design or marketing firm. Part of their time may be spent in workshops where they assemble and paint various display props. In smaller stores, they tend to work alone or with a partner, while in large chains and department stores they work on a team. Full-time employees typically work about forty hours a week, including some night and weekend hours. Overtime hours may be occasionally necessary to meet project deadlines.

Profile

Working Conditions: Work Indoors
Physical Strength: Light Work, Medium Work
Education Needs: On-The-Job Training, High School Diploma or G.E.D., Junior/Technical/Community College
Licensure/Certification: Usually Not Required
Opportunities For Experience: Internship, Volunteer Work, Part-Time Work
Holland Interest Score*: AES

* See Appendix A

Occupation Interest

The work performed by visual merchandisers attracts people who are creative, detail-oriented, and interested in market research or sales. They may stop to admire the way a mannequin is posed or a colorfully set table. They keep up with fashion trends and advertising, and view consumer goods as a way to make a statement. Creativity and artistic ability are among the most important skills for this position. Visual merchandisers need to be resourceful, physically fit enough to lift mannequins and display materials, well organized, and able to meet deadlines.

A Day in the Life—Duties and Responsibilities

Visual merchandisers usually accent the newest products, or older products that need an extra boost. In larger stores and chains, they might assemble displays based on guidelines or plans devised by their managers or a team of professionals. In other cases, visual merchandisers have full creative control. They often begin by sketching an idea on paper or in a design program. While seasonal and holiday themes drive many designs, they glean other inspiration from current events, fads, popular leisure time activities, and many other sources. In general, displays should not only be eye-catching, but also accurately reflect the ambience of the store.

To promote fashions, the visual merchandiser selects suitable mannequins, dresses them with clothing and accessories, applies wigs and makeup, and situates the mannequins in appealing poses. He or she might also create mini-theatrical sets, complete with furniture, props, and backgrounds. Visual merchandisers assemble stands and props from kits, build them from scratch, or obtain items from used furniture stores or elsewhere. They choose the lighting and, in some cases, audio or multimedia components. Some also create graphic designs for the backgrounds.

Those merchandisers who help sell home furnishings will typically dress beds, coordinate table settings, and arrange towels, pillows, and other merchandise in striking, colorful displays.

Visual merchandisers also hang products from ceilings, decorate for holidays, and arrange displays for mall courtyards, trade shows, special events, and other occasions.

They also dismantle displays, maintain inventories, and order supplies when needed.

Duties and Responsibilities

- Consulting with advertising and sales officials to find out which merchandise to feature in a display
- Designing the layout and selecting the theme, props and colors of the display
- Constructing or assembling display props from wood, fabric, glass, paper and plastic
- Placing prices and descriptive information in the display
- Arranging props such as furniture, mannequins and merchandise

OCCUPATION SPECIALTIES

Display Managers

Display Managers develop advertising displays for windows or interior use and supervise display workers as they lay out and build displays.

Decorators

Decorators prepare and install decorations and displays from blueprints or drawings for trade and industrial shows, expositions, festivals and other special events.

WORK ENVIRONMENT

Relevant Skills and Abilities

Communication Skills
- Speaking effectively
- Writing concisely
- Creative/Artistic Skills
- Being skilled in art, music or dance

Interpersonal/Social Skills
- Cooperating with others
- Working as a member of a team

Organization & Management Skills
- Making decisions
- Paying attention to and handling details

Research & Planning Skills
- Creating ideas
- Predicting
- Selling ideas or products
- Using logical reasoning

Physical Environment

Visual merchandisers typically work in comfortable environments. They are at a slight risk for injuries related to climbing ladders, using various hand and power tools, and from kneeling, bending, and working in awkward positions. Paint and other art supplies could cause a health risk if not used with adequate ventilation.

Human Environment

Visual merchandisers report to a supervisor or manager and might supervise assistants. They interact with other visual merchandisers

Technical Skills
- Working with machines, tools or other objects

Unclassified Skills
- Performing work that produces tangible results

and/or sales associates and sometimes collaborate with graphic designers, marketing experts, and merchandising teams.

Technological Environment

Visual merchandisers use various hand and power tools to build props, including saws, sanders, hammers, staple guns, and painting tools. Display equipment might include audio systems and various types of lighting. Irons are used for clothing and textiles. Some visual merchandisers might also use illustration, design, and layout computer software.

EDUCATION, TRAINING, AND ADVANCEMENT

High School/Secondary

A high school diploma is required. Students should take a well-rounded academic program, with electives in art, crafts, computer design, drafting, and/or woodworking, and, if offered, interior decorating, consumer education, or fashion design. Business math and geometry will provide the mathematical skills necessary for budgeting and planning displays, while English and other related courses will teach written and oral communication skills necessary for relating with associates and promoting design ideas. Experience in building theatrical sets, staging fashion shows, or other extracurricular activities and seasonal or part-time employment in retail stores will also provide a good foundation.

Suggested High School Subjects
- Arts
- Business Math
- College Preparatory

- Crafts
- Drafting
- English
- Graphic Communications
- Interior Design
- Merchandising
- Ornamental Horticulture

Famous First

The first "reality" based store window display was put on in 2009 by the clothing and accessories retailer XOXA in New York City. The display featured two women, sometimes scantily clad, going about their daily business in a faux apartment setting.

College/Postsecondary

Most visual merchandisers learn on the job, although employers today also typically expect some postsecondary coursework, and sometimes an Associate's or Bachelor's degree. While visual merchandising and fashion merchandising are the programs most closely related to visual merchandising, other desirable majors include art, interior decorating, and graphic design. Retail management, marketing, and business, with electives or a minor in art or visual merchandising, are also useful, especially for those with management or self-employment goals. Students should include courses in psychology, as well. An internship can provide excellent hands-on experience.

Related College Majors

- Design & Visual Communications
- Home Furnishings & Equipment Installation & Consultants

Adult Job Seekers

Adults with a retail, interior decorating, or an arts background will have an advantage when changing careers. Skills can be updated by taking classes or through on-the-job training. As many jobs require some nights and weekend work, the hours might not always be conducive to parenting and other personal responsibilities.

Advancement is dependent upon the size of the business, experience, and/or a college degree, and may result in promotions to supervisory or management positions, or, if employed by a retail chain, taking on responsibility for a larger territory or more prestigious locations, or focusing more on the design of displays rather than hands-on work. Experienced visual merchandisers might also choose to teach or establish their own consulting or design firms.

Professional Certification and Licensure

No licenses or certifications are needed. Some visual or fashion merchandising programs offer certification upon completion.

Additional Requirements

A driver's license is required for visual merchandisers who work at multiple locations. Good eyesight, including the ability to see colors, and good manual dexterity are also required.

Fun Fact

During World War II, female mannequins wore dark clothes and somber expressions. But as troops returned at the end of war, they looked happier, and more voluptuous.
Source: https://mannequinmadness.wordpress.com/the-history-of-mannequin/

EARNINGS AND ADVANCEMENT

Earnings depend on the size and geographic location of the employer, the type of work done and the level of responsibility, ability and experience of the individual. Median annual earnings of visual merchandisers were $26,590 in 2014. The lowest 10 percent earned less than $18,800, while the highest 10 percent earned more than $45,300.

Visual merchandisers may receive paid vacations, holidays, and sick days; life and health insurance; and retirement benefits. These benefits are usually paid by the employer. Most visual merchandisers receive a discount on their purchases.

Metropolitan Areas with the Highest Employment Level in This Occupation

Metropolitan area	Employment	Employment per thousand jobs	Annual mean wage
Phoenix-Mesa-Glendale, AZ	3,920	2.15	$28,340
New York-White Plains-Wayne, NY-NJ	3,480	0.65	$39,350
Atlanta-Sandy Springs-Marietta, GA	3,180	1.33	$29,290
Houston-Sugar Land-Baytown, TX	2,440	0.86	$25,720
Santa Ana-Anaheim-Irvine, CA	2,110	1.42	$27,370
Dallas-Plano-Irving, TX	2,070	0.93	$29,870
Minneapolis-St. Paul-Bloomington, MN-WI	1,920	1.05	$28,300
Seattle-Bellevue-Everett, WA	1,830	1.23	$29,940
Baltimore-Towson, MD	1,560	1.20	$32,320
Los Angeles-Long Beach-Glendale, CA	1,500	0.37	$33,610

Source: Bureau of Labor Statistics

EMPLOYMENT AND OUTLOOK

Visual merchandisers held about 85,000 jobs nationally in 2014. They are usually employed by department stores or retail shops. Employment is expected to grow about as fast as the average for all occupations through the year 2024, which means employment is projected to increase 4 percent to 9 percent. Most jobs will result from the need to replace workers who retire, transfer to other occupations or leave the labor force for other reasons.

Employment Trend, Projected 2014–24

Visual merchandisers: 7%

Retail salespersons: 7%

Total, all occupations: 7%

Note: "All Occupations" includes all occupations in the U.S. Economy. Source: U.S. Bureau of Labor Statistics, Employment Projections Program.

Related Occupations

- Commercial Artist
- Designer
- Fashion Coordinator
- Floral Designer
- Florist
- Industrial Designer
- Interior Designer
- Sign Painter and Letterer

Conversation With . . .
JUDY BELL

CEO, Energetic Retail
Minneapolis, Minnesota
Visual merchandising, 30 years

1. What was your individual career path in terms of education/training, entry-level job, or other significant opportunity?

My first jobs were retail positions in sales and store management, working for a variety of department stores, specialty stores and boutiques. After eight years, I landed my first visual merchandising position, working as the only visual merchandiser for the Herberger's department store in Albert Lea, Minnesota. I was responsible for fourteen storefront windows and three floors of displays. I had only minimal visual background, so I duplicated windows in visual trades magazines to learn the basics. I also handprinted all of the store pricing signs on a tabletop roller printing press!

After two years, I was hired as a visual merchandiser by Braun's Fashions in Minneapolis and seven years later was promoted to visual merchandising director. I was traveling to different stores every day to do displays and noticed that there was no consistent presentation of apparel and accessories. So, on my own time over several weekends, I wrote the company's first visual merchandising guidelines manual and emphasized the importance of consistent presentation. When I presented it to my boss, he was delighted. A vocational school student who was working with us showed the manual to one of her instructors, who contacted me about using it in class. I told her that wasn't possible because it was owned by Braun's Fashions, but said I would go ahead and write a textbook for schools. The result, "Silent Selling: Best Practices and Effective Strategies in Visual Merchandising," was first published in 1986. A fourth edition was published in 2012.

Based on my textbook, I was hired by Target Corporation to develop both a visual merchandising team and training for the stores. For the next twenty-two years, I led a variety of teams in visual merchandising, innovation, and competitive insights. In 2012, when I left Target, I started my own company, Energetic Retail (www. energetic-retail). I call myself the CEO: Chief Energetic Officer! I'm now marketing a half-day workshop—"What's Your Energy Quotient?"—that draws on my years of evaluating retail competitors for Target. I've also done a series of television segments for Fox. Over the years, I've received several national retail design awards recognizing the work that I've done.

2. **What are the most important skills and/or qualities for someone in your profession?**

The most important skills are a passion for creative thinking, the ability to easily engage and collaborate with others, and a desire to go "above and beyond" every day.

3. **What do you wish you had known going into this profession?**

I wish I had known the importance of random meetings in elevators, lunchrooms, etc., from the very start. Always be prepared to take advantage of an opportunity. My most valuable tip to young people starting out is to get involved with the larger industry by attending national conferences like GlobalShop, joining committees, and getting elected to the boards of professional trade organizations.

4. **Are there many job opportunities in your profession? In what specific areas?**

Multitudes. Visual merchandising is important not just to people who work in merchandise presentation, but to so many retail professions: product design and buying and marketing.

5. **How do you see your profession changing in the next five years? What role will technology play in those changes, and what skills will be required?**

I think visual merchandising will gain even more importance in retail stores as they compete with online merchants. But online venues will also present visual merchandising opportunities. The same skills used in brick and mortar stores can be applied online. Design is design, on a screen or in a physical space.

6. **What do you enjoy most about your job? What do you enjoy least about your job?**

When you find a profession that you love, you "play" every day: collaborating with others from the very beginning of a project, setting goals together, building a new store experience that will engage shoppers, and ultimately relishing improved sales results. I thoroughly enjoyed all aspects of my career in visual merchandising, but if there was one thing I could tweak it would be the ever-expanding review process in corporate settings. Rather than continually reporting on the work my team and I accomplished, I would have preferred creating and producing more exciting new projects.

7. **Can you suggest a valuable "try this" for students considering a career in your profession?**

If there are any retail corporate offices near where you live, there may be opportunities to shadow someone for a half or full day. In the meantime, experiment with different design techniques in your dorm room or apartment. Every space is an opportunity to create a visually stimulating environment ripe with design principles.

SELECTED SCHOOLS

Most community colleges and four-year universities offer programs related to careers in business, advertising, or sales. Completion of such a program is not necessary in most cases to obtain a job in visual merchandising, but it may give the job seeker an advantage over other applicants.

MORE INFORMATION

National Association of Display Industries (NADI)
3595 Sheridan Street, Suite 200
Hollywood, FL 33021
954.893.7225

Retail Design Institute
25 North Broadway
Tarrytown, NY 10590
800.379.9912
www.retaildesigninstitute.org

Visual Merchandising and Store Design
P.O. Box 1060
Skokie, IL 60076-9785
847.763.4938
http://vmsd.com

Sally Driscoll/Editor

Wholesale Sales Representative

Snapshot

Career Cluster(s): Business, Sales & Service

Interests: Sales, interpersonal communication, business, customer service, economics, traveling

Earnings (Yearly Average): $55,020

Employment & Outlook: Average Growth Expected

OVERVIEW

Sphere of Work

Wholesale sales representatives sell products or services on behalf of the manufacturer or wholesaler. They sell to a variety of organizations, including businesses and government agencies. Some wholesale sales representatives are employed by independent agencies whose clients are wholesalers or manufacturers. A representative demonstrates the products or services to the client and explains how they will be beneficial. Representatives target specific customers based on their needs, specifications, and regulations.

Work Environment

Wholesale sales representatives are typically assigned a territory in which to sell. Some have large territories, such as entire regions of the United States, while others have smaller ones, such as a city or county. Because of this, a representative may need to spend a significant amount of time traveling. Representatives generally work indoors, meeting with clients and putting together presentations using computers and other materials. They also utilize computers and the Internet to communicate with clients.

Profile

Working Conditions: Work Indoors
Physical Strength: Light Work
Education Needs: Junior/
Technical/Community College,
Bachelor's Degree
Licensure/Certification:
Recommended
Opportunities For Experience: Part-
Time Work
Holland Interest Score*: ESA

* See Appendix A

Occupation Interest

Wholesale sales representatives are outgoing people who enjoy working with others. The job entails a great deal of travel, so the profession tends to attract individuals who are comfortable working away from home. Representatives need to have good communication skills in order to thoroughly express how their product will be beneficial to their clients. Because their job security and income usually depend on the amount of products they sell, sales representatives also need to be able to work under pressure.

A Day in the Life—Duties and Responsibilities

The most important aspect of a wholesale sales representative's job is communicating with clients. Representatives must understand the needs of their clients in order to be able to explain to them how specific products and services can meet those needs. Some representatives work in specialized fields such as science, agriculture, or mechanical equipment. Others deal in clothing, food, or office supplies.

To search for clients, a representative follows leads from established clients, attends conferences, and uses business directories. Once a potential client has been contacted, the representative discusses the client's needs and explains how the products and services on offer can meet those particular needs. If the client is interested, the representative may travel to his or her location for a meeting. Sometimes the representative may be able to present products and services remotely, using video chat or e-mail.

When making a presentation to a potential client, a representative highlights the features of the products and services that are capable of satisfying the client's needs. Any questions the client may have regarding cost, availability, or service agreements are addressed by the representative. Clients also negotiate the price and contract through the representative. After making a sale, the representative stays in touch with the client to answer questions and resolve any issues.

Representatives may collaborate with each other to exchange sales strategies and other marketing information.

Duties and Responsibilities

- Soliciting orders by phone or in person
- Monitoring inventory levels
- Processing orders
- Promoting product lines
- Providing technical information and assistance
- Assisting in resolving customer problems
- Recording and reporting on sales

OCCUPATION SPECIALTIES

Food Products Sales Representatives

Food Products Sales Representatives sell food to grocers, restaurants, hotels or institutions.

Chemical and Drug Sales Representatives

Chemical and Drug Sales Representatives sell chemicals or pharmaceuticals to businesses.

Petroleum Products Sales Representatives

Petroleum Products Sales Representatives sell fuel and lubricants to vehicle service stations.

Home Furnishings Sales Representatives

Home Furnishings Sales Representatives sell items for homes to retailers and other outlets.

Communication Equipment Sales Representatives

Communication Equipment Sales Representatives sell electronic communication equipment.

Animal Feed Sales Representatives

Animal Feed Sales Representatives sell animal feed products to farmers and retail stores.

Motor Vehicle and Parts Sales Representatives

Motor Vehicle and Parts Sales Representatives sell vehicles and parts to dealers and service stations.

Recreation and Sporting Goods Sales Representatives

Recreation and Sporting Goods Sales Representatives sell to retailers and park managers.

General Merchandise Sales Representatives

General Merchandise Sales Representatives sell various dry goods and housewares to retailers.

WORK ENVIRONMENT

Physical Environment

Wholesale sales representatives spend a great deal of time traveling, so their work environment may include trains, airplanes, and cars. Client locations can include a variety of commercial, industrial, and government buildings. Office environments are typical in this field.

Relevant Skills and Abilities

Communication Skills
- Persuading others
- Speaking effectively
- Writing concisely

Interpersonal/Social Skills
- Being able to remain calm
- Being able to work independently
- Cooperating with others
- Respecting others' opinions
- Working as a member of a team (SCANS Workplace Competency – Interpersonal)

Organization & Management Skills
- Selling ideas or products

Research & Planning Skills
- Analyzing information
- Solving problems

Technical Skills
- Working with data or numbers
- Working with machines, tools or other objects

Human Environment

Wholesale sales representatives communicate and collaborate daily with clients, other sales representatives, managers, and business owners. Communication and collaboration with others in the profession is essential for keeping up to date with marketing and product information.

Technological Environment

Wholesale sales representatives use a variety of technologies, depending on the industry they are working in. They also use computers, projectors, and software to communicate and to prepare presentations for clients.

EDUCATION, TRAINING, AND ADVANCEMENT

High School/Secondary

Wholesale sales representatives are normally required to have a high school diploma or the equivalent. High schools usually offer several basic courses that a student will find beneficial for a job in sales, including basic mathematics, computer science, and courses such as English that develop interpersonal communication skills. Representatives may work with scientific and technical products, so any courses related to those would also be beneficial.

Suggested High School Subjects
- Applied Communication
- Bookkeeping
- Business Math
- English
- Merchandising
- Speech

Famous First

The first wholesale ice cream business was started in Baltimore in 1851 by C. Jacob Fussell, who got his start as a seller of "country fresh" dairy products in York County, Penn. Fussell sold his ice cream at the wholesale rate of 25 cents per quart. The retail rate was 60 cents per quart.

College/Postsecondary

Although it may not be required for some wholesale sales representatives, those working with scientific, pharmaceutical, industrial, or technical products are usually required to have a bachelor's degree. A degree in any related field, such as chemistry, biology, or engineering, would be helpful. Representatives in less technical and scientific fields may benefit from a degree in business or economics. Being a wholesale sales representative involves a wide range of subjects, so students should pursue a multidisciplinary approach to education.

Some technical and vocational schools offer courses and training programs related to the products and services typically represented by wholesale sales representatives. These programs last anywhere from several months to a year. Such schools offer an excellent way for an individual to network with more experienced people in the field, and some offer job-placement programs.

Related College Majors
- Agricultural Supplies Retailing & Wholesaling
- Fashion Merchandising
- Food Products Retailing & Wholesaling Operations
- General Retailing & Wholesaling Operations & Skills
- Home Furnishings & Equipment Installation & Consultants
- Hospitality & Recreation Marketing Operations

Adult Job Seekers

Being a wholesale sales representative requires a great deal of travel to and from clients. Aspiring sale representatives should also consider that their job security and income are determined by their success in the field. A person with no background in sales or a related field should consider enrolling in a college or a technical or vocational school that offers relevant degrees or programs.

Professional Certification and Licensure

A wholesale sales representative can become certified through the Manufacturers' Representatives Education Research Foundation. This organization offers different certifications, including Certified Sales Professional and Certified Professional Manufacturers' Representative certificates. These certification programs instruct professionals in a wide range of related topics, including business ethics, strategy, and legal concerns. Certification normally involves the successful completion of a written exam and a demonstration of technical skills. Becoming certified will give a representative a competitive advantage when seeking a job and when pursuing advancement.

Several companies have formal training programs for representatives. These programs, which typically last up to one year, instruct representatives on all aspects of the industry they are working in, including the manufacture, installation, and distribution of their product or service. Once a representative has completed training, he or she is usually allowed to work with less or no supervision.

Additional Requirements

Sales and customer-service skills are extremely important for wholesale sales representatives. They need to be able to communicate clearly and persuasively to clients in order to demonstrate how their product or service will satisfy their clients' needs. They also need to be confident in their abilities and knowledge when making presentations and speaking with clients.

Fun Fact

Half of all sales go to the first salesperson to contact a prospect.
Source: http://www.slideshare.net/JakeAtwood1/20-shocking-sales-stats/13-Email_Marketing_has2x_higher_ROI

EARNINGS AND ADVANCEMENT

Earnings depend on the type of goods and services sold, and the individual's experience and ability. Most employers pay a combination of salary plus commission or salary plus bonus. Commissions are usually based on the amount of sales, whereas bonuses may depend on individual performance, on the performance of all wholesale sales representatives in the group or district, or on the company's overall performance. Because sales patterns fluctuate, many companies pay wholesale sales representatives an advance or draw against commissions.

Median annual earnings of wholesale sales representatives, including commission, were $55,020 in 2014. The lowest ten percent earned less than $26,790, and the highest ten percent earned more than $116,230.

Wholesale sales representatives may receive paid vacations, holidays, and sick days; life and health insurance; and retirement benefits. These are usually paid by the employer. Wholesale sales representatives are usually reimbursed for their expenses, such as transportation, meals, hotels, and entertaining customers.

Metropolitan Areas with the Highest Employment Level in This Occupation

Metropolitan area	Employment	Employment per thousand jobs	Annual mean wage
New York-White Plains-Wayne, NY-NJ	60,740	11.27	$78,770
Chicago-Joliet-Naperville, IL	47,750	12.73	$71,200
Los Angeles-Long Beach-Glendale, CA	46,110	11.37	$62,830
Houston-Sugar Land-Baytown, TX	36,370	12.79	$77,040
Atlanta-Sandy Springs-Marietta, GA	36,130	15.13	$62,880
Dallas-Plano-Irving, TX	32,020	14.30	$76,110
Philadelphia, PA	23,710	12.73	$68,870
Minneapolis-St. Paul-Bloomington, MN-WI	23,470	12.86	$76,750
Seattle-Bellevue-Everett, WA	21,570	14.45	$73,380
Denver-Aurora-Broomfield, CO	20,100	15.16	$71,860

Source: Bureau of Labor Statistics

EMPLOYMENT AND OUTLOOK

There were approximately 1.5 million wholesale sales representatives (nontechnical sales) employed nationally in 2014. Employment is expected to grow about as fast as the average for all occupations through the year 2024, which means employment is projected to increase 5 percent to 10 percent. This continued job growth is due to the increasing variety and number of goods to be sold. Many job openings will occur because of the need to replace workers who transfer to other occupations or retire.

Employment Trend, Projected 2014–24

Sales representatives, wholesale and manufacturing, technical and scientific products: 7%

Wholesale and manufacturing sales representatives: 7%

Total, all occupations: 7%

Sales representatives, wholesale and manufacturing, except technical and scientific products: 6%

Sales and related occupations: 5%

Note: "All Occupations" includes all occupations in the U.S. Economy. Source: U.S. Bureau of Labor Statistics, Employment Projections Program.

Related Occupations

- Insurance Sales Agent
- Manufacturers Representative
- Online Merchant
- Purchasing Agent
- Real Estate Sales Agent
- Retail Salesperson
- Sales Engineer
- Services Sales Representative
- Technical Sales Representative
- Wholesale & Retail Buyer

SELECTED SCHOOLS

Most colleges and universities offer programs related to careers in business, marketing, and sales; the student may also get started in a technical or community college. For a list of some of top schools with programs in sales, visit the website of the Sales Education Foundation (see below).

MORE INFORMATION

Manufacturers' Agents National Association
16-A Journey, Suite 200
Aliso Viejo, CA 92656
877.626.2776
www.manaoline.org

Manufacturers' Representatives Education Research Foundation
999 S. Monaco Parkway, #200
Denver, CO 80224
303.463.1801
www.mrerf.org

Retail, Wholesale and Department Store Union
30 East 29th Street
New York, NY 10016
212.684.5300
www.rwdsu.org

Sales and Marketing Executives International
P.O. Box 1390
Sumas, WA 98295-1390
312.893.0751
www.smei.org

Sales Education Foundation
3123 Research Boulevard, Suite 250
Dayton, OH 45420
937.610.4369
www.salesfoundation.org

Patrick Cooper/Editor

What Are Your Career Interests?

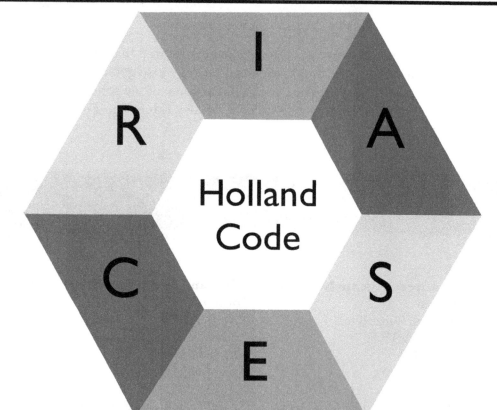

This is based on Dr. John Holland's theory that people and work environments can be loosely classified into six different groups. Each of the letters above corresponds to one of the six groups described in the following pages.

Different people's personalities may find different environments more to their liking. While you may have some interests in and similarities to several of the six groups, you may be attracted primarily to two or three of the areas. These two or three letters are your "Holland Code." For example, with a code of "RES" you would most resemble the Realistic type, somewhat less resemble the Enterprising type, and resemble the Social type even less. The types that are not in your code are the types you resemble least of all.

Most people, and most jobs, are best represented by some combination of two or three of the Holland interest areas. In addition, most people are most satisfied if there is some degree of fit between their personality and their work environment.

The rest of the pages in this booklet further explain each type and provide some examples of career possibilities, areas of study at MU, and co-curricular activities for each code. To take a more in-depth look at your Holland Code, take a self-assessment such as the SDS, Discover, or a card sort at the MU Career Center with a Career Specialist.

This hexagonal model of RIASEC occupations is the copyrighted work of Dr. John Holland, and is used with his permission. The Holland Game is adapted from Richard Bolles' "Quick Job Hunting Map." Copyright 1995, 1998 by the MU Career Center, University of Missouri-Columbia.

Realistic *(Doers)*

People who have athletic ability, prefer to work with objects, machines, tools, plants or animals, or to be outdoors.

Are you?		**Can you?**	**Like to?**
practical	independent	fix electrical things	tinker with machines/vehicles
straightforward/frank	ambitious	solve electrical problems	work outdoors
mechanically inclined	systematic	pitch a tent	be physically active
stable		play a sport	use your hands
concrete		read a blueprint	build things
reserved		plant a garden	tend/train animals
self-controlled		operate tools and machine	work on electronic equipment

Career Possibilities
(Holland Code):

Air Traffic Controller (SER)	Dental Technician (REI)	Laboratory Technician (RIE)	Property Manager (ESR)
Archaeologist (IRE)	Farm Manager (ESR)	Landscape Architect (AIR)	Recreation Manager (SER)
Athletic Trainer (SRE)	Fish and Game Warden (RES)	Mechanical Engineer (RIS)	Service Manager (ERS)
Cartographer (IRE)	Floral Designer (RAE)	Optician (REI)	Software Technician (RCI)
Commercial Airline Pilot (RIE)	Forester (RIS)	Petroleum Geologist (RIE)	Ultrasound Technologist (RSI)
Commercial Drafter (IRE)	Geodetic Surveyor (IRE)	Police Officer (SER)	Vocational Rehabilitation
Corrections Officer (SER)	Industrial Arts Teacher (IER)	Practical Nurse (SER)	Consultant (ESR)

Investigative *(Thinkers)*

People who like to observe, learn, investigate, analyze, evaluate, or solve problems.

Are you?		**Can you?**	**Like to?**
inquisitive	intellectually self-confident	think abstractly	explore a variety of ideas
analytical	Independent	solve math problems	work independently
scientific	logical	understand scientific theories	perform lab experiments
observant/precise	complex	do complex calculations	deal with abstractions
scholarly	Curious	use a microscope or computer	do research
cautious		interpret formulas	be challenged

Career Possibilities
(Holland Code):

Actuary (ISE)	Chemical Engineer (IRE)	Geologist (IRE)	Physician, General Practice (ISE)
Agronomist (IRS)	Chemist (IRE)	Horticulturist (IRS)	Psychologist (IES)
Anesthesiologist (IRS)	Computer Systems Analyst (IER)	Mathematician (IER)	Research Analyst (IRC)
Anthropologist (IRE)	Dentist (ISR)	Medical Technologist (ISA)	Statistician (IRE)
Archaeologist (IRE)	Ecologist (IRE)	Meteorologist (IRS)	Surgeon (IRA)
Biochemist (IRS)	Economist (IAS)	Nurse Practitioner (ISA)	Technical Writer (IRS)
Biologist (ISR)	Electrical Engineer (IRE)	Pharmacist (IES)	Veterinarian (IRS)

<u>A</u>rtistic *(Creators)*

People who have artistic, innovating, or intuitional abilities and like to work in unstructured situations using their imagination and creativity.

Are you?
creative
imaginative
innovative
unconventional
emotional
independent
Expressive

original
introspective
impulsive
sensitive
courageous
complicated
idealistic
nonconforming

Can you?
sketch, draw, paint
play a musical instrument
write stories, poetry, music
sing, act, dance
design fashions or interiors

Like to?
attend concerts, theatre, art
   exhibits
read fiction, plays, and poetry
work on crafts
take photography
express yourself creatively
deal with ambiguous ideas

Career Possibilities
(Holland Code):

Actor (AES)
Advertising Art Director (AES)
Advertising Manager (ASE)
Architect (AIR)
Art Teacher (ASE)
Artist (ASI)

Copy Writer (ASI)
Dance Instructor (AER)
Drama Coach (ASE)
English Teacher (ASE)
Entertainer/Performer (AES)
Fashion Illustrator (ASR)

Interior Designer (AES)
Intelligence Research Specialist
   (AEI)
Journalist/Reporter (ASE)
Landscape Architect (AIR)
Librarian (SAI)

Medical Illustrator (AIE)
Museum Curator (AES)
Music Teacher (ASI)
Photographer (AES)
Writer (ASI)
Graphic Designer (AES)

<u>S</u>ocial *(Helpers)*

People who like to work with people to enlighten, inform, help, train, or cure them, or are skilled with words.

Are you?
friendly
helpful
idealistic
insightful
outgoing
understanding

cooperative
generous
responsible
forgiving
patient
kind

Can you?
teach/train others
express yourself clearly
lead a group discussion
mediate disputes
plan and supervise an activity
cooperate well with others

Like to?
work in groups
help people with problems
do volunteer work
work with young people
serve others

Career Possibilities
(Holland Code):

City Manager (SEC)
Clinical Dietitian (SIE)
College/University Faculty (SEI)
Community Org. Director
   (SEA)
Consumer Affairs Director
   (SER)Counselor/Therapist
   (SAE)

Historian (SEI)
Hospital Administrator (SER)
Psychologist (SEI)
Insurance Claims Examiner
   (SIE)
Librarian (SAI)
Medical Assistant (SCR)
Minister/Priest/Rabbi (SAI)
Paralegal (SCE)

Park Naturalist (SEI)
Physical Therapist (SIE)
Police Officer (SER)
Probation and Parole Officer
   (SEC)
Real Estate Appraiser (SCE)
Recreation Director (SER)
Registered Nurse (SIA)

Teacher (SAE)
Social Worker (SEA)
Speech Pathologist (SAI)
Vocational-Rehab. Counselor
   (SEC)
Volunteer Services Director
   (SEC)

<u>E</u>nterprising *(Persuaders)*

People who like to work with people, influencing, persuading, leading or managing for organizational goals or economic gain.

Are you?		**Can you?**	**Like to?**
self-confident	ambitious	initiate projects	make decisions
assertive	agreeable	convince people to do things	be elected to office
persuasive	talkative	your way	start your own business
energetic	extroverted	sell things	campaign politically
adventurous	spontaneous	give talks or speeches	meet important people
popular	optimistic	organize activities	have power or status
		lead a group	
		persuade others	

**Career Possibilities
(Holland Code):**

Advertising Executive (ESA)
Advertising Sales Rep (ESR)
Banker/Financial Planner (ESR)
Branch Manager (ESA)
Business Manager (ESC)
Buyer (ESA)
Chamber of Commerce Exec
  (ESA)

Credit Analyst (EAS)
Customer Service Manager
  (ESA)
Education & Training Manager
  (EIS)
Emergency Medical Technician
  (ESI)
Entrepreneur (ESA)

Foreign Service Officer (ESA)
Funeral Director (ESR)
Insurance Manager (ESC)
Interpreter (ESA)
Lawyer/Attorney (ESA)
Lobbyist (ESA)
Office Manager (ESR)
Personnel Recruiter (ESR)

Politician (ESA)
Public Relations Rep (EAS)
Retail Store Manager (ESR)
Sales Manager (ESA)
Sales Representative (ERS)
Social Service Director (ESA)
Stockbroker (ESI)
Tax Accountant (ECS)

<u>C</u>onventional *(Organizers)*

People who like to work with data, have clerical or numerical ability, carry out tasks in detail, or follow through on others' instructions.

Are you?		**Can you?**	**Like to?**
well-organized	practical	work well within a system	follow clearly defined
accurate	thrifty	do a lot of paper work in a short	procedures
numerically inclined	systematic	time	use data processing equipment
methodical	structured	keep accurate records	work with numbers
conscientious	polite	use a computer terminal	type or take shorthand
efficient	ambitious	write effective business letters	be responsible for details
conforming	obedient		collect or organize things
	persistent		

**Career Possibilities
(Holland Code):**

Abstractor (CSI)
Accountant (CSE)
Administrative Assistant (ESC)
Budget Analyst (CER)
Business Manager (ESC)
Business Programmer (CRI)
Business Teacher (CSE)
Catalog Librarian (CSE)

Claims Adjuster (SEC)
Computer Operator (CSR)
Congressional-District Aide (CES)
Cost Accountant (CES)
Court Reporter (CSE)
Credit Manager (ESC)
Customs Inspector (CEI)
Editorial Assistant (CSI)

Elementary School Teacher
  (SEC)
Financial Analyst (CSI)
Insurance Manager (ESC)
Insurance Underwriter (CSE)
Internal Auditor (ICR)
Kindergarten Teacher (ESC)

Medical Records Technician
  (CSE)
Museum Registrar (CSE)
Paralegal (SCE)
Safety Inspector (RCS)
Tax Accountant (ECS)
Tax Consultant (CES)
Travel Agent (ECS)

BIBLIOGRAPHY

General, E-Commerce, and Technical

Bettger, Frank. *How I Raised Myself from Failure to Success in Selling*, rpt. ed. New York: Touchstone, 1991.

Calderone, Brian. *Front of the Class to Top of the Sales Rankings: Practical Advice for College Graduates Starting Their Sales Career from 36 Top Sales Professionals*. North Charleston, SC: CreateSpace, 2011.

Care, John, and Aron Bohlig. *Mastering Technical Sales: The Sales Engineers Handbook*. Norwood, MA: Artech House, 2014.

Klein, Ruth. *The Everything Guide to Being a Sales Rep*. Avon, MA: Adams Media, 2006.

Laudon, Kenneth C. *E-Commerce*. Upper Saddle River, NJ: Prentice Hall, 2014.

Ruff, Tom. *How to Break into Pharmaceutical Sales*. New York: Waverly Press, 2007.

Ziglar, Zig. *Selling 101: What Every Successful Sales Professional Needs to Know*. Nashville, TN: Thomas Nelson, 2003.

Insurance

Atkinson, David B. *Life Insurance Products and Finance: Charting a Clear Course*. Schaumberg, IL: Society of Actuaries, 2000.

Hungelman, Jack. *Insurance for Dummies*. Hoboken, NJ: Wiley, 2009.

Reavis, Marshall Wilson, III. *Insurance: Concepts & Coverage*. Victoria, BC: Friesen Press, 2012.

Real Estate

Cook, Frank. *21 Things I Wish My Broker Had Told Me: Practical Advice for New Real Estate Professionals*. Chicago: Dearborn Financial, 2002.

Irwin, Robert. *Tips & Traps for Getting Started as a Real Estate Agent*. New York: McGraw-Hill Educational, 2006.

Keller, Gary, et al. *The Millionaire Real Estate Agent*. New York: McGraw-Hill Educational, 2004.

Zeler, Dirk. *Your First Year in Real Estate*, 2d ed. New York: Crown Business, 2010.

Zeller, Dirk. *Success as a Real Estate Agent for Dummies*. Hoboken, NJ: Wiley, 2013.

Financial

Little, Jeffrey. *Understanding Wall Street*. New York: McGraw-Hill Educational, 2009.

Rockefeller, Barbara. *Technical Analysis for Dummies*. Hoboken, NJ: Wiley, 2014.

Thomsett, Michael C. *Getting Started in Stock Analysis*. Hoboken, NJ: Wiley, 2015.

INDEX

WITHDRAWAL